Palgrave Studies in Language, Gender and Sexuality

'By exploring the entire gamut of the representation of masculinity in both old and new media and across a wide range of disciplines, Baker and Balirano get readers really thinking about what it means to be a man in today's liquid society. Guaranteed to raise awareness about the diverse ways of being and performing masculinity, the book provides a novel contribution to an exciting new field opening up new avenues for other researchers.'

—Delia Chiaro, *Professor of English Linguistics and Translation, University of Bologna, Italy, and President of the International Society of Humor Studies*

'Exploring the interface of queer studies with the fields of linguistics, anthropology, semiotics, critical discourse analysis, literary and film studies, the articles in this collection draw a multi-faceted picture of the discursive construction and representation of queer masculinities in a range of text genres and contexts. They engage in fascinating analyses of various aspects of queer masculinities, including issues such as consumer culture, representation in TV series, films, literature and art, intersectionality with trans and racial identities, homophobic discourse and subordination through hegemonic masculinity.'

—Heiko Motschenbacher, *Western Norway University of Applied Sciences, Bergen*

Language, Gender and Sexuality is a new series which highlights the role of language in understanding issues, identities and relationships in relation to genders and sexualities. The series will comprise innovative, high quality research and provides a platform for the best contemporary scholarship in the field of language, gender and sexuality. The series is interdisciplinary but takes language as it central focus. Contributions will be inclusive of both leading and emerging scholars in the field. The series is international in its scope, authorship and readership and aims to draw together theoretical and empirical work from a range of countries and contexts.

More information about this series at
http://www.palgrave.com/series/15402

Paul Baker • Giuseppe Balirano
Editors

Queering Masculinities in Language and Culture

palgrave
macmillan

Editors
Paul Baker
Linguistics and English Language
Lancaster University
Lancashire, UK

Giuseppe Balirano
Literary, Linguistic and Comparative Studies
University of Naples "L'Orientale"
Naples, Italy

Palgrave Studies in Language, Gender and Sexuality
ISBN 978-1-349-95795-8 ISBN 978-1-349-95327-1 (eBook)
https://doi.org/10.1057/978-1-349-95327-1

Cover illustration: Westend61 GmbH / Alamy Stock Photo

Printed on acid-free paper

This Palgrave Macmillan imprint is published by Springer Nature
The registered company is Macmillan Publishers Ltd.
The registered company address is: The Campus, 4 Crinan Street, London, N1 9XW, United Kingdom

Contents

Notes on Contributors

Emilio Amideo is a PhD student in Literary, Linguistic, and Comparative Studies at the University of Naples "L'Orientale", Italy, where he is researching contemporary black queer narratives as embodied politics of resistance. He has previously carried out research on the linguistic representation of "racial otherness" in the British Press and on issues of gender and "race" performativity in Afro-diasporic literary and visual productions. He was a visiting pre-doctoral fellow at the Northwestern University, USA, in 2015 and at Goldsmiths University of London, UK, in 2016.

Paul Baker is Professor of English Language at Lancaster University, UK. His research interests include language, gender and sexuality, discourse analysis, and corpus linguistics. He has written 14 books including *Using Corpora to Analyze Gender* (2014), *Sexed Texts: Language, Gender and Sexuality* (2008), *Using Corpora in Discourse Analysis* (2006), *Public Discourses of Gay Men* (2005), and *Polari: The Lost Language of Gay Men* (2002). He is the commissioning editor of the journal *Corpora.*

Giuseppe Balirano (PhD in English) is Associate Professor of English Linguistics and Translation at the University of Naples "L'Orientale", Italy. His research interests and publications lie in the fields of multimodal critical discourse analysis, humour, masculinity studies, and audio visual translation. He is the Director of the inter-university research centre, I-LanD, for the linguistic investigation of identity and diversity in discourse. His recent publications include *Humosexually Speaking: Laughter and the Intersections of Gender* (2016, co-edited with Delia

Chiaro); *Languaging Diversity* (with Nisco M.C., 2015); *Language, Theory and Society* (with Nisco M.C., 2015); *Masculinity and Representation: A Multimodal Critical Approach to Male Identity Constructions* (2014); *Variation and Varieties in Contexts of English* (with Bamford J. and Vincent J., 2012); and *The Perception of Diasporic Humour: Indian English on TV* (2008).

Vincenzo Bavaro is Assistant Professor of American Literature at the University *"L'Orientale"* in Naples, Italy. He holds an MA in Cultural Studies from Dartmouth College, NH, USA, and a PhD in English from the University of Rome "La Sapienza". He is the author of *Una Storia Etnica?* (Pitagora, 2013) and his recent publications include work on lesbian, gay, bisexual, and transgender (LGBT) cultural history, community activism in New York City, and twentieth-century American drama. He has recently co-edited, with Shirley Geok-Lin Lim, a forthcoming issue of *Anglistica* on the representation and the performance of "mess" in contemporary Anglophone culture.

Andrea Bernardelli is Senior Lecturer in Semiotics at the University of Perugia, Italy. His main research areas are narratology and literary theory, media studies, and semiotics. He is the author of various volumes on narratology and semiotics, among which are *Semiotica. Storia, teorie e metodi* (Carocci 2014), *Che cos'è l'intertestualità?* (Carocci 2013), and *Il testo narrativo* (with. R. Ceserani, Il Mulino 2005). He edited the volumes *Il trionfo dell'antieroe nelle serie televisive* (Morlacchi 2012) and *La rete intertestuale* (Morlacchi 2010). Two forthcoming books are *Cos'è una serie televisiva?* (with G. Grignaffini, Carocci) and *Cattivi seriali. Personaggi atipici nelle produzioni televisive contemporanee* (Carocci).

Andrew Brindle is an Assistant Professor at the St. John's University in Taiwan. His research interests include masculinities, right-wing populist discourse, discourses of racism and homophobia, and political discourse. His work on media constructions of a democracy movement in Taiwan has been published in the journal *Discourse and Society* and he studies the discursive constructions and online strategies of a far-right Islamophobic group in the UK, the English Defence League.

Paola Di Gennaro holds a PhD in English and Comparative Literature. After completing her BA in Comparative Studies at the University of Naples "L'Orientale", she went on to receive an MA in Comparative Literature from the School of Oriental and African Studies (SOAS)—University of London. At present, she teaches English literature at the University "Suor Orsola Benincasa", Naples, Italy. Her research interests include studies in the field of English and comparative literature and theory with particular reference to European,

Anglo-American, and Japanese contexts, as well as poems and short stories. Her publications include *Wandering through Guilt. The Cain Archetype in the Twentieth-Century Novel* (2015).

Emilia Di Martino (PhD in English for Specific Purposes) is Associate Professor of English Language and Translation at the Università di Napoli Suor Orsola Benincasa, Italy. She is the author of numerous articles and volume publications, and has presented at many local and international conferences on a variety of topics, mostly focusing, in terms of linguistic issues, on the nexus between language, identity, and power. She is currently editing a Special Issue of the *International Journal of the Sociology of Language* (De Gruyter Mouton) on transgender language with Luise von Flotow.

Annalisa Di Nuzzo (PhD in Cultural Anthropology, Migration Processes, and Human Laws) has recently obtained habilitation as Associate Professor of Cultural Anthropology and is Adjunct Professor of Geography of Languages and Migration at the Università di Napoli Suor Orsola Benincasa, Italy and a research fellow at the Università di Salerno, Italy. Her main research interests are anthropology of migrations, anthropology of tourism, anthropology and gender, and anthropology and literature. She is a member of the anthropology workshop for intercultural communication and tourism directed by Simona De Luna at the Università di Salerno. Her publications include *Fuori da casa. Migrazioni di minori non accompagnati*, Carocci, Roma, (2013), and *Napoletanità e identità post-moderne. Riplasmazioni del femminiello a Napoli., in Genere: femminielli. Esplorazioni antropologiche e psicologiche (a cura di Zito, Valerio)*, Libreria dante & Decartes Ed (2013).

Eleonora Federici (MA and PhD, University of Hull, UK) is Associate Professor of English and Translation Studies at the University of Naples "L'Orientale", Italy. Her main areas of research are translation studies, gender studies, utopian studies, and science fiction and Language for Specific Purposes (especially the language of advertising and tourism). Among her publications are *The Translator as Intercultural Mediator* (2006), *Translating Gender* (2011), and *Quando la fantascienza è donna. Dalle utopie del XIX secolo all'età contemporanea* (Carocci 2015). She co-edited *The Controversial Women's Body: Images and Representations in Literature and Arts* (2003, with V. Fortunati and A. Lamarra), *Nations, Traditions and Cross-Cultural Identities* (2009 with A. Lamarra), and *Bridging the Gap Between Theory and Practice in Translation and Gender Studies* (2013 with Vanessa Leonardi). She is currently working in translation and transnational studies in Italy.

Serena Guarracino's research interests encompass performance studies and postcolonial literature, gender, and cultural studies, with a particular focus on the relationship between literature and performativity. She authored *La primadonna all'Opera. Scrittura e performance nel mondo anglofono* (2010), and *Donne di passioni. Personagge della lirica tra differenza sessuale, classe e razza* (2011). More recently, she has written a series of articles on the role of the postcolonial writer in the public arena, featuring Salman Rushdie, J.M. Coetzee, Caryl Phillips, and Chimamanda Ngozi Adichie as case studies. She is currently teaching a course on English literature of the eighteenth and nineteenth centuries at the University of Naples "L'Orientale", Italy.

Tommaso M. Milani is Professor of Multilingualism at the University of Gothenburg, Sweden. His broader areas of research encompass media discourse, multimodality, and language, gender and sexuality. He is the co-editor of the journals *Gender and Language*, and *African Studies*. Among his most recent publications is the edited collection *Language and Masculinities: Performances, Intersections, Dislocations* (2015).

Maria Cristina Nisco holds a PhD in English Linguistics and is Senior Lecturer of English linguistics at the University Parthenope, Naples. Her current research areas include media studies, news discourse, language, identity and migration, and corpus-based discourse analysis. Her most recent publications include *Agency in the British Press. A Corpus-Based Discourse Analysis of the 2011 UK Riots* (2016), *Languaging Diversity* (co-edited with G. Balirano, 2015), and *Language, Theory and Society* (co-edited with G. Balirano, 2015). She has also researched and written on varieties of English—having authored *The Routes of English. (Un) Mapping the Language* (2010)—and translation as intercultural communication.

Laura Tommaso holds a PhD in English from the University "G. D'Annunzio" of Pescara, Italy, since 2009, and has been working as Lecturer in English Language and Literature at the University of Molise, Italy. Her main research interests are in the fields of cultural gerontology, medical discourse, and televisual genres. She is also interested in early modern and contemporary British theatre. Her recent publications include *Disorderly Families: La teatralizzazione dell'incesto da Shakespeare a Ford* (2016), "Old Age and Motherhood in April De Angelis's *After Electra*" (2016), and "The Construction of Age Identity in an Online Discourse Community: The Case of *Boomer Women Speak*" (2015).

List of Figures

List of Tables

1

Introduction

Giuseppe Balirano and Paul Baker

1 Queer masculinities: By Way of Introduction

This collection brings together diverse experiences, views, and studies stemming from original interdisciplinary research on different linguistic and cultural representations of queer masculinities in new and old media. It is a timely contribution towards ongoing research on changing representations of men and masculinities in contemporary academic studies. Each of the self-contained chapters in the volume is bound into a specific frame of reference enhancing a series of examinations on the ways that

G. Balirano (✉)
Literary, Linguistic and Comparative Studies,
University of Naples "L'Orientale", Naples, Italy

P. Baker
Linguistics and English Language,
Lancaster University, Lancashire, UK

P. Baker, G. Balirano (eds.), *Queering Masculinities in Language and Culture*,
Palgrave Studies in Language, Gender and Sexuality,
https://doi.org/10.1057/978-1-349-95327-1_1

masculinities intersect with queer identities and practices. The diverse authors who contributed to the book have analysed the representation of "queer" social actors from the perspective of gender studies, with the benefit of approaches and insights from masculinity and queer studies, linguistics, anthropology, and semiotics. Queering masculinities aims to promote a range of integrated approaches, particularly those relating to emerging ways of signifying contemporary masculinities and relating constraints, stereotypes, and prejudices within English-speaking contexts by addressing issues concerning gender in linguistic, literary, social, and cultural contexts. Hence, the book entails several analytical approaches spanning from critical discourse analysis and multimodal analysis to literary criticism and anthropological and social research.

The editors' original idea was to spark academic discourse relating to the existence of and/or resistance to non-hegemonic masculinities in order to acknowledge and foster further analyses of diverse, complementary, and/or contrasted gender identities (Connell 1995). Since masculinity is traditionally seen as one half of a mutual and binary identity construal (along with femininity), it is only through its relationship with other linguistically, semiotically, and socially construed instances of identity that contemporary dominant tropes on masculinity can be produced. The representation of hegemonic masculinity as a form of power by consent and/or power through dominance can, indeed, only gain real authority via its dichotomous interaction with the very concept of femininity, mainly in the ways that femininity serves to outline what masculinity is not (Balirano 2014). Therefore, when "kindliness", "mildness", and "passivity" are stereotypically labelled as feminine attributes, the typical masculine traits will necessarily be marked by corresponding antonyms such as "harshness", "aggressiveness", and "domination". Those forms of gender stereotypes and roles are damaging to men as maintained by one of the earliest studies dealing with the negative consequences of gender stereotypes and roles:

> The male machine is a special kind of being, different from women, children, and men who don't measure up. He is functional, designed mainly for work. He is programmed to tackle jobs, override obstacles, attack

> problems, overcome difficulties, and always seize the offensive. He will take on any task that can be presented to him in a competitive framework. His most positive reinforcement is victory.
>
> He has armor plating that is virtually impregnable. His circuits are never scrambled or overrun by irrelevant personal signals. He dominates and outperforms his fellows, although without excessive flashing of lights or clashing of gears. His relationship with other male machines is one of respect but not intimacy; it is difficult for him to connect his internal circuits to those of others. In fact, his internal circuitry is something of a mystery to him and is maintained primarily by humans of the opposite sex. (Fasteau 1975: 2)

According to Fasteau, men are socially expected to be strong, aggressive, confident, and in control of all situations at all times. Since many men find it difficult to live up to this masculine ideal, they may feel a loss of self-esteem, overcompensate with "machismo" or super-masculinity, or constantly pretend to be something they are not. Men are allowed less flexibility in gender role modelling than women: pre-pubescent females can be "tomboys", but it is still not acceptable for males of the same age range to act like "sissies". Consequently, boys must learn not to cry when they are hurt and are often pushed into "male" activities regardless of their talents or preferences. Men are forced to prove—to themselves and to others—over and again—that they are masculine.

According to Messerschmidt (2012), masculinity is not always the consequence of physical power or male brutality; it can also be seen as a discursive form of persuasion, a status each man should try and adopt in order to be empowered with those typical male features. Yet, this theorisation does not necessarily apply to those men who do not wish to align themselves with such a restrictive definition. Consequently, non-aligned forms of masculinity result in a constant re-interpretation of models at odds with prearranged schemes. Such dissident voices contribute to the construction of different stances which tend to undermine the very concept of masculinity. Novel and divergent processes of representation and re-configuration of the *nature* of manliness, seen as a social semiotic and widely shared construct, predictably mark a crisis point for hegemonic men.

When analysing masculinity as a relational construct, the hierarchies of power encompassing the different types of relationships among men must also be clearly identified. Kaufman (1994: 145) maintains that,

> [p]atriarchy exists as a system not simply of men's power over women but also of hierarchies of power among different groups of men and between different masculinities.

Conceptually, in any given society, men maintain hierarchical social roles over other men, as well as over other gender identities. Therefore, an investigation of masculinity cannot hinge on the study of a unique or homogeneous male identity unless we wish to incur the same charges made against some strands of feminist research. As Butler (1990: 3) has observed,

> there is a political problem that feminism encounters in the assumption that the term *woman* denotes a common identity. Rather than a stable signifier that commands the assent of those whom it purports to describe and represent, *women*, even in the plural, has become a troublesome term, a site of contest, a cause for anxiety.

Early masculinity theory has been frequently accused of essentialism since only the "essential" qualities of men were studied as those unique properties that make a man what he is. By privileging the concerns of white heterosexual middle-class men, terms like "men's experience" and "masculinity" reify an over-generalised, homogeneous male population.

Hegemony, then, concerns all possible kinds of masculinity, both those who make up its constituent members and those who either support or challenge it from the flanks. For that reason, Mort (1988: 195) aptly observed that "we are not dealing with masculinity, but with a series of *masculinities*" (*his emphasis*), since important factors such as class, race, sexual orientation, and many others are all *essential* in the construction of a man's identity. Consequently, the very term "masculinities" must contemplate the fact that any two performances of so-called masculine traits will never perfectly overlap. As the sociologist Connell (2005: 37–38) asserts:

> [t]o recognize diversity in masculinities is not enough. We must also recognize the relations between the different kinds of masculinity: relations of alliance, dominance, and subordination. These relationships are constructed through practices that exclude and include, that intimidate, exploit, and so on. There is a gender politics within masculinity.

Perceiving diverse forms of masculinity is only a first step towards the recognition of manifold male representations. It is also necessary to observe the relations occurring among men. Men, and their diverse forms of masculinities, cannot only be defined in relation to other men and other masculinities, but also through the study of women or femininities. Consequently, masculinities are perhaps more accurately understood in terms of complex associations of traits belonging to multiple social actors.

The acknowledgement that there are several forms of masculinities must be combined with the recognition that, as, in his seminal study on masculinities, *The Men and the Boys*, Connell (2000: 10) puts it,

> different masculinities do not sit side-by-side like dishes on a smorgasbord. There are definite social relations between them. Especially there are relations of hierarchy, for some masculinities are dominant, while others are subordinated, marginalized.

In much the same way as the identities, experiences, and practices of different groups of men and boys may vary widely, depending on factors such as age, race, culture, class, and sexual orientation, so too will their interests and forms of representation.

Male power and dominance is not typically attained by means of brute force or by issuing threats, it is *embedded*, to use Connell's expression, in society and its apparatuses and institutions such as the mass media, church, and school. Any form of dominance entails persuasion—and here the media plays a significant role—the bulk of the population that certain social institutions are acceptable because they are seen as "normal" or even natural. Connell (2005: 77) argues that, at any particular point in time, "one form of masculinity rather than others is culturally exalted", consequently the concept of "hegemonic masculinity" to refer to a particular variety of masculinity to which all others are subordinated.

Studies of hegemonic masculinity normally set out to identify a specific typology of men who thrive on power and wealth. Such research also attempts to explicate how the legitimacy of social relationships based on dominance often goes unquestioned. Culturally idealised forms of masculinity may not align with more standard forms generally practiced within a given society's history, at a particular time. Furthermore, the actual personalities of the majority of men may have little in common with the cultural ideals of masculinity. Hegemony may, in fact, resort to fantasy characters to embody its particular variety of masculinity. In later works, Connell retains the use of the concept of hegemonic masculinity as essential, since it provides "a way of theorizing gendered power relations among men, and understanding the effectiveness of masculinities in the legitimation of the gender order" (2005: xviii).

Some critics have argued that hegemonic masculinity is too stable a concept in that it suggests a static, fixed masculine identity. Caution is required, however, when claiming that "hegemonic masculinity" is always contestable and susceptible to variations in time and place. In this regard, hegemonic masculinity is not necessarily the most common pattern of masculinity, as other forms may emerge concurrently. Connell's notion of hegemonic masculinity does, after all, emphasise power relations among diverse forms of masculinities: some are dominant and others are complicit, subordinate, or marginalised.

It is essential, at this point, to specify the way in which the multifarious and diachronically baffling meaning of the word "queering" is adopted throughout this volume as a premodifier of the term *masculinities*. It is only by retrieving its original semantic value, devoid of any potentially threatening implication, that we can grant the term a new denotative and connotative value. According to the *Online Etymology Dictionary*, (Harper, D.), the term, most probably, derives from Scottish (c.1500) and originally meant "strange", "peculiar", "eccentric", a derivation from Low German (Brunswick dialect) "queer" ("oblique", "off-centre") and related to German "quer" ("oblique", "perverse", "odd"); from Old High German "twerh" ("oblique"), from PIE root *terkw- ("to turn", "twist", "wind"). Since the early twentieth century, "queer" has mainly had the meaning of "gay" or "lesbian" and for much of the time has been used with disparaging intent and perceived as insulting. Since the 1980s, the term *queer* has increasingly been adopted as a linguistic act of re-appropriation and re-signification among younger members of the gay and lesbian community as a positive term of self-reference. *Queer* has more recently come to include any person whose sexuality or gender identity falls outside the heterosexual mainstream or the gender binary: the use of *queer* avoids any specific label. For several scholars, the term *queer* does not apply to any categorical identity since it is customarily employed to refer to a wide range of social or personal events and phenomena (Halperin 1995: 61–62). Queer theory, in particular, developed alongside and out of post-structuralism, and has been extensively informed and re-contextualised by Judith Butler's theory of gender performativity (1990), whose central concept considers gender as a construction of the subject's personal repetitive performance of gender. Predictably, queer theory has stemmed out of a constellation of diverse positions since its beginning; Milani (2014) clearly summarises this critical position, putting the term *queer* in relation to several institutions and discourses, including laws, social pressure, violence, ceremonies, religious decree, and medicine.

Throughout this volume, "queer" is not employed with the primary purpose of seeking and establishing acceptance, freedom, or any sort of recognition for somewhat questionable and questioning categories of men. All of the authors in the collection, in fact, have tried to demonstrate how the common social practice of placing people and their relationships into pre-established groups or categories based on typical binary sexual/gender divide is impracticable since identities are always multiple, fluid, and thus positively *odd*. Hence, since identities necessarily tend to advance and adjust to society's continuous changes, the different studies within the collection have adopted Kulick's suggestion to push queer linguistics "beyond the study of the linguistic behavior of people we know to be, or suspect might be, gay, lesbian, bisexual, or transgendered" (2002: 68).

Some people find the refusal of queer to name what it is to be confusing and difficult to understand. Others refuse to use "queer" because the word is still associated with an insult and they cannot get behind the reclaimed and politically disruptive use of the term. Some people disagree on what queer actually means, and it has been argued that, for some scholars, it is just a fashionable word to refer to gay or lesbian, while some other people, who employ (or even abuse) the term, do not necessarily engage in the theory behind it. In addition, queer theory does not involve a specific moral, humanistic view of sexuality—Is it acceptable to say that someone who desires children or wants to rape people is "queer"? What about men who buy sex? All could be seen as "against the normal". As Baker (2008: 220–221) asks, do we draw lines based on our own values? As an off-shoot of post-structuralism, queer could even lead to nihilism.

Against this backdrop, the editors' choice of premodifying the term *masculinities* with the several meanings of "queering" arose almost naturally from the fact that many of the chapters deal with men who perform their gender identity in a way which goes against what was seen as "normal" or socially acceptable for the time period and society that they were in. All of the chapters, in fact, question mainstream society's idea of what it means to be a man. Additionally, queer voices are often marginalised, ignored, laughed at, or not given priority in society, so drawing attention to these types of men is an act of queering in itself. Some questions the authors in the collection were asked to consider were:

How could their analyses disrupt, question, or complicate traditional notions of what it means to be a man?

How could their analyses "queer" the idea of people possessing single, fixed, or stable identities or desires?

How could their analyses give a voice to an identity that is normally ignored or invisible, or how does it give a different perspective on an identity that is normally viewed as problematic?

While questioning the political implications of these claims, we posit that it is crucial to recognise the social contexts within which these questions are usually raised. Therefore, although this study is not driven by a sociological framework, it is unquestionably socio-linguistically concerned with how social context informs the claims to queer that have pervaded contemporary media representations of men over the last decades. The central purpose of this collection of chapters is not so much to question whether the process of queering masculinity is indeed taking place, but rather to inspect how the notion of queer is being articulated and mediated in portrayals of social actors. The aim, therefore, is to examine the political and social stances of these "queering" discourses when applied to male representation as a relational construct.

Queering masculinity means, above all, engaging with different points of view and with the various gazes of different men, that is, with the way men, and of course women, look out upon the world, a process notably studied by multimodal discourse analysts and found in the discourses of mainstream mass media. Representations change over time, and forms endorsed by previous generations are today threatened, under considerable pressure since contemporary social structures increasingly privilege new processes, such as consumption over production.

Queering masculinity draws on various implications and men can adopt one of its forms on the basis of their interactional needs. Those same men can, however, opt out when they feel that it does not suit their purposes. Consequently, "masculinity" is not applicable to a specific, clearly delineated, type of man but, rather, it refers to the way that men position themselves through discursive practices. It becomes evident that when such a blurred concept of masculinity intersects with other social groups, the critical ways in which discursive constructions of masculinity resonate with the reproduction of power discrimination merely serve to generate an even more complex representation (Milani 2011). As a result, it becomes impossible to detach masculinity from the overlapping cultural and political contexts in which it is regularly produced and maintained.

2 Overview of the Collection

The chapters in the book do not fall neatly into discrete "topics" which naturally suggest sections, but instead each chapter references multiple themes: neo-liberalism, normativity, intersectionality, hegemonic masculinity, marginalisation, complicity, trans identity, homophobia, stereotyping, and subordination. Additionally, the authors draw on examples from newspapers, adverts, novels, film, television episodes, and online discourse, making this a book which broadly covers a range of different types of old and newer media. It should also be noted that the majority of our contributors are from Italy, with almost all of the chapters coming from a conference which took place in Naples in 2015. While two of the chapters deal specifically with the Italian context (the pasta advert in

Chap. 3 and the discussion of Valentina OK in Chap. 9), other chapters examine data from the UK (Chap. 5's analysis of the sitcom *Vicious*, and Chap. 11's consideration of newspaper articles), or the USA (the advert for engagement rings discussed in Chap. 3, the police drama *Starsky & Hutch* in Chap. 4, and the women's prison series *Orange is the New Black* in Chap. 8). Other chapters, particularly those which deal with online data, cannot so readily be assigned to a single nationality. Our ordering of the chapters thus reflects a progressive narrative, with each chapter acting as links in chain, rather than being assigned into specific categories.

Chapters 2 and 3 in this collection relate to the relationship between queer masculinity and neo-liberal culture as articulated through advertising. Tommaso Milani, in Chap. 2, begins with a critique of the current state of queer as a theoretical concept, in light of what resistance to the normal looks like in the context of queer institutionalisation. He then moves on to provide an analysis of websites which either sell or advocate the use of prostrate massagers, ostensibly marketed towards heterosexual men. In order to carry out what is a consumerist exploitation of the rectum for the purposes of male pleasure, and bearing in mind taboos around male penetration with its associations with a homosexual or female sexual identity, to say that the advertisers have a discursive uphill struggle is something of an understatement. Following from studies which have examined how products which challenge traditional notions of masculinity (e.g. make up or plastic surgery for men) have been marketed, Milani takes a critical discourse analysis approach to consider the way that language is used to strategically legitimate the use of anal massagers by straight men while enabling them to retain heterosexual masculinity, yet also sustaining the capitalist imperative for goods and money to exchange hands.

Chapter 3 (Eleonora Federici and Andrea Bernardelli) also considers advertising that could be seen as "strategically" queer, this time relating to two mainstream television adverts (aired in Italy and America) aiming to sell pasta and engagement rings respectively. While Milani's chapter looked at how to sell a queer sexual practice to heterosexual men, this chapter focuses on the normalisation (and commodification) of same-sex relationships in a context of increasing liberalisation. The authors note some cross-cultural differences in terms of the way that such relationships are discursively constructed, although argue that despite the messages of acceptance and equality which the adverts advocate, they can also be read as fundamentally homonormative—featuring handsome, similar-looking, domesticated, masculine white men who can afford the comfortable lifestyles on display. The adverts are both inclusive and exclusionary then, inviting a subset of gay men some relief from the subordination afforded to them by hegemonic masculinity, although assuming they are willing to "buy in", not just to the product on offer, but a committed domestic partnership.

We move on to two chapters which examine queered representations of masculinity in television programmes, with both chapters focusing on a central intimate relationship between two men, although in some ways each chapter acts as an inverse image of the other. First we have Vincenzo Bavaro's chapter (Chap. 4) on the "bro-mance" relationship between two American detectives Dave Starsky and Kenneth "Hutch" Hutchinson. Both men are exemplars of hegemonic masculinity, tempered somewhat through a 1970s cultural context which was beginning to make space for more ambiguous, nuanced, and subversive types of masculinity to emerge. Indeed, Starsky and Hutch are early examples of mainstream television deflecting the male gaze to instead have the male body be the one which is looked at. While the heterosexuality of both men is firmly reiterated, it is also backgrounded, with the connection between the two men being the most explored and developed relationship in the series. Bavaro's analysis keenly shows how other forms of masculinity are also given airtime in the programme, in the unremarkable ways that a butch woman and a black man are represented and denoted as "the good guys". Perhaps ironically, Starsky and Hutch can be read as a more successful queering of masculinity than the more self-consciously "queer" texts examined in the earlier chapters.

The counterpoint to Starsky and Hutch are the two bickering camp queens in the British sitcom *Vicious*, discussed by Laura Tommaso in Chap. 5. While Starsky and Hutch are young, virile, heterosexual men, Freddie and Stuart are an elderly gay couple who spend a lot of screen time commenting in detail on how unattractive they find each other. Both couples consist of two men in strongly committed relationships, intimate rather than overtly sexual. One reading of *Vicious* is that it is complicit in the subordination of gay identities, particularly in terms of what it has to say about gay relationships, ageing, and masculinity, indulging in old stereotypes of the older gay man as effeminate and bitchy. The sitcom, in terms of the way it is filmed and its static indoor sets, brings to mind earlier British comedies from the 1970s and 1980s like *Mind Your Language*, *Are You Being Served*, and *George and Mildred*. On the other hand, Tommaso's analysis of the scripts indicates that Freddie and Stuart's relationship has stood the test of time, locating moments of genuine affection which cut deeper than the humorous barbs. It should also be borne in mind that almost all British situation comedy is concerned with unlikeable failures who never learn and grow. Additionally, the fact that two older and less than physically perfect gay men have a place on mainstream British television indicates a move away from the more sanitised and safe advertising depictions discussed earlier. Freddie and Stuart offer no apologies for who they are, and they are more than capable of responding viciously with a well-stocked arsenal of put-downs for anyone who does not like them.

A third pair of men are the subject of Chap. 6, which considers the fraternal relationship between what are traditionally seen as the original brothers—Cain and Abel. Paola Di Gennaro explores several iterations of this literary archetype, linking its development across time and over different cultures in order to chart changing understandings of masculinity. Di Gennaro argues that in certain contexts both brothers can be read as queer—Cain typically is the villainous monster, the marginalised one who is cast out, although at times Abel is represented as the more feminine of the pair, the passive victim whose voice and identity are erased. Using examples from the original Biblical text as well as medieval Christian art, Shakespearian plays, through to modern day literature, comics, and films we see how the representations of the two brothers reveal something about the ways that different cultures and time periods have conceptualised the line between normal and not normal, and how the distinction is more complex than Cain, Evil, and Abel, Good.

Chapter 7 continues the theme of examining fictional texts, but this time moves to consider representations of masculinity from the perspective of trans identities, the first of three consecutive chapters to do so. Serena Guarracino takes the 2014 novel by Kim Fu, *For Today I Am a Boy*, examining how the central character transforms from Peter to Audrey. The analysis unpicks a web of intertextual references within the novel, encompassing song, theatre, and film, with a particular focus on the way that male high voices have been historically signified as indexing a queer form of masculinity. Additionally, Guarracino considers queer masculinity from an intersectional perspective, taking into account the context of Chinese immigration to North America, and the feminisation of Asian American men through the trope of the "transvestite Oriental". Guarracino shows how the narration style of the book is deftly used to distinguish between the different identities which the main character takes on, and how this is both hampered and realised through relationships with other characters who embody more traditionally gendered characteristics—Chef and Margie, or who could be identified as queer themselves—Peter and Claire. The analysis ends with a consideration of what constitutes an authentic voice, arguing that the novel's multiple voices—a musical embodied voice and one which is literary and disincarnated reflect multiple gendered and racialised discourses, ultimately advancing a progressive message which boils down to the importance of being heard, no matter what you sound like.

In Chap. 8, Emilia Di Martino considers the African-American trans actress Laverne Cox, best known for her portrayal as a trans inmate in the critically acclaimed women's prison television series *Orange is the New Black*. Di Martino looks at the ways that Cox's identity as a black trans woman is represented in a number of different public texts—magazine covers, interviews, and dialogue from the television series. Using visual analysis, she examines how Cox's stance, her physical features, facial expression, and gaze are used to index a combination of masculine and feminine traits which subvert assumptions about gender. Di Martino focuses on the attention paid to Cox both in real life and through the way that her character Sophia interacts with others in *Orange is the New Black*, showing how Cox combines a strong "masculine" stance with a message of universal love to reverse the othering practices that are the province of dominant gendered discourses. Cox accepts her loss of privilege which is compounded through the intersections between her stigmatised and marginalised identities—she experiences a unique form of hostility which also gives her insight. Di Martino argues that in both explicit and implicit ways Cox is a queer diplomat, her personal achievements afforded a distinctly political dimension.

The third trans person in this collection is the intriguingly named Valentina OK (Chap. 9). Annalisa Di Nuzzo situates this chapter within the context of the unique city of Naples and its adoration of a local daytime television celebrity in the 1990s. Valentina OK was a trans woman who took live phone call requests and dedications from members of the public. She used the programme's simplistic format as a way of connecting with her community, through a form of interaction which could be superficially interpreted as phatic, banal, or repetitive, but also projected a reassuring sense of propriety and affection which resulted in a wide fan base, including mothers, young men, and children. By analysing screenshots and dialogue from her phone-in programme, along with interview transcripts, Di Nuzzo explains Valentina's success, but crucially links her popularity to the social conditions within Naples—its status as a liminal space which absorbs rather than rejects diversity, integrating racial, class, and gender distinctions in a way which marks the city itself as queer. As with Cox, Valentina aimed for universal love, while rejecting mainstream society's stereotyping of trans identity as sexualised or hyper-feminine. Linking Valentina's identity to the traditional *femminiello*, Di Nuzzo notes how aspects of masculinity and femininity combine in different ways—with Valentina projecting a masculine role as a social guide and community leader with one which appeared maternal and caring, and how her physical appearance incorporated elements of male and female. While Valentina was unlikely to have been aware of queer theory, Di Nuzzo shows how in her final interview statement, she was remarkably prescient and self-aware, embodying a completely queer perspective on her own identity.

In Chap. 10, Emilio Amideo focuses on the 1989 film *Looking for Langston*, directed by Isaac Julien. This chapter echoes Chaps. 8 and 9 in that it takes an intersectional perspective on queer masculinity, with its focus on an interracial love affair between two men which is set in 1920s America. Amideo's chapter proposes a new reading of the film, based on a semiotic approach, drawing on Kress and van Leeuwen's multimodal analysis and the tradition of the Caribbean diaspora. By positioning the film within the historical context of representations of black masculinity in cinema and art, Amideo argues that Julien's choice to show beautiful black male bodies is a way of countering stereotypes, aiming for the audience to experience visual pleasure rather than feeling threatened or menaced. The analysis focuses on the director's use of close-up, light and shadow, sound, gaze, body pose, and camera movement in order to create aestheticised black male bodies which challenge the idea of objective reality. Amideo also emphasises the role of water in the film, from the sound track featuring sea waves to the use of a conch shell, as a way of symbolising black queer desire, signifying the crossing of the Atlantic, from Africa to America, and creating an overlap between past and present. The conclusion focuses on the fluidity of interpretation within the film, which rejects monolithic and reductionist homophobic conceptions of black masculinity, instead enabling the possibility of sexual healing.

The final two chapters in the collection also focus on homophobic discourses as they relate to masculinity. They are both based on news stories, but in two very different contexts. In Chap. 11, Maria Cristina Nisco considers the ways that the British press reported on asylum seekers who claimed to be gay. Nisco shows how initially, the asylum-seeking process was based on a model of homosexuality which assumed all gay people (no matter where they were from) would be familiar with aspects of stereotyped western "gay culture" like knowing the playwright Oscar Wilde or liking the music of Kylie Minogue. This occurred alongside questions which focused on penetrative anal sex. It is against this backdrop that the analysis then moves to consider a set of newspaper articles about gay asylum seekers, published in July 2010, which report on a ruling which was seen as a key point in asylum policy, when a decision to deny two gay men asylum was overturned. Nisco shows how British newspapers were critical of the decision, but that the negative reporting was compounded by a focus on stereotyping remarks made by the judge, who described gay men as drinking multi-coloured cocktails and going to Kylie concerts—a linking of effeminacy with homosexuality which echoed the earlier asylum tests. Rather than taking a critical view of the judge's comments, most of the newspapers instead reified this stereotyping, complaining that the decision would "open the floodgates" to any asylum seeker who wanted to "cry gay". Nisco argues that the reporting represented a lost opportunity for a more complex discussion around stereotyping, and that future asylum testing could do more to focus on abuse rather than attempting to associate homosexuality with a handful of clumsy cultural tropes.

Finally, in Chap. 12, Andrew Brindle considers homophobic discourse articulated in the online far-right "white supremacist" internet forum Stormfront. He analyses responses to a news story about an attack by a Muslim man in a gay nightclub in 2016 which resulted in the deaths of 49 innocent people. Considering that Stormfront is heavily invested in maintaining hegemonic masculinity, Brindle examines how its members construct and orient towards different types of masculinities, focusing particularly on the contestations and ambiguities that members raised. He finds that gay men were subordinated and associated with sexual deviancy, spreading disease and paedophilia, while Muslims were labelled as a violent, savage out-group. However, some posters were supportive of the attack, viewing the attacker as having the "strength of his convictions", while others argued that the gay men in the club were human beings with families and did not deserve to be killed. On the other hand, white men were alternatively viewed as victims, repressed by a Jewish-controlled government, and preyed on by gay men, but paradoxically represented by others as powerful and at the pinnacle of civilisation. Brindle argues that hegemonic masculinity only gains meaning in relation to what it is not, and that such distinctions must be constantly reaffirmed. The differing of opinions and contestation found in the forum is likely to be attributed to multiple localised hegemonic masculinities colliding in an online environment, but also demonstrates fluidity and ambiguity in terms of how these men understand masculinity. Brindle concludes by pointing out that hegemonic masculinity sustains itself through subordination, but that it is the act of subordination rather than who is subordinated, which is key—and engaging in debate about who to subordinate constitutes a performance of hegemonic masculinity in itself. Ultimately then, Brindle notes that queer theory, in refusing to name the object and allowing for any identity to be against the normal, mirrors the tendency of hegemonic masculinity to be equally versatile in terms of loosely defining its subordinated groups.

We hope that the chapters in this collection will provoke debate, inspire further study, and raise awareness about the diverse and ever-changing ways of being a man.

References

Baker, P. (2008). *Sexed Texts: Language, Gender and Sexuality*. London: Equinox.

Balirano, G. (2014). *Masculinity and Representation. A Multimodal Critical Discourse Approach to Male Identity Constructions*. Naples: Iniziative Editoriali.

Butler, J. (1990). *Gender Trouble: Feminism and the Subversion of Identity*. New York: Routledge.

Connell, R. W. (1995). Sociology and Human Rights. *Australian and New Zealand Journal of Sociology, 31*(2), 25–29.

Connell, R. W. (2000). *The Men and the Boys*. Sydney: Allen & Unwin.

Connell, R. W. (2005). *Masculinities* (2nd ed.). Berkeley: University of California Press.

Fasteau, M. F. (1975). *The Male Machine*. New York: Dell.

Halperin, D. M. (1995). *Saint Foucault: Towards a Gay Hagiography*. New York: Oxford University Press.

Harper, D. (n.d.). *Online Etymology Dictionary*. Dictionary.com http://www.dictionary.com/browse/queer

Kaufman, M. (1994). Men, Feminism, and Men's Contradictory Experiences of Power. In H. Brod & M. Kaufman (Eds.), *Theorizing Masculinities* (pp. 142–165). Thousand Oaks, CA: SAGE.

Kulick, D. (2002). Queer Linguistics? In K. Campbell-Kibler, R. J. Podesva, S. J. Roberts, & A. Wong (Eds.), *Language and Sexuality: Contesting Meaning in Theory and Practice* (pp. 65–68). Stanford: CSLI Publications.

Messerschmidt, J. W. (2012). Engendering Gendered Knowledge: Assessing the Academic Appropriation of Hegemonic Masculinity. *Men and Masculinities, 15*(1), 56–79.

Milani, T. (2011). Introduction: Re-casting Language and Masculinities. Special Issue of *Gender and Language, 5*(2): 175–186.

Milani, T. (2014). Queering Masculinities. In S. Ehrlich, M. Meyerhoff, & J. Holmes (Eds.), *The Handbook of Language, Gender and Sexuality* (2nd ed., pp. 260–277). Malden: Wiley Blackwell.

Mort, F. (1988). Boy's Own? Masculinity, Style and Popular Culture. In R. Chapman & J. Rutherford (Eds.), *Male Order: Unwrapping Masculinity* (pp. 193–224). London: Lawrence & Wishart.

2

Is the Rectum a Gold Mine? Queer Theory, Consumer Masculinities, and Capital Pleasures

Tommaso M. Milani

1 Introduction

While witnessing the deaths and concomitant homophobic debates surrounding the AIDS epidemic in the 1980s, the American queer theorist Leo Bersani importantly asked: is the rectum a grave? This question was the starting point of an insightful critique of discourses about gay men's promiscuous anal sexual practices and their pathologisation—demonisation even—in the wake of the AIDS outbreak. Bersani provocatively concluded the essay saying that "if the rectum is a grave in which the masculine ideal [...] of proud subjectivity is buried, then it should be celebrated for its very potential for death" (1987: 222). Judging from the burgeoning male sex toy industry, one might begin to wonder whether the condition of the male rectum might be very different thirty years later, having turned from the potential grave of masculinity into a gold mine of neo-liberal masculine identities.

T.M. Milani (✉)
Department of Swedish, University of Gothenburg, Gothenburg, Sweden

P. Baker, G. Balirano (eds.), *Queering Masculinities in Language and Culture*,
Palgrave Studies in Language, Gender and Sexuality,
https://doi.org/10.1057/978-1-349-95327-1_2

It is an investigation of this potential shift in the representational regimes, and the attendant consumerist exploitation, of a male body part that this chapter aims to present. The analysis is based on a set of media texts that seek to promote sex toys said to improve the health of the male prostate, as well as produce sexual enjoyment. The chapter also seeks to re-purpose a queer theoretical approach to discourse analysis in light of a neo-Marxian commitment to unveiling the economic rationale underpinning neo-liberal regimes of consumer culture (see in particular Mieli 1980; Kirsch 2000; Penney 2014). I begin with an overview of the theoretical framework that undergirds the chapter; I then move on to give some background to research on masculinities and consumption practices in the age of neo-liberalism, before delving into a detailed analysis of relevant data. The chapter concludes with some considerations about the importance of a queer approach to global materiality for the field of language and sexuality, and masculinities more specifically (see also Peck and Stroud 2015; Bucholtz and Hall 2016; Borba 2016).

2 Re-purposing Queer Theory

Simultaneously cherished by some and loathed by others as the disobedient child of the humanities and social sciences, the notion of *queer* was born in the 1980s out of a sense of dissatisfaction among activists with sexual identity categories (e.g. gay and lesbian) as a means through which to achieve political emancipation and provide social critique. In the academic world, the originally infamous slur queer was wed to the significantly more respectable word "theory" (Kulick 2005) as a heuristic lens that ultimately resists any definition, and hence negates its very essence as theory. Such reticence against precise categorisation emerges repeatedly in the foundational texts of what would later become the field of queer studies. There, queer is presented as "whatever is at odds with the normal, the legitimate, the dominant. There is nothing in particular to which it necessarily refers. It is an identity without essence" (Halperin 1995: 61–62). Also, as Michael Warner explains, queer embodies "an aggressive impulse of generalization; it rejects a minoritizing logic of toleration or simple political interest-representation in favour of a more thorough resistance to regimes of the normal" (Warner 1993: xxvi). Differences notwithstanding, the proponents of queer theory would agree that *anti-normativity*—whatever this may mean and be in different contexts—is what differentiates queer from other concepts and approaches to understanding social texts.

Unsurprisingly, queer theory has come under fire from a variety of positions since its inception. I have summarised these critiques elsewhere (Milani 2014), so I will limit myself here to the ones that are directly relevant to the arguments mounted in this chapter. While queer was indeed born out of an anti-establishment spirit, in thirty years of life it has become so institutionalised—through conferences, journals, and even academic jobs specifically dedicated to it—that one might begin to wonder whether such institutional entrenchment is not at odds with the very spirit of queer as a form of insubordination against normative and normalising forces. In this respect, Judith Butler, one of queer theory's most authoritative voices, strongly proposes that queer

> will have to remain that which is, in the present, never fully owned, but always and only redeployed, twisted, queer from a prior usage in the direction of urgent and expanding political purposes, and perhaps also yielded in favour of terms that do [its] political work more effectively. (Butler 1993: 19)

In light of this recommendation, it might be time to re-think what a resistance to the regimes of the normal would entail in the context of queer institutionalisation. While some commentators say that we should just accept that queer is dead and is not worth reviving (see e.g. Penney 2014), others are less pessimistic and argue for the preservation of queer as an important "common good" for critical scholarship (Sicurella 2016). Cognizant of these disagreements, I believe that we should not necessarily throw the queer baby out with the institutional bath water; yet I also believe that the queer project would benefit greatly from some serious reconsideration, which might even lead to the renewed possibility of a radical politics of sexuality.

A possible way forward is offered by a "southern" perspective on queer recently advocated by a group of Brazilian scholars of sexuality (see in particular Borba et al. 2014; Miskolci 2014; Pelúcio 2014). These critical voices not only question the North American bias of queer scholarship, and the concomitant erasure of radical work on sexuality in the Global South, they also interrogate the very relevance of the notion of queer in contexts like Brazil where this word does not really have any traction. As a provocative alternative, Larissa Pelúcio draws upon the work of the Spanish thinker Beatriz Preciado in order to suggest a *teoria cu*—a theory of the anus (*cu* means *asshole* in Brazilian Portuguese)—which "is more than an attempt to translate 'queer' [...] [than] to highlight our anthropophagy by placing a certain structural emphasis on assholes and mouths; assholes and marginal production" (2014: 47). While this is a standpoint from which Pelúcio seeks to (re)launch Brazilian scholarship as a worthy margin in the global geopolitics of knowledge on sexuality, a return to the anus, in my view, might also be germane to injecting some much-needed anti-normative force into the queer academic project (see, however, Wiegman and Wilson 2015 for a critique of anti-normativity in queer).

Not only will a focus on the anus bring back some dirt to the more sanitised areas of queer inquiry, because, as Preciado aptly notes, "[h]istorically, the anus has been considered to be an abject organ, never clean enough, never silent. It is not and never will be politically correct" (Preciado 2009: 172 in Pelúcio 2014: 47), but, as this chapter demonstrates, paying attention to the anus will also force us to consider current consumerist trends which seek to incorporate the rectum into the logic of global capitalism. Finally, bringing the anus into analytical spotlight is in line with current proposals about "embodied sociolinguistics" (Bucholtz and Hall 2016) or "corporeal sociolinguistics" (Peck and Stroud 2015), which highlight how a focus on the body will bring up "topics that may be viewed as marginal to or entirely outside of some branches of sociocultural linguistics yet are crucial to the advancement of the field as a whole" (Bucholtz and Hall 2016: 174; see also Borba 2016 about the "dystopic body").

The anti-normative mantra I espouse here is not without its critics, who accuse queer theory of violating its own anti-essentialist principles and its distrust of any form of identity consolidation (e.g. Wiegman 2012; Hall 2013; Jagose 2015; Wiegman and Wilson 2015). According to these scholars, queer theory operates by reifying an anti-identitarian, anti-foundationalist, and anti-normative enterprise. As Wiegman puts it,

> Through its own self-animating antinormative intentions, then, Queer Studies gets to have its cake and eat it too: it can function as an organizing referent for queer theory while simultaneously forging an interdisciplinary critique of it; it can promise to fulfill queer theory's anti-identitarian commitments while proliferating identity commitments of its own; it can refuse institutionality while participating in and generating its own institutionalized forms. (2012: 332)

To paraphrase Wiegman, the underlying anti-normative positioning of queer theory has itself become a norm, against which both scholarly and political projects are evaluated and judged (though cf. Duggan 2015 and Halberstam 2015 for trenchant critiques of this argument). Of course, we should be wary of dispensing too easily the label of queer to, say, sexual promiscuity or sadomasochistic sex while critiquing monogamy and same-sex marriage as inherently "homonormative" institutions and practices. That being said, if queer has something that distinguishes from other approaches to the study of gender and sexuality, then its distinctiveness lies in its ability to

> create anxiety and discomfort, and a feeling that theorists and researchers are going where they shouldn't go, lighting lights that ought to stay dark, examining what many would prefer be ignored, and waking up bears that should have been left sleeping. (Kulick 2012: 31; my translation)

In a time when neo-liberalism has become hegemonic, perhaps the bear "that should have been left sleeping" is capitalism and its ability to rope gender and sexual anti-normativity into its logic. In arguing for the importance of accounting for the relationship between regimes of representations and the economic conditions that underpin them, I concur with Michael Penney (2014) that it might be worth re-discovering the ideas of Mario Mieli (1980), an Italian thinker and activist who has been largely ignored by US-based queer scholarship. In Mieli's (1980) view, radical sexual politics cannot be achieved simply through textual deconstruction of representational arrangements, but requires a critical monitoring of how capitalism incorporates non-normative identities and desires in order to reproduce itself. According to this perspective, "humanity will not be emancipated until human labour [...] ceases to be alienated in the production of falsely liberated perverse commodities" (Penney 2014: 102). So, while, in an anti-normative spirit, we might fall into the temptation of celebrating the presence of non- or anti-normative gender and sexual identities, practices and performances in mainstream media, a neo-Marxian perspective à la Mieli raises questions about the economic stakes that that very queer visibility serves for the well-functioning of global capitalism (see also Barnhurst 2007 about paradoxes of visibility, and Kirsch 2000 for a critique of queer theory in relation to class struggle).

Those who are sceptical of the possibility of the demise of capitalism would argue that we should reap the representational dividends that visibility may bring to queer constituencies rather than waste unnecessary energy critiquing a socio-economic system that will not go away so easily. But, as critical discourse analysts have pointed out ad nauseam, any form of representation—no matter how queer it seeks to be—can never be fully inclusive because of the semiotic choices made, which inherently entail the backgrounding or erasure of some elements or participants in order to foreground others (Fairclough 1995). Furthermore, even considering that we might never be able to step outside of capitalism into a different socio-economic system, the more we recognise our "capital enjoyments" (Penney 2014: 106), that is, the affective bondages between commodities, consumers, and their identities, the more likely it is that we gain critical distance from "the dictates of commodity relations" (Penney 2014: 110). But let us first take a look at the gender identity affordances that have been recently sold—quite literally—to male consumers through a variety of media sites.

3 Consumer Masculinities and Neo-liberalism

In the field of language, gender, and sexuality, Bethan Benwell has produced a thoroughgoing and acute analysis of the links between economic imperatives, the emergence of men's magazines, and the production and circulation of new masculine identities (Benwell 2002, 2003, 2004, 2005). Studying the rise of men's lifestyle products in the UK, Benwell carefully illustrates how the advent of the image of the

"New Man" in British popular culture closely tracks the expansion of the body grooming industry towards heterosexual male constituencies. Heterosexual men, who according to the prevailing stereotype were supposed not to worry about their appearance lest they were viewed as less masculine and therefore "gay," began to be hailed as the prime consumers of beauty products. The conundrum between economic growth and gender stereotyping is overcome through careful semiotic choices on the part of the advertisers of body grooming products. The men in the ads, often half-naked, photographed staring directly into the camera, are not looking at potential consumers with a same-sex desiring eye—they do not interpellate the viewer as "gay"—because a no less scantily clad woman is also pictured with the male model, warmly embracing him, thus reassuring the viewer of the heterosexual nature of her partner (see in particular Benwell 2002).

In a similar vein, Claire Harrison's (2008) analysis of advertisements of men's make-up products such as "guyliner" and "manscara" demonstrates how the producers of the ads simultaneously encourage "men to be consumers of feminine-style products while also allowing them to maintain the qualities that have traditionally been gendered as masculine" (Harrison 2008: 55). Benwell's and Harrison's works unveil the double binds engendered, on the one hand, by a growing male lifestyle industry, and, on the other, by ideas about what men should do in order not to lose their masculinity while purchasing their "new look." Such quandaries also emerge very clearly when analysing what British lads say about the products they buy, including the magazines they read (Benwell 2005). Irony, in particular, is a key rhetorical device that enables young male consumers to participate in the "feminised" domain of consumption while at the same time expressing sexist and homophobic views through which they can inhabit powerful masculine discursive positions (Benwell 2003).

An ambiguous and slippery tension between the potential threat of feminisation and the reproduction of chauvinist male dominance not only characterises the British lifestyle industry of male make-up products and lads mags, but can also be found in other areas of popular culture such as the so-called guy-lit, "'romantic sexual comedies' (Thompson 2013), written by men and with a central heterosexual male character, who is struggling with life/growing up, and looking—albeit ambivalently—for love"

(Gill 2014: 187). In these novels, male characters might appear to be unheroic, self-deprecating, or innocent; they are however no less invested in male privilege, and may even embody a post-feminist transmutation of hegemonic masculinity, one that enables men to simultaneously "hold on to social power, while presenting them as harmless and troubled victims of a world where women rule" (Gill 2014: 200).

Most crucially, the changing faces of contemporary masculinities are not simply cultural and/or discursive, but are underpinned by a neo-liberal economic rationale that is often forgotten by post-structuralist approaches to textual deconstruction. Granted, neo-liberalism has become a rather unhelpful buzzword in much scholarship, which in the fervour to define itself as critical often forgets to explain what the connotations of "neo" are in neo-liberalism. Is it just a resurgence of old ideas? Or is it a revival of old tenets under new guises? The former alternative seems to be assumed in the American economist Joseph Stiglitz's definition of neo-liberalism as "that grab-bag of ideas based on the fundamentalist notion that markets are self-correcting, allocate resources efficiently and serve the public interest well" (2008: 1). Such a characterisation is very similar to Adam Smith's (1977 [1776]) original explanation of economic liberalism. In my view, a more useful and nuanced understanding of neo-liberalism can be found in Nikolas Rose's (1999) theorisation of what he calls "advanced liberal governmentalities." Drawing on the Foucaultian notion of technologies of the self, Rose (1999) points out that neo-liberalism is not just about an ever increasing expansion of markets—for example selling grooming products to men when the demand of such goods by female constituencies is about to become saturated—but also involves a more subtle array of technologies of self-government through which the consuming individual internalises a fallacious sense of being a "sovereign subject" (Davidson and Rees-Mogg 1999), who can make his or her own choices and hence become whoever she/he wants to be. In reality she/he is simply following what the producers want him/her to do.

Overall, neo-liberal governmentality can be defined as a "global normative framework which, in the name of liberty and relying on the leeway afforded individuals, orientates their conduct, choices and practices in a new way" (Dardot and Laval 2013: 3). What should be noted in this context is the role played by "experts" in this new orientation of the conduct of the entrepreneurial self under neo-liberal conditions. As Foucault (1990 [1978]) points out, academic expertise and its knowledge production has been bound up with the emergence of the modern state. Under neo-liberal dispensations though there is a proliferation of those who count or present themselves as experts, which in turn gives rise to a cacophony of voices, each vying for hegemony in a concerted attempt "to install the capacities for self-determination and self-mastery" (Rose 1999: 89). Among these "experts" are pharmaceutical and other companies that market products to be ingested, spread over the skin, or inserted into the body, which have given rise to what Preciado (2013 [2008]) calls "pharmacopornographic capitalism," "a kind of totalized pharmaceutical control of pleasure and pain through the production of new forms of prosthetic subjectivity" (Halberstam 2013: np).

As we will see below, prostate massagers and the promotional discourses surrounding them are key "epistemological sites" (Sunderland 2004) in which heterosexual male pleasure is re-configured via a prosthetic device in the interest of their pleasures, and of capitalism's expansion. In the same way that men's grooming products "threaten" heterosexual masculinities, so do sex toys for men that involve penetration. In order to make these objects desirable for heterosexual male constituencies, then, an interdiscursive net of promotional messages and medical advice is marshalled together with the aim of foregrounding the "normality" of anal penetration as a healthy and pleasurable experience, and its compatibility with the lifestyle of a heterosexual man.

4 Prostate Massagers and the "Queering" of Heterosexual Masculinities

We saw earlier that the main aim of any approach informed by queer theory is to disrupt normality and provide counter-narratives to "common sense" ideas about gender and sexuality. Sex toys might not have become mainstream yet, but they are certainly not an idiosyncratic kink of a few enthusiasts. According to recent statistics, the annual worldwide sex toy industry revenue in 2013 amounts to over 15 billion US dollars. A comprehensive sociological analysis of who buys what and why has yet to be done on the global sex toy market. However, an investigation of the UK's most popular online retailer *Lovehoney.co.uk* (Millward 2013) might be useful in order to contextualise the analysis of prostate massagers in this chapter. Journalist John Millward analysed the sales of 1 million sex toys over a period of five months in 2013, and demonstrated that the most frequently purchased items are lube and other essentials (22%), followed by vibrators (18%) and lingerie (12%). Anal sex toys like prostate massagers and butt plugs come fourth (7%), just before cock rings (6%), jiggle balls (4%), and dildos (3%). If we then go on and see who buys anal sex toys in terms of their gender, relationship status, and sexual orientation, we discover that single men buy anal sex toys more than those in a relationship, while female customers are more equally distributed between relationship categories. If we add sexual identity into the picture, the most eager buyers are quite unsurprisingly single gay/bi men (34%), followed by gay/bi men in a relationship (29%). However, single and attached heterosexual men are not too far away, with 21% and 19%, respectively. And it is precisely how heterosexual men are targeted for the sale of anal sex toys that the present study seeks to understand. In this context, allow me to introduce Bob, the prostate massager who is the protagonist of this chapter.

Introducing Bob: "A Gentleman's Pleasure"

With its deep blue or red oblong shape, Bob is part of a "family" of no less colourful anal toys that also includes Billy, Bruno, Hugo, and Loki. They are all produced by the Swedish company Lelo, which presents itself on its website as "the world's leading designer brand for intimate lifestyle products" (https://www.lelo.com/company/about-lelo). These products are sold throughout the world not only on Lelo's own website and other specialised sites such as *Lovehoney.co.uk, Lovetreats.in, Stagshop.com*, and others, but also on general online retailers such as *Amazon.com*, which invites potential buyers with the following description (Extract 1):

Extract 1

BOB is a **gentleman's** pleasure object elegantly sculpted, with LELO's customary attention to detail, to provide exquisite tension and profound pleasure. As a gentleman's plug for deep internal stimulation, including male G-spot massage, **he** helps the user sustain sensation and **reach a new intensity of release.** Hygienic, stylish and ready for play, **he** is smooth and designed **with a ring for full control** of the sensual experience. Use BOB as you wish, whether it be with a **partner** for **added enjoyment** or as **a secret companion, worn discreetly**. Comes presented in an elegant gift box, includes a user manual, satin pouch for stylish storage and a 1-year LELO warranty. (https://www.amazon.com/LELO-Prostate-Massager-Deep-Blue/dp/B0029ZALCQ; bold emphasis added.)

Obviously inanimate objects—beers, muffins, or prostate massagers—are not inherently sexed; they do not have a penis, a vagina, or any other sexual organ. However, as scholars of gender and language have pointed out, it is interesting to tease out the processes through which objects become *gendered*, and are thus associated with either men or women and imbued with masculine or feminine traits (see e.g. Baker 2008 for the gendering of muffins, and Milani and Shaikjee 2013 for beer).

Discursive processes of gendering are quite patent in the extract above. Through a nomination strategy—Bob—and the usage of the third-person singular pronoun "he," the prostate massager is simultaneously gendered and personified, and hence partly loses its nature as an object. Furthermore, the usage of a hypocorism—the shortening and diminutive form of Robert—contributes to adding an affective layering typical of an intimate acquaintance or relationship. That this form of intimacy is "between men" (Sedgwick 1993) is made clear in the very first sentence of the product description saying that Bob is a pleasure object for a "gentleman," not a "lady."

Critical discourse analysis has taught us that speakers and writers have to make specific linguistic choices when labelling reality. The English language in its many varieties offers a plethora of options through which to refer to male bodied individuals: man/men, guy/s, dude/s, lad/s, bloke/s, bro/s, bruh/s, oke/s, and so on. Whether intentional or not, these choices are ideological because of the very different connotations that similar labels for one of the same referent carry with them. In the case of *gentleman*, the word has an aura of formality and politeness; moreover, a quick glance at its patterns of collocations in the 100 million word British National Corpus indicates that it indexes a specific type of masculinity, one that, in the context of the British parliament, is *aware*, *honourable*, *knowledgeable*, and to which other MPs are generally *grateful*. A similar search for the collocates of *gentleman* on the Corpus of Contemporary American English illustrates how this word strongly co-occurs with the following: *English*, *distinguished-(looking)*, *chivalry*, *portly*, and *dignified*, as well as with adjectives indicating old age (*older*, *elderly*, *white-haired*). I am not implying in any way that, by association with gentlemen, Bob is being advertised to British male MPs, or older, stout, distinguished, and chivalrous men. Rather, the point I want to make is that the choice of the label "gentleman" brings with it a range of generally positive associations with respectability, dignity, knowledge, and honour. I will return later on to the issue of honour in relation to shame and heterosexual erotic practices (Extracts 2 and 3).

What should also be highlighted at this juncture is how Bob is presented as bringing a "new intensity of release," which implies new levels of ejaculation for the gentlemen who buy the product. Male customers, however, are reassured that they are in charge of the situation and that the achievement of such a remarkable ejaculatory ability is always under their control. Here we can see how the trope of male sexual potency is more or less subtly reiterated and revamped at the same time as the self-determining trait of masculine subjectivity is guaranteed with the assurance of the existence of a "ring for full control" (see also below for the reproduction of hegemonic masculinity). Admittedly, it is mentioned in the following sentence that Bob can also be used with an otherwise gender-neutral "partner" for "added enjoyment." It is ambiguous here whether (1) the usage with a partner would give added value to the experience of the product; or (2) Bob would give "added enjoyment" to other sexual activities with a partner. Alternatively, Bob can fill the void of such a partner, becoming himself a "companion" to be carried around or worn "discreetly."

While self-controlled potency typical of masculine hegemony seems to be reproduced, sexual identities remain rather vague. Ultimately, we do not know whether the gentleman in the extract above is identified as heterosexual, bisexual, gay, or none of the above. On the other hand, with regard to sexual practices, there is a gesture—albeit a discreet one—towards a re-territorialisation of the domain of the erotic. Writing about the Victorian period and its historical legacy, Foucault famously pointed out that "[s]exuality [...] moved into the home. [...] A single locus of sexuality was acknowledged [...] at the heart of every household [...]: the parents' bedroom" (Foucault 1990 [1978]: 3). This is what ultimately made sex in public not only illegal but also a form of moral deviance which would breach public decency, whatever this may mean. Obviously, there is no incitement to public sex in the description of Bob above. However, the fact that it can be worn anywhere unsettles normative assumptions that (self-)erotic practices can only be conducted in the home. Though inconspicuously, Bob brings anal stimulation and pleasure into the public realm. And while the gentleman who wears it does not lose his respectability, the inconspicuousness of his enjoyment perturbs the very nature of what counts as "public indecency."

In order to unveil how more traditional hegemonic masculinity is interlinked with a more fluid treatment of sexual identities, pleasures, and practices, we need to explore other sites intertextually and interdiscursively connected to Bob and other prostate massagers.

When Anti-normative Erotic Pleasures Need to Come Out While Heterosexuality Stays Put

Like many other online retail companies, Lelo has embedded into its website a corporate blog called *Volonté*, which defines itself as a "pleasure project"; it consists of a variety of posts from condom innovation and sadomasochist sex to sexually transmitted infections. One of the most recent articles at the time of writing this chapter (July 2016) is entitled "Why Anal and Prostate Play is Worth Exploring." There the sex and relationship therapist Dr Joe Kort "discusses the benefits of prostate play and some of the societal reasons that make straight men hesitate to try anal play." One of these is that

> Extract 2
>
> Sometimes, men themselves **worry** that—because they're interested in anal play—it automatically means they're gay … or perhaps even bisexual. I like to tell them: "In the state where I am a board certified sex therapist, your **anus doesn't have a sexual orientation**." That **calms them down**. (Bold emphasis added. The underlining indicates a hyperlink that takes the web user to a webpage on "bicuriosity.")

Against this backdrop, Dr Kort goes on to suggest that

> Extract 3
>
> **Before discussing anal play with a partner, men first have to come to terms with their own shame**. They have to own the fact that this is something they like. If they come into a conversation with their partner with shame, it will only upset her more. He already has to feel that **there's nothing gay about this.**
>
> There are some great books out there that help men come to terms with their own shame. Jack Morin, Ph.D., for example, wrote Anal Pleasure and Health: A Guide for Men, Women and Couples. In it, he writes about how men can come to confront the taboo around anal pleasure, and to understand **the difference between sexual orientation and erotic orientation. You can be straight and enjoy anal sex. What we like isn't related to who we are.** If you enjoy anal sex, it's just because you experience erotic pleasure there.
>
> Once you have dealt with your own shame, you can perhaps share with your partner the prevalence of websites that exist showing women giving anal sex to men. **Its commonality may be able to help establish its normalcy**. (https://www.lelo.com/blog/why-anal-and-prostate-play-is-worth-exploring/; bold emphasis added. The underlining indicates a hyperlink that takes the web user to an Amazon webpage where they can buy the book in question.)

To begin with, it is important to point out how in these examples academic expertise works in the service of consumerism. The writer's voice on sexual matters is made authoritative through several discursive devices.

First and foremost is the usage of an honorific ("Dr"), which foregrounds his academic credentials. Another discursive strategy of authority is the reliance on the arguments made by another expert, also identified by his educational achievements ("PhD"), who has written a book on the matter. A third discursive device of authority is the rather legalistic turn of phrase "In the state where I am a board certified sex therapist," which implies that the US state apparatus stands as a warrant of the veracity of the doctor's statement. Granted, there is nothing inherently wrong in the usage of legalistic language and academic titles. What is worth questioning though is how academic knowledge gets incorporated into consumerist discourse, and is thus employed to legitimate the sale of prostate massagers.

Issues of discursive authority aside, both extracts may appear as textbook examples of what queer theorists have been preaching for the past thirty years, namely that sexual *identities* should be distinguished from erotic *practices*. In a queer fashion, Dr Kort debunks the myth according to which what you *do* in bed or elsewhere—the realm of practice—makes who you *are* sexually—the domain of identity. Indeed the human anus does not have a sexual orientation per se. It is its usage for male same-sex practices across time and contexts that have created an indexical tie between male anal sex and homosexuality. In this way, the extracts counter dominant discourses that conflate specific erotic acts with either heterosexual or homosexual identities, thus offering a counter-discourse that complicates too simple views of sexual experience.

However, such an apparently queer distinction between identities and practices fails to produce the radical re-thinking of the boundaries between heterosexuality and same-sex desire that queer theorists have been aiming for. Quite the contrary: heterosexual men are reassured that their heterosexuality remains unquestioned. The rescuing of a heterosexual identity is operated discursively via the distinction between sexual and erotic orientations. So, in line with Sarah Ahmed, we might wish to ask ourselves: "What does it mean for sexuality to be lived as oriented? What difference does it make what or who we are oriented toward in the very direction of our desire?" (Ahmed 2006: 543). And what does it mean to distinguish between erotic and sexual orientation? What Dr Kort does is encourage heterosexual men to separate their sexual orientation towards specific gendered bodies—women—from their erotic orientation towards their own bodily part—their rectums. But there is a discursive, and emotional, hindrance that must be overcome for this to happen. Prostate massagers may be marketed as a "gentleman's pleasure," as in the case of Bob, but Western masculine values of dignity and honour encoded in the very word "gentleman" are at odds with a heterosexual man openly acknowledging his enjoyment of stimulating his own prostate. This mismatch, crucially, creates the feeling of shame about men's interest in their arses.

Interestingly, the expert's suggestions about defeating shame are highly reminiscent of the advices given to lesbian and gay individuals in the so-called coming out literature (see e.g. Kaufman and Raphael 1996). In the "coming out" genre, the defeat of shame about one's sexual desires typically goes hand in hand with the embracing of a previously repressed or disavowed identity category—gay/lesbian/bisexual (see also Chirrey 2015 for critical work on the "coming out" advice genre). In contrast, in the extract above, heterosexual men are not advised to come out as anyone but themselves. There is no bottled-up identity category that needs to pop out like a jack-in-the box; rather it is their desires and enjoyments that they need to speak about openly. Unlike in Extract 1 where the word *partner* remained genderless, here it is posited as female, and nowhere in the text is it mentioned that men's pleasurable experiences of their rectums could be generated by another man manoeuvring the prostate massager. Moreover, the reference to "the prevalence of websites that exist showing women giving anal sex to men" *normalises* what at a first glance may appear as a "queer" anti-normative erotic practice. In this way, heterosexuality can stay put very solidly. But what about masculinity? While men who get penetrated by women may still be heterosexual, are they still "real" men?

"Woman Fucks Man" Reconfigures Heterosexual Intimate Life—or Perhaps Not?

In a later section of the blog post, Dr Kort addresses the issue of gender roles in the context of penetration, offering interesting views about male/female power relationships as well as mentioning the value of reversing dominant/dominated positions:

Extract 4

For some men, it may never occur to them to experiment with anal and/or prostate play. Others, however, discover the possibilities for pleasure on their own. They may have used their own fingers to explore their own areas. They may have tried using a dildo or other toy or object. Eventually, **they come to realize that solo play is not enough. It occurs to them that, in receiving anal or prostate pleasure, they can be vulnerable. They can feel submissive. They like that idea. They're just afraid to approach their female partner with their desires because they don't want to feel humiliated by it.**

When I can convince a female to try this with her partner, to perhaps use a strap-on, she is sometimes pleasantly surprised. **Many women report back to me that they've never been so wet in their life. That they felt dominant. That they were never so turned on before. He, meanwhile, was able to be submissive and vulnerable, often for the very first time. It can be a very positive experience for both partners.**

In addition to this shift in the power dynamic, many men find the prostate to be a source of great pleasure. In experimenting with prostate play, **they end up experiencing more intense, longer lasting orgasms. Sometimes they even find they can have multiple orgasms.** (https://www.lelo.com/blog/why-anal-and-prostate-play-is-worth-exploring/; underlined sections in original; bold emphasis added.)

Once again, men's anxieties about discovering the pleasures of exploring their own rectums are the backdrop against which new intimate heterosexual experiences can be enjoyed. What is particularly notable is how heterosexual men are portrayed here. They are far from being the decisive selves so common to the many dominant discourses of masculinities. Instead, they are tentative: they might start by playing with their anus on their own, before recognising that it might be more enjoyable with a female partner (see also Extract 1 above). Besides the hesitation, what goes against the dominant grain here is that these men also enjoy being submissive and being pleasured by a more agentive woman. All this suggests a re-signification of the very meaning of "fucking." It is no longer the case that "man fucks woman. Subject, verb, object" as Catherine MacKinnon (1982) cogently put it, a statement that was later buttressed quantitatively by Elizabeth Manning's (1997) corpus linguistic study of verbs denoting sexual or romantic acts. Rather, it is the woman that does the penetration, and we are told that this action not only produces pleasure for the recipient, but is also gratifying for the agent to the point that women have "never been so wet" before. Moreover, the reversal of the dominant/dominated role is said to be a beneficial experience for heterosexual intimate life in general.

That being said, is it the case that "to be penetrated is to abdicate power," as Bersani (1987: 212) argued? In my view, we should be careful about celebrating the reversal of the gender order in the promotion of prostate massagers. Women indeed become the penetrators, and they might enjoy doing it. But the submissive and vulnerable man who gets penetrated by a woman does not necessarily "abdicate power." Analogous to the post-feminist masculinities in "guy lit" analysed by Gill (2014), the submissive man in the extract above is no less masculine because of the act of penetration. Rather, the prostate stimulation not only generates more pleasure, but also enhances his sexual potency. The "more intense," "longer lasting," and "even multiple" orgasms that prostate massagers can help achieve are based on the assumptions of a "poor man" discourse (see also Sunderland 2004 for the "poor boy" discourse) that positions men as subjects in need of attention and advice; they are not exploiting their bodies to their full potential, unlike their female counterparts, whose multiple orgasms have filled the columns of lifestyle magazines such as *Cosmo* for years. One could argue then that we are witnessing here a form of colonisation of gendered discourse; what has previously been discussed around the female body has now been transferred to the male one; and this is with a view to selling prostate massagers, so that the capitalist machinery is kept well lubed.

That men do not really abdicate power in contexts of promotion of prostate massager can be illustrated with the help of another example taken from a website completely dedicated to the topic of the male orgasm:

Extract 5

Prostate Massager: Achieve the Ultimate Orgasm

The male sexual orientation is changing. For the first time in over a thousand years, it's becoming common for men to explore the pleasures of the anus and more specifically the prostate. While **gay men** have obviously

> been keen on this for a long time, **straight men** often ran for the hills when the topic of anal sex came up. Now with the interest in the prostate gland, **men around the world** are exploring a new type of sexual pleasure.
>
> What has drawn men to prostate massage is the stories of intense orgasms that men have experienced with the aid of the technique. Without a doubt that is the number one selling point for prostate massager toys. **With the help of these toys, men are able to have much longer and more satisfying orgasms than they could have through normal means. Whether using the toys during masturbation or while actually having sex, these super male orgasms are the perfect way to end any sexual session.** (http://www.mangasm.com/; bold emphasis added.)

Unlike Extracts 3 and 4, where the boundaries between same-sex desire and heterosexuality are kept watertight, the first paragraph in Extract 5 seems to suggest a diachronic progression from a time when gay and heterosexual men were divided in their very different attitudes to the erotics of the rectum, to a more recent moment of discovery where an all-encompassing category of "all men around the world" irrespective of sexual identification seem to have begun to explore a "new type of sexual pleasure." No matter how undifferentiated these men are in terms of their sexual identities, their masculine subjectivity seems to show the traits typically associated with hegemonic masculinity. The prostate massager is a prosthetic device that allows these men to achieve what had previously been impossible. Real men not only wear mascara (Harrison 2008), they also let themselves be penetrated by their female partners, and prostate massagers turn them into *sexual supermen*.

5 Conclusion

This chapter was born out of the suggestion made by some Southern scholars (Preciado 2009; Pelúcio 2014) that a focus on the anus could allow a queering of queer theory in new ways. A rectal perspective, in turn, is in line with recent proposals about (re)discovering the body as an entry point for understanding the role played by language in social processes as well as re-thinking sociolinguistic inquiry more broadly (Peck and Stroud 2015; Bucholtz and Hall 2016; Borba 2016). Looking at the male anus and its pleasures enables us to tap into the ways in which neo-liberalism operates by re-shaping heterosexual intimate life; it does so by reproducing old stereotypes of masculinity, but re-packaging them in new ways that both contest and reproduce neat divisions between sexual identity categories, sexual practices, and erotic pleasures (see also the contributors to Cornwall et al. 2016 for a series of studies about masculinities under neo-liberal conditions).

A complex nexus of producers' online advertising material and experts' advice offered a plethora of views about sexual identities and orientations, and affective concerns with the enhancement of erotic pleasure. All these discursive ingredients mixed together are not only manifestations of a new "incitement to discourse" (Foucault 1990 [1978]) about sexuality, but also indicators of that "pharmacopornographic capitalism," which, according to Preciado (2013 [2008]), polices bodies and their desiring potential among other things via a radical hybridisation of the public/private divide. In the case of sex toys for men analysed above, an individualistic male consumer is encouraged to buy prostate massagers in order to fully explore the potentials of his rectum and thus pursue a more satisfying sexual life. For this purpose, he is advised to "come out," talk about his erotic orientation towards his anus, and actively explore the pleasures of the rectum with a female partner. Doing so might imply a momentary loss of sovereignty and a temporary abdication of power, but his heterosexual identity remains intact, and he does not relinquish his masculinity. Quite the reverse: the prostate massager is a prosthetic device that allows heterosexual men to finally get back to the top of the erotic pecking order, at least where orgasms are concerned.

Most importantly, such discourses of heterosexual masculinity are tied to economic imperatives. The purchase of prostate massagers and the incitement to discourse about heterosexual men's discovery of their rectum ultimately satisfy the pleasures of the capital. From a queer perspective, we might be tempted to acclaim the appearance of historically anti-normative forms of male sexual enjoyment. But in doing so, we are actually paying lip service to the very logic of capitalism and its chameleon-like ability "to prey upon dissident desires" (Penney 2014: 101) and sexual practices, turning them into "the squalid fetishes of sex marketed by the system" (Mieli 1980: 101). Heterosexual men are encouraged to explore new erotic pleasures; through these men's uptake of this alluring promise, capitalism enjoys it too. The rectum seems to have indeed turned into one of capitalism's newly discovered gold mines.

References

Ahmed, S. (2006). Orientations: Towards a Queer Phenomenology. *GLQ: A Journal of Lesbian and Gay Studies, 12*(4), 543–574.

Baker, P. (2008). *Sexed Texts: Language, Gender and Sexuality*. London: Equinox.

Barnhurst, K. (2007). *Media Queered: Visibility and Its Discontents*. Frankfurt: Peter Lang.

Benwell, B. (2002). Is There Anything 'New' About These Lads? The Construction of Masculinity in Men's Magazines. In L. Litosseliti & J. Sunderland (Eds.), *Discourse Analysis and Gender Identity* (pp. 149–174). Amsterdam: John Benjamins.

Benwell, B. (2003). Ambiguous Masculinities: Heroism and Anti-heroism in the Men's Lifestyle Magazine. In B. Benwell (Ed.), *Masculinity and Men's Lifestyle Magazines* (pp. 151–168). Oxford: Blackwell.

Benwell, B. (2004). Ironic Discourse. *Men and Masculinities, 7*(1), 3–21.

Benwell, B. (2005). "Lucky This Is Anonymous!" Men's Magazines and Ethnographies of Reading: A Textual Culture Approach. *Discourse & Society, 16*(2), 147–172.

Bersani, L. (1987). Is the Rectum a Grave? *AIDS: Cultural Analysis/Cultural Activism, 43*, 197–222.

Borba, R. (2016). Posfácio—O corpo distópico. In G. Bonfante (Ed.), *A erótica dos signos em Aplicativos de Pegação* (pp. 313–320). Rio de Janeiro: Multifoco.

Borba, R., Lewis, S. E., Falabella Fabricio, B., & de Souza Pinto, D. (2014). Introduction: A Queer Postcolonial Critique of (Queer) Knowledge Production and Activism. In S. E. Lewis, R. Borba, B. Falabella Fabricio, & D. de Souza Pinto (Eds.), *Queering Paradigms IV: South-North Dialogues on Queer Epistemologies, Embodiments and Activisms* (pp. 1–10). Frankfurt: Peter Lang.

Bucholtz, M., & Hall, K. (2016). Embodied Sociolinguistics. In N. Coupland (Ed.), *Sociolinguistics: Theoretical Debates* (pp. 173–200). Cambridge: Cambridge University Press.

Butler, J. (1993). *Bodies that Matter: On the Discursive Limits of Sex*. New York: Routledge.

Chirrey, D. A. (2015). Formulating Dispositions in Coming Out Advice. *Discourse Studies, 13*(3), 283–298.

Cornwall, A., Karionis, F. G., & Lindisfarne, N. (Eds.). (2016). *Masculinities Under Neoliberalism*. Chicago: Zed Books.

Dardot, P., & Laval, C. (2013). *The New Way of the World: On Neoliberal Society*. New York: Verso.

Davidson, J. D., & Rees-Mogg, W. (1999). *The Sovereign Individual: Mastering the Transition to the Information Age*. New York: Touchstone.

Duggan, L. (2015). Queer Complacency Without Empire. Retrieved August 1, 2016, from https://bullybloggers.wordpress.com/2015/09/22/queer-complacency-without-empire/

Fairclough, N. (1995). *Media Discourse*. London: Arnold.

Foucault, M. (1990 [1978]). *The Will to Knowledge: The History of Sexuality Vol. 1*. London: Penguin.

Gill, R. (2014). Powerful Women, Vulnerable Men and Postfeminist Masculinity in Men's Popular Fiction. *Gender and Language, 8*(2), 185–204.

Halberstam, J. (2013). Charming for the Revolution: A Gaga Manifesto. *E-Flux, 44*(4). Retrieved August 1, 2016, from http://www.e-flux.com/journal/charming-for-the-revolution-a-gaga-manifesto/

Halberstam, J. (2015). Straight Eye for the Queer Theorist. Retrieved August 1, 2016, from https://bullybloggers.wordpress.com/2015/09/12/straight-eye-for-the-queer-theorist-a-review-of-queer-theory-without-antinormativity-by-jack-halberstam/

Halperin, D. (1995). *Saint Foucault: Towards a Gay Hagiography*. New York: Oxford University Press.

Harrison, C. (2008). Real Men Do Wear Mascara: Advertising Discourse and Masculine Identity. *Critical Discourse Studies, 5*(1), 55–74.

Jagose, A. (2015). The Trouble with Antinormativity. *Differences: A Journal of Feminist Cultural Studies, 26*(1), 26–47.

Kaufman, G., & Raphael, L. (1996). *Coming Out of Shame: Transforming Gay and Lesbian Lives*. New York: Main Street Books.

Kirsch, M. H. (2000). *Queer Theory and Social Change*. New York: Routledge.

Kulick, D. (2005). Four Hundred Thousand Swedish Perverts. *GLQ: A Journal of Gay and Lesbian Studies, 11*(2), 205–235.

Kulick, D. (2012). En unken och beklaglig människosyn: män, sex och fuktionshinder. In L. Gottzén & R. Jonsson (Eds.), *Andra män—maskulinitet, normskapande och jämställdhet* (pp. 25–44). Lund: Gleerups.

MacKinnon, C. (1982). Feminism, Marxism, Method and State: An Agenda for Theory. *Signs, 7*(3), 515–544.

Manning, E. (1997). Kissing and Cuddling: The Reciprocity of Romantic and Sexual Activity. In K. Harvey & C. Shalom (Eds.), *Language and Desire: Encoding Sex, Romance and Intimacy* (pp. 43–59). London: Routledge.

Mieli, M. (1980). *Homosexuality and Liberation: Elements of a Gay Critique*. London: Gay Men's Press.

Milani, T. M. (2014). Queering Masculinities. In S. Ehrlich, M. Meyerhoff, & J. Holmes (Eds.), *The Handbook of Language, Gender and Sexuality* (2nd ed., pp. 260–277). Malden: Wiley Blackwell.

Milani, T. M., & Shaikjee, M. (2013). A New South African Man? Beer, Masculinity and Social Change. In L. L. Atanga, S. E. Ellece, L. Litosseliti, & J. Sunderland (Eds.), *Gender and Language in sub-Saharan Africa: Tradition, Struggle and Change* (pp. 131–148). Amsterdam: John Benjamins.

Millward, J. (2013). Down the Rabbit-Hole: What One Million Sex Toy Sales Reveal About Our Erotic Tastes, *Kinks and Desires*. Retrieved August 1, 2016, from http://jonmillward.com/blog/studies/down-the-rabbit-hole-analysis-1-million-sex-toy-sales/

Miskolci, R. (2014). Queer Epistemologies. In S. E. Lewis, R. Borba, B. Falabella Fabricio, & D. de Souza Pinto (Eds.), *Queering Paradigms IV: South-North Dialogues on Queer Epistemologies, Embodiments and Activisms* (pp. 13–30). Frankfurt: Peter Lang.

Peck, A., & Stroud, C. (2015). Skinscapes. *Linguistic Landscape, 1*(1–2), 133–151.

Pelúcio, L. (2014). Possible Appropriations and Necessary Provocations for a *Teoria Cu*. In S. E. Lewis, R. Borba, B. Falabella Fabricio, & D. de Souza Pinto (Eds.), *Queering Paradigms IV: South-North Dialogues on Queer Epistemologies, Embodiments and Activisms* (pp. 53–66). Frankfurt: Peter Lang.

Penney, J. (2014). *After Queer Theory: The Limits of Sexual Politics*. New York: Pluto Press.

Preciado, B. (2009). Terror Anal: apuntes sobre los primeros dias de la revolución sexual. In G. Hocquenghem (2009 [1972]) *El Deseo Homosexual* (pp. 133–174). Barcelona: Melusina.

Preciado, B. (2013 [2008]). *Testo Junkie: Sex, Drugs, and Biopolitics in the Pharmacopornographic Era*. New York: The Feminist Press.

Rose, N. (1999). *Powers of Freedom: Reframing Political Thought*. Cambridge: Cambridge University Press.

Sedgwick, E. K. (1993). *Between Men: English Literature and Male Homosocial Desire*. New York: Columbia University Press.

Sicurella, F. G. (2016). The Approach That Dares Speak Its Name: Queer and the Problem of 'Big Nouns' in Academia. *Gender and Language, 10*(1), 73–84.
Smith, A. (1977 [1772]). *An Inquiry into the Nature and Causes of the Wealth of Nations*. Chicago: University of Chicago Press.
Stiglitz, J. (2008). The End of Neo-liberalism. *Project Syndicate*. https://www.project-syndicate.org/commentary/the-end-of-neo-liberalism?barrier=true
Sunderland, J. (2004). *Gendered Discourses*. Basingstoke: Palgrave Macmillan.
Warner, M. (1993). Introduction. In M. Warner (Ed.), *Fear of a Queer Planet* (pp. vii–xxxi). Minneapolis: University of Minnesota Press.
Wiegman, R. (2012). *Object Lessons*. Raleigh: Duke University Press.
Wiegman, R., & Wilson, E. A. (2015). Introduction: Anti-normativity's Queer Conventions. *Differences: A Journal of Feminist Cultural Studies, 26*(1), 1–25.

3

Masculinity and Gay-Friendly Advertising: A Comparative Analysis Between the Italian and US Market

Eleonora Federici and Andrea Bernardelli

1 Introduction

It is acknowledged that advertising has a social and cultural influence on contemporary society (e.g. Cook 1992; Goddard 1998; Hermeren 1999; Kelly-Holmes 2005). Advertising also has an effect on women's and men's identity formation, as well as their wider representation in different media (e.g. Goffman 1979; Cortese 2004; Parkin 2006; Cronin 2000; Carter and Steiner 2004). Every day we are surrounded by images which refer to

Federici was the lead author for parts 1, 3.2 and 4 while Bernardelli led on parts 2 and 3.1.

E. Federici (✉)
Dipartimento di Studi Letterari, Linguistici e Comparati, Università degli Studi di Napoli "L'Orientale", Napoli, Italy

A. Bernardelli
Dipartimento di Filosofia, Linguistica e Letterature, University of Perugia, Piazza dell'Università, Perugia, Italy

P. Baker, G. Balirano (eds.), *Queering Masculinities in Language and Culture*,
Palgrave Studies in Language, Gender and Sexuality,
https://doi.org/10.1057/978-1-349-95327-1_3

specific gender models and are accompanied by a language which draws on discourses which legitimize gendered social relations, identities and the notions of masculinity and femininity. Adverts and commercials contribute towards common representations of gender which often refer to stereotypes, assigning individuals to pre-established roles. Such representations are socially and historically determined (Connell 1995) and embedded both in images and words. Socially sanctioned male and female behaviours in society are mirrored in printed adverts and commercials because gender in itself is a meaning system influencing visual and verbal codes.

Because they both reflect and reproduce current social and cultural values, it is interesting to think about the many changes which have occurred in advertising through time, especially in recent decades. There have been numerous changes in advertising since Erving Goffman's touchstone study on gender in adverts in 1979. His semiotic analysis revealed how these texts were reflections of specific social themes and values. If adverts are still the results of cultural practices based on shared meanings it is clear that customs and habits have been deeply transformed. As a consequence, images of femininity and masculinity must be considered in light of cultural expectations which are continuously changing (see MacKinnon 2003; Whitehead 2002; Talbot 2000). More recent adverts demonstrate a change in thought, if not a "de-gendering" process, that is to say, nowadays we witness an ideological recycling of fixed notions of femininity and masculinity towards an idea of multiple femininities/masculinities.

Starting from these premises the analysis of adverts alluding to the LGBT community should take into account also the debate on different theoretical perspectives dealing with "queer masculinity" (Kirsch 2000; Penney 2013; Poole 2014). Keeping in mind the recent debate within Queer Studies our aim here is to analyse how the recent fluidity of gender roles and expressions in Western society has been affecting the advertising world by considering a relatively new market segment: gay and lesbian consumers (see Tuten 2005; Tsai 2004). This is a segment that has been identified as "dream consumers" (Wardlow 1996) and seen as good targets for advertisers due to having fewer financial responsibilities and large disposable incomes (although Badgett 2001 disputes the idea that gay and lesbian consumers are as affluent as they are sometimes portrayed).

Thus some recently printed adverts and commercials have represented non-heterosexual orientations in a positive way (see Baker 2008). However, the appearance of LGBT people in advertising raises further issues. For example, it is important to avoid treating gay consumers as a homogenous group with monolithic preferences and perceptions because, as scholars have already underlined, there are differences between and among gay men and women, for example the socio-political nature of lesbian identity (see Clarke 2000; Stein 1989). While adverts featuring positive representations of LGBT people can be viewed as raising visibility and thus part of the fight for social rights and legitimization (Chasin 2000), we also need to bear in mind that the primary motivation for advertising is to sell products and make profits—and this may result in discourses within advertising which conflict in subtle ways.

In this chapter we look at the representations of masculinity in gay-friendly printed adverts and commercials, focusing on the tensions between marketing and socio-political discourses that occur within them. We also offer a comparative perspective between gay-friendly advertising in Italy and in the USA, starting from two specific campaigns: "Findus Piramide" which consists of a series of commercials for the brand Findus broadcast in Italy in 2014 and Tiffany's campaign "Will You?" appearing in commercials and printed adverts in the USA in 2015. Bearing in mind that advertising reflects culturally specific practices and discourses, our goal is to foreground differences between two social contexts by analysing the extent to which Italian and North American cultures react differently to gay-friendly advertising and to map out the possible reasons for that. Despite the fact that in the North American context it is possible to recognize a recent and interesting theme, that is to say, representations of gay families, we have decided to choose examples where the focus is on the couple. This is due mainly to the fact that in our context (Italy), because of the lack of a legal recognition of gay couples and the lack of legislation for gay people who want to adopt a child, brands have not yet created adverts for gay families with children.

We have focussed on mainstream advertising rather than adverts aimed specifically for an LGBT audience. The Italian case study is from a food company campaign aimed at the general public and for which the chosen commercial is only one from a series for the same product while the American example is from a jewellery company and is also part of a wider campaign of printed and broadcast commercials about engagement rings.

Before starting the analysis it is useful to consider in more detail what is meant by the term *gay-friendly advertising* While two main typologies have been identified (the so-called "gay window advertising" (Bronski 1984) and the more recent and explicit "out of the closet" commercials and printed adverts (Kates 2000) aimed at the LGBT market), we divide LGBT advertising into three main areas:

1. the use and abuse of gay images for the heterosexual market. This means that gay images are used for heterosexual consumers and usually depict various caricatures of gay men (e.g. gay men as effeminate), drag queens (nowadays more accepted in the mainstream imagination), transvestites presented through a comic register or lesbian chic (almost used as a pornographic heterosexual image). Two examples of this kind are from the car brand Renault which in its Italian 2009 campaign presented a commercial with a drag-queen father protagonist and in 2010 portrayed a female couple flirting and blinking at the heterosexual consumer.
2. gay window advertising, which is allusive, non-explicit and non-direct; it leaves the viewer in doubt about the presence of homosexuality. In this case advertisers do not reference a homophobic sensibility, while on the other hand, they use subtle signs that could lead gay consumers to recognize themselves as the target of the message. The message is encoded: gay symbolism and codes are used for minimum risk of alienating the heterosexual consumer (see Choong 2010). In this case we have two levels in reading the adverts: one for the LGBT market and the other for heterosexual consumers. For example, Volkswagen's 1997 advert for the Golf, titled "Sunday Afternoon", managed to be memorably ambiguous with a pair of representative twenty-somethings who may or may not have been a couple, driving the car looking for old furniture.

3. "Out-of-closet advertising" which is explicit and direct, addressing the gay target immediately without leaving any doubt. The product is sold for a gay market segment, like for example, Chevrolet commercial for the 2014 Winter Olympics Opening Ceremony which features gay families together with heterosexual ones. This example could also be representative of a fourth category, that is adverts where an explicit use of LGBT people in a positive context is used also for a general market.

Taking into account commercials and adverts aimed at the LGBT community there is another distinction to be drawn: the one between commercial advertising and social campaigns. On the one hand, social campaigns are created by institutions (e.g. charities, pressure groups or political parties) in order to promote awareness and understanding about equality issues relating to gender and sexuality. On the other hand, commercial advertising refers to homosexuality for marketing reasons, aimed at (certain types of) gay consumers to connect the brand to a specific target, for example, younger and progressive consumers.

Having acknowledged this, our main question is does gay-friendly advertising advocate cultural change? In order to answer this question we will start from the assumption that advertising is connected to the brand and to the product's valorization (i.e. to say the meanings added to the product beyond its characteristics, see Floch 1990 and Kapferer 2000). In order to positively represent a product, typically controversial topics will be avoided. However, the representation of controversial topics has been used in advertising to convey specific valorizations to the product. For example, in the 1980s Oliviero Toscani and the brand Benetton proposed a series of printed advertising campaigns which directly referred to social issues such as AIDS and terminally ill patients, a kiss between a priest and a nun, and a war cemetery (see Semprini 1996). Benetton/Toscani tested conventional advertising breaking advertising rules with a series of "catastrophe" adverts recycling photographic material of TV news footage and newspapers (oil-stained birds, an Albanian boat full of would-be immigrants on the Italian coast and a burning car in a street, see Falk 1997).

It is also worth considering how the adverts relate to the concept of normativity (see Kates 1999; Wiegman and Wilson 2015). If a core aspect of Queer Theory is to take a critical stance towards the idea of fixed and stable identity categories, which are then viewed through a lens of normativity, we are interested in the ways that the adverts uphold and/or challenge models of mainstream masculinities (see Baker 2008; Milani 2014). In order to analyse our case studies from a linguistic and discursive point of view with a special attention to the ideological and cultural aspects of adverts we have found an approach that considers semiotics to be fruitful.

2 Semiotics of Advertising

Semiotics has been used to analyse different typologies of social discourse, such as journalistic, political or media discourse, including advertising discourse. A useful methodology for advertising texts is the model envisaged by Algirdas Julien Greimas (1917–1992) directly connected to Structural Analysis (particularly to L. T. Hjelmslev's theory). From this perspective, advertising has a narrative structure and can be interpreted as a sort of fairy tale or dream world. In any commercial a subject wants to achieve a goal and this occurs through the relationship between a Subject and an Object of value which the Subject wants to acquire (we are referring to Greimas's actantial narrative schema where actants are narrative roles; see Greimas 1987, 1990). The Subject is aided by a Helper in carrying out this operation, for instance, in the fairy tale Pinocchio, the Blue Fairy transforms the protagonist (a puppet) into a child, that is to say, permits the actant Subject (Pinocchio) to achieve his Object of value (being a real child). In advertising a Subject (represented by the protagonist of the printed ad or commercial) wants to obtain a specific objective, or in semiotic terms, an Object of value (seduction, beauty and success). In order to achieve this goal they need a Helper, which in advertising is represented by the product, the magic object of the fairy tale world. The actantial model can be summarized in three couples of six actants: Subject/Object, Helper/Opponent and Sender/Receiver. The Sender is the narrative role requesting the establishment of the junction between Subject and Object (e.g. the King asks the Prince to rescue the Princess) while the Receiver is the narrative role for which the quest is being undertaken (e.g. at the end of the fairy tale the King recognizes the success of the Prince's action).

In advertising, the value is given to the Object through a series of discursive and textual semantic operations. Thanks to these mechanisms, Object (product/brand) determinate values not necessarily substantial to the product (e.g. freedom, youth and success) are given. The advertised object, in its substance, becomes thus marginal, the important issues are the values that the brand/agency assigns to it or "charges" it with. For example, in order to analyse these mechanisms, Jean Marie Floch outlined a semantic model which he defined as a "grid of consumption values" (see Danesi 2013). Analysing car advertising, and then applying the same schema to other product typologies and services (furniture, hypermarket users and underground travellers), Floch created a first opposition between "basic values" and "use values" that characterize the object. With the term "use values" he means practical and utilitarian values which represent everyday actions, while "basic values" refer to existential values related to desires and troubles (existential matter). From this opposition between basic and use values Floch outlines four types of valorization of the object: (1) practical valorization, which corresponds to utilitarian values (in the case of cars to comfort, stability and reliability); (2) utopian valorization, which corresponds to existential values (e.g. identity, adventure and vitality); (3) ludic valorization, which is the negation of practical valorization (such as luxury, class and speed); and (4) critical valorization, which represents the negation of utopian valorization (based on the relationship quality/price or innovation/cost). The semiotic square is a graphic representation of a semantic micro-universe; it can be considered both from a static point of view (semantic aspects) and a dynamic point of view (syntactical aspects). Floch's categories can be so represented in Fig. 3.1 (see Floch 2001: 120).

We will refer to this schema in our analysis of the case studies here presented.

3 Analysis

Case Study 1: Findus Piramide Campaign 2014–2015[1]

As with many other countries in the early twenty-first century, attitudes to and laws around LGBT people are changing. While homosexuality has

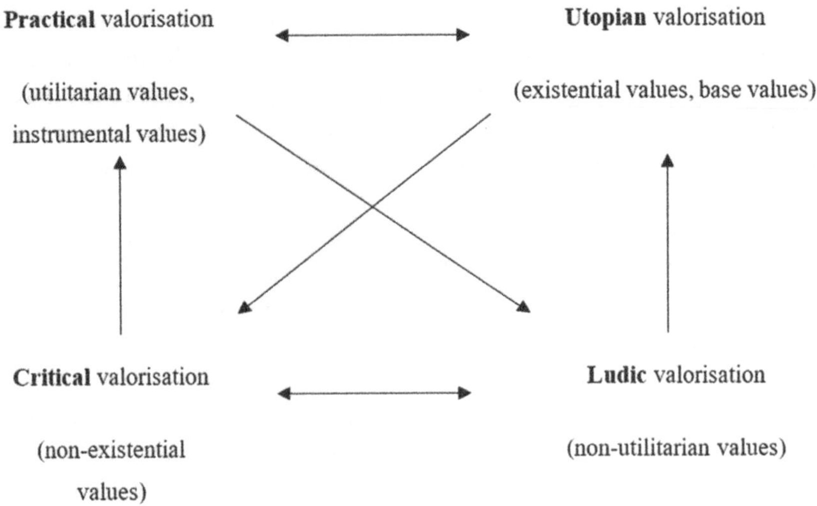

Fig. 3.1 The semiotic square

been legal in Italy since 1887, it was only in June 2016 that a law allowing civil unions for same-sex couples was passed. According to a Eurispes survey in 2016, 71.1% of Italy's residents identify as Catholic.[2] The Catholic Church opposes same-sex unions, believing homosexuality to be a "moral disorder".[3]

In Italy, adverts for the LGBT community are not common, becoming an object of discussion after Guido Barilla's declaration in 2013 that implied that the market of his brand of pasta was only for the traditional heterosexual family. This declaration had many effects worldwide especially in the North American market where Barilla is one the major Italian brands. When adverts for the LGBT community are shown they result in controversies. For example, the Tiffany's campaign that we analyse in part 3.2 was at the centre of political debate and controversy in Italy. The advertising campaign of the Findus Piramide (Pyramid) product aroused a series of strong reactions in Italy.[4] The advert introduces Luca, who invites his mother to the apartment he shares with his flatmate Gianni. After surprising her with his skill in whipping up a delicious (frozen) meal, Luca says (translated to English) "Mum, there is another little surprise. Gianni is not just my flatmate, he is my partner". The mother replies fondly "Darling, I already knew" and touches her son's hands. The coming out is not unexpected for the mother who seems more interested in the product and its novelty (reading in-between the lines what the advertiser wants to underline is that the product itself helped the mother to positively accept her son's sexuality). But to what extent does this "coming out" reflect the real-life experiences of LGBT people? And does the advert's use of a political issue feel like an overly exploitative commercial strategy? Therefore, the questions which drive our analysis of this commercial is what social and cultural valorizations are conveyed through the representation of a homosexual couple in the Italian context? Related to this, we ask who is the target advertisers aim at by their allusion to homosexuality?

We will start from the analysis of the narrative structure of the 30-second commercial. It begins with an introductory still shot (with the brand image overlapped to the shot) where a voice-over—external to the story—says: "Findus *Quattro salti* presenta..." (Findus *Quattro salti* presents..."; see Fig. 3.2).[5] The same voice-over closes the "frame" story effect at the end with a new still shot, that visually shows the product, that is to say two different types of packaging, while declaiming the brand's claim: "Findus, il sapore della vita" (Findus, the flavour of life). The story is developed within these initial and final shots. The main sequence is represented from the audio track perspective by a dialogue between two young men and the mother of one of them, a dialogue where we witness the coming out of the son. From the visual point of view the shots of this sequence seem to tell another story—apparently more neutral and banal—from the dialogue. The relevance of the dialogue over the actions represented is highlighted by the technical characteristics of the shots.

First, it is important to underline that the shots are trembling and blurred—which is technically caused by the low depth of field. Faces do not appear in the shots (see Fig. 3.2), and at the centre of the shots, perfectly in focus, is the product in its manifestations: the packaging, the plastic pyramid where the food is contained and cooked and the product's image in the dish. The subjects in the scene are identified only through their hands, the only body part which is sharpened through the close-up shot or extreme close-up (e.g. when the mother's hand is tenderly overlapping her son's hand). The fact that faces do not appear could be interpreted as a form of censorship, since we are dealing with a controversial

Fig. 3.2 Still of Findus advert

(for some) issue (homosexuality) but the same technique of not shooting the faces of the protagonists (a sort of visual rhetoric figure of *reticentia*) is used also in another commercial dedicated to the same product (where the issue of homosexuality is not at stake). What equates both commercials is the theme of seduction reflected in the product, in fact in the second one a young man seduces his girlfriend with his culinary skills, by cooking the pyramid, that is the product.

How can we interpret the audio-visual story of this commercial containing a direct allusion to homosexuality? Let's start with the voice-over. It is contemporarily meta-diegetic and extra-diegetic—it is the voice of the brand which authenticates what is within the story frame, that is to say, the diegetical part of the dialogue during the preparation of the meal. From the point of view of Greimas's actantial model this voice in the introduction has the role of the Sender: it invites the Subject—both the viewer of the commercial and the protagonist of the story—to achieve a goal. In the conclusion the same voice acquires the role of the Receiver and this confirms the success of the Subject's mission: the product (the Helper) has obtained the desired effect in helping the Subject to achieve his goal, that is to say, to convince the mother that the product is good (and that he is able to cook by himself following the national stereotype of the Italian mother cooking for her son).

What is interesting is that the voice-over—the brand that is both Sender and Receiver in this story—ratifies the novelty of the product, but only incidentally, as an unexpected consequence of what has occurred in the social sphere, that is to say, the gay couple's coming out. From the beginning the voice-over clarifies that at the centre of the viewer's attention is the product and not the social issue.

In order to corroborate this hypothesis there is a further aspect present in the dialogue sequence between mother and son, the fact of listening to voices without looking at the speakers' faces. Listening to voices without seeing faces is a typical cinematic strategy of the thriller genre and through this audio-visual technique it is possible to create tension towards a revelation or discovery (*anagnoresis*). In this commercial the shots are never focused on the speakers' faces, therefore they do not reveal the identity of the subjects in the dialogue, but only focus on the product. The real surprise, the revelation or *anagnoresis* of the story, is not the boy's outing but the novelty of the product. The mother asks her son: "Allora Luca, qual è la sorpresa?" ("So Luca what is the surprise?"). And consequently, the viewer also asks himself, what is the surprise? It is the revelation of her son's homosexuality—that she is clearly aware of, as witnessed by her answer: "Tesoro mio, l'avevo capito" ("Darling, I already knew"). The product is both at the centre of the shots and of the story. The gay couple and the revelation to the mother—a second agnoresis—is additional (in the dialogue the boy says "Mamma c'è un'altra sorpresa", "Mum, I have another little surprise") which guarantees the product a specific thematic characterization, that is to say, a valorization. The issue of the gay couple and their coming out is utilized to delineate the young and transgressive character of the product. The mother's reaction to her son's coming out could perhaps be seen as unusual, considering that some Italian parents may find it difficult to accept homosexuality. It is not by chance that recently Agedo and CondividiLove, two private associations for LGBT rights, produced an advert for 2015's Coming Out Day entitled "Amore dimmelo" (My love, please tell me) where parents talk about the coming out of their sons and daughters (https://www.youtube.com/watch?v=9O3EOmmVNdc).

The novelty of the Piramide Findus product is represented through a theme, a series of values, which belong to a determinate consumer target.

This is the answer to our initial question: who are the targets advertisers are aiming at through the allusion to homosexuality? The answer is probably highly educated, socially progressive young consumers and gay people, who could be the consumers of a ready-made meal. The idea is to market something new (a product) and link it to a contemporary social debate. The key terms which refer both to the consumer and to the cultural/social issue are novelty, transgression, youth and difference.

If we want to identify which marketing strategy is utilized in this commercial according to Floch's semiotic square and his valorizations we can map out a positioning between the utopian and ludic, because on the one hand it defines a specific consumer's identity (the product's image characterizes the consumer's existence, his self-perception), but also recalls the novelty and the transgression of a stereotyped social order (highlighted by the final claim "Findus the flavour of life"). This positioning of the product underlines how the presence of the gay couple in this commercial shows a normalization of this issue. This representation does not hurt the sensibility of the conservative audience; on the contrary it helps to sell the product. Notably, the advert represents the gay couple in a homonormative context, constructing them as similar to traditional heterosexual couples, putting them in a domestic family setting in a comfortable-looking and tastefully decorated home. Although we do not fully see the faces of the couple, they are clothed in a similar way, appear to be the same age and have similar body shapes. The family is thus signified as respectable members of the middle-class with only sexuality being a marker of difference from the norm.

Case Study 2: Tiffany's "Love Without Limits" Commercial 2013

While in Italy adverts for the LGBT community have only recently been shown, Corporate America spends billions of dollars each year targeting members of the LGBT population in the market place, believing in the lucrative potential of this marketing segment. Corporate policies have included a public stance as advocates for equal treatment for LGBT individuals under the law and businesses have given financial donations to gay causes (see Oakenfull 2013). These brands have been recognized as progressive and are aimed at the so-called "pink dollar" (a term which describes the apparent purchasing power of the gay community). Out of the closet marketing on the American market began relatively early, as can be seen from a 1994 Ikea commercial which utilized a quasi-documentary format (giving the appearance of a real couple and real life) about a gay couple shopping for home furnishings. The tagline of the commercial was "It's a big country. Someone's got to furnish it". Four years later, in 1998, Virgin Cola presented a campaign entitled "Say Something" which represented a gay marriage.[6] The 1990s were a period where the coming out of celebrities in the US became more common, so there was a public recognition of sexual identity in spite of the anti-gay conservative politics of the time. In the current context, same-sex marriage was legalized in June 2015 in the US. In 2011 a Gallup poll found that 42% of Americans identified as Protestant and 23% as Catholic.[7] The US has a longer history of LGBT representations in contexts like advertising, and is not as influenced by the views of the Catholic Church as Italy, but we also note that conservative Christianity opposes rights for LGBT people in the US too and same-sex marriage was legalized only recently.

The commercial we have chosen for the analysis is part of a wider Tiffany campaign begun in 2011 that is still ongoing at the time of writing, focussing on love relationships and inclusiveness. All the adverts in the campaign have the title "Will You Marry Me?" (2011, 2013, 2015). In its 2011 advert Tiffany presented a commercial made of a series of interviews about New York love stories told by different couples (including one gay couple, one interracial couple, one senior citizen couple and one African-American couple). It is a short film (6.32 minutes in length) directed by Edward Burns. This campaign has been the starting point for a series of adverts and commercials for Tiffany's products until the recent campaign "Will You?" planned by Ogilvy & Mather, New York (launched in 2015, 1.14 minutes in length) where different kinds of couples are shown (including an interracial couple, a gay couple (see Fig. 3.3) and a couple where they was a significant age difference).[8] This commercial was preceded by a print advert campaign about real-life couples amongst which there was a gay couple.

Fig. 3.3 Still from 'Will You?' Tiffany advert

The commercial we are analysing is entitled "Love without Limits", produced in 2013 by Blakeley Jones as copy-writer; Matt Reamer as photographer; and Karlin Lichtenberg as director—all part of the VCU Brandcenter in Richmond. The commercial is about an engagement ring specifically produced for men. Can it be seen as a smart marketing decision by the brand, or is it a sign of changing times and shifting cultural values? In this advert it seems that the video and the audio tell the viewer different stories that run in parallel: on the one hand a voice-over telling a story of love and on the other images which run shot after shot building up a visual love story. The soundtrack and the images are built up as two parallel narrative lines, a verbal story and a visual one and never overlap until they converge at the end of the commercial through the image of the product. It is the product which links the audio-visual stories. The voice-over expresses essential concepts and values of an absolute and true love connected to the brand in order to characterize the campaign "Will You?". Only at the end does the voice reveal for whom the product is, a gay couple. The revelation of the main target consumer occurs when the brand Tiffany appears on the screen and the voice-over states the commercial headline: "The first engagement ring for men". It is at this moment that the voice-over and the images converge. The visual story shows a man dressing up for a ceremony, wearing a shirt and a tie, reading aloud from a letter and then grabbing a small gift box before going out. The commercial features a series of close-up shots of two major objects (a gift box and a piece of paper containing the speech he is going to read aloud, see Fig. 3.4), and of a series of medium-long shots focussing on the subject. The editing of the different shots is suggestive of the subject's tense mood and focuses the viewer's attention on the two objects that become the co-protagonists of the scene. In the second sequence of the commercial the gift box is revealed to be a ring case while the letter is a declaration of love. We could call the first sequence of the commercial "preparatory" (where the subject acquires competence), and define the second sequence as "performative", where the subject makes clear what was virtually presented in the first part of the commercial. We can also observe a topological distinction[9]: the space of the first sequence is a closed one, it is a house in which the subject acquires the competence (the gift and the letter), while the space of the action and of the identification and agnition (both for the viewer who understands the target of the commercial and for the subjects involved in the action) is an open one. Moreover, this space is public and the couple is visible to everyone present in that

Fig. 3.4 Still from 'Love without Limits' Tiffany advert

space. The space, which is a shrine, has a glass window opened to the external world and can be seen as a metaphor of the coming out and at the same time of a desired recognition of the relationship. The idea of public recognition for gay couples is a recurring one in Tiffany's printed adverts and commercials clearly referring to the social and political context of those years.

At the beginning of the commercial the viewer is unlikely to realize that the man is gay, for 46 seconds (over the 1 minute of the entire commercial) he could be heterosexual. The truth emerges only at the end, as a revelation, like in the Italian commercial. However, the inclusion of a gay couple in a campaign about engagement rings and their story told as a love story developing through time can be considered as a means to affirm that any form of love is true and love can express itself in different forms.

The turning point in the commercial takes place inside the shrine, the background being the Virginia War Memorial, known as "Shrine of Memory" in Richmond, Virginia, built in 1956 and dedicated to fallen soldiers from WWII to the Gulf War; a monument famous for its architecture and importance to American history. This choice of location is significant as it indexes a change of attitude towards homosexuality in the US military which has come into being in the last few years. In June 2013 Chuck Hagel, at the time Secretary of Defense, acknowledged equal rights for same-sex military couples. In January 2014 President Obama positively remarked the Supreme Court ruling in favor of legalising same-sex marriage nationwide and welcomed the end of a policy which banned gay and lesbian service personnel in the army.

The gay target audience is made clear in the last 15 seconds of the commercial, and becomes an "out of the closet" example where there is no ambiguity about addressing the gay market. The ring, the product, mediates the revelation for the viewer. From the point of view of the actantial structure the product is the instrument (the Helper) for obtaining the value object (love, engagement). In the commercial the man is at the centre of the stage, looks at the engagement ring and turns when a second man enters the scene. The traditional marriage proposal is put on the stage with the man proposing on his knee (see Fig. 3.5). At this point the brand overlaps with the image of an embrace between the two men.

Fig. 3.5 Still from 'Love without Limits' Tiffany advert

Looking at Floch's valorizations we can say that they are used in a very similar way if compared to the previous case study. Once again we have a utopian valorization of the product and the product mirrors the gay couple's life. In this example the utopian valorization is aimed at a gay target, as a matter of fact the product is very specific.

The commercial is in black and white, so that we do not have a chromatic effect or, following Greimas's idea, we have a non-colour effect. Black and white gives an aura of nostalgia to the commercial and represents a timeless action; moreover, it renders the images essential and clear; the actors' faces seem endowed with more character. Similarly, places are shown in a shadow and light effect. Therefore, the use of black and white creates a romantic atmosphere and charges the action with pathos. We believe that the advert offers a new representation of masculinity which is now possible in the North American context due to increased acceptance of gay identity, although this representation partly conveys an idea of homonormativity (Duggan 2002: 179): "a politics that does not contest dominant heteronormative assumptions and institutions but upholds and sustains them while promising the possibility of a demobilized gay constituency and a privatized, depoliticized gay culture anchored in domesticity and consumption". In Fig. 3.3 the couple are both handsome, well-groomed, white, middle-class men. Apart from the fact that they are touching, they resemble the heterosexual models of hegemonic masculinity from numerous mainstream advertising campaigns such as Banana Republic, Marlboro cigarettes or Lacoste aftershave.

4 Conclusion

From the case studies analysed it is clear that the use of gay couples results in new masculinities being represented in printed adverts and commercials, both in the American and the Italian context. Advertising mirrors what is socially accepted in the context where it is presented, thus reflecting contemporary social values in the two different cultural contexts through fictional representations. The Italian example underlines a somewhat muted form of social acceptance of gay relationships, evident from the fact that there is no physical contact between the couple, and the partners are not shown to be married or engaged. Certainly there is a market for engagement rings and gay marriages in Italy but there is still social and political resistance; Italy is one of the most resistant countries within the European community against gay marriage and same-sex relationships recognition. This helps to explain why the Tiffany commercial was not shown in the Italian media. Moreover, the Italian commercial encloses the issue of homosexuality in a family atmosphere with narrative tension being created around whether the mother will show her acceptance of the son's relationship. The mother acts as a mediator with the rest of the world (and the commercial's audience). The need for a mediator figure is not present in the American commercial where the acceptance of cultural, ethnical and racial differences has probably grown more than within the Italian context. Here, nobody but the couple themselves are required to "accept" the relationship, and instead the tension arises from whether the engagement ring will be accepted.

From these examples we can affirm that the representation of gay-friendly advertising is connected to marketing strategies but structured differently according to the cultural context and the acceptance of LGBT issues. In the Italian advert the representation of the same-sex couple is still presented in an implicitly controversial way, while in the American advert we have a clearer assertion of homonormativity, due to the different political and social contexts. Moreover, in the Italian example, the representation of homosexuality is connected to the selling of a general item (food), while in the American example, the representation is strictly connected to same-sex marriage. So, in the first case study homosexuality is "used" to promote a product which has nothing to do with LGBT issues, while in the second case study marketing strategies are connected to these issues.

From a queer perspective notwithstanding the differences among the two case studies, the representation of homosexuality in both adverts is homonormative, proposing once again a traditional model of masculinity which mirrors heteronormativity. If this representation is connected to marketing strategies, and acceptable social values, it is, however, a first step in the introduction of LGBT issues in a commercial domain, and thus in the social sphere. But it should be seen as a beginning towards a wider range of diverse representations of queer people, rather than an end.

Notes

1. The campaign was produced by Havas Worldwide and planned by Havas Media, Milan.
2. http://riforma.it/it/articolo/2016/02/01/litalia-e-le-religioni-nel-2016
3. *Letter to the Bishops of the Catholic Church on the pastoral care of homosexual persons* http://www.vatican.va/roman_curia/congregations/cfaith/documents/rc_con_cfaith_doc_19861001_homosexual-persons_en.html
4. Different newspapers commented on the ad, for example, *Il Fatto Quotidiano* (B. Ballardini, "Findus, 4 schiaffi a Barilla" "Findus 4 slaps to Barilla" June 11, 2014 where the title clearly refers to Barilla's chairman's declaration that gay families did not represent his company's values prompting a boycott of Barilla's products), *Il Giornale* (G. Masini, "Findus sfratta il capitano per far posto alle coppie gay" "Findus fires the Captain to give a job to gay couples" August 11, 2014 where the title refers to the previous testimonial of the brand who was an old sailor), *Il Corriere della sera* (E. Tebano, "Il posto del barbuto capitano Findus? L'hanno preso due ragazzi gay" "The place of bearded Captain Findus? It has been taken by two gay young men) both referring to the old image of the sea captain used for the brand, which was traditional and part of a classic image of

masculinity, changed with the representation of a gay couple, but only for these new products.
5. "Quattro salti" is the name of the product line.
6. For more examples of LGBT commercials and adverts see www.commercialcloset.com
7. http://www.gallup.com/poll/1690/religion.aspx
8. In Italy this campaign has caused a strong reaction by the Conservative Party (NcD Nuovo Centro Destra) who affirmed that the printed ad showing the gay couple cannot be utilised because it will contrast with the identity of Italian people (meaning being gay means being anti-Italian). See M. Winkler's article "Tiffany, la campagna gay-friendly? Per il governo è passibile di denuncia" *Il Fatto quotidiano* Jan 13, 2015.
9. Greimas's (1989) visual semiotics distinguishes between *figurative* and *plastic* levels of analysis of an image. Figurative categories permit the identification of objects, figures and representations carrying a recognisable signifier (the figure of a man, an object). The concept of plastic signifier is used to analyse images from the point of view of three main subcategories: *topological* categories (*rectilinear* like upper/lower or felt/right and *curvilinear* like peripheral/central and closing/enclosed), *chromatic* categories (colours, brightness and saturation) and *eidetic* categories (shapes and forms).

References

Badgett, M. L. V. (2001). *Money, Myths and Change—The Economic Lives of Lesbians and Gay Men*. Chicago: University of Chicago Press.

Baker, P. (2008). *Sexed Tetxs. Language, Gender, and Sexuality*. London: Equinox.

Bronski, M. (1984). *Culture Clash: The Making of Gay Sexuality*. Boston: South End Press.

Chasin, A. (2000). *Selling Out: The Gay and Lesbian Movement Goes to Market*. New York and Basingstoke: Palgrave.

Choong, K. (2010). Targeting Gay Men: The Cryptic Approach. www.ANZMAC.org

Clarke, D. (2000). Commodity Lesbianism. In H. Abelove et al. (Eds.), *The Lesbian and Gay Studies Reader* (pp. 186–201). New York: Routledge.

Danesi, M. (2013). *Encyclopedia of Media and Communication*. Toronto: University of Toronto Press.

Duggan, L. (2002). *The Incredible Shrinking Public: Sexual Politics and the Decline of Democracy*. Boston: Beacon Press.

Falk, P. (1997). The Benetton-Toscani Effect: Testing the Limits of Conventional Advertising. In M. Nava, A. Blake, I. MacRury, & B. Richards (Eds.), *Buy This Book: Studies in Advertising and Consumption* (pp. 64–83). London: Routledge.

Floch, J. M. (2001). *Semiotics, Marketing, and Communication: Beneath the Signs, the Strategies*. Basingstoke (UK), Palgrave (first edition: *Sémiotique, marketing et communication: sous les signes, les stratégies*. Paris: PUF, 1990).

Goffman, E. (1979). *Gender Advertisements*. London: Macmillan.

Greimas, A. J. (1987). *On Meaning: Selected Writings in Semiotic Theory* (P. Perron & F. Collins, Trans.). London: Pinter.

Greimas, A. J. (1989). Figurative Semiotics and the Semiotics of the Plastic Arts. *New Literary History, 20*(3), 627–649.

Greimas, A. J. (1990). *Narrative Semiotics and Cognitive Discourses* (P. Perron & F. Collins, Trans.). London: Pinter.

Kapferer, J. N. (2000). *Les marques à l'épreuve de la pratique*. Paris: Editions d'Organisation.

Kates, S. (1999). Making the Ad Perfectly Queer: Marketing 'Normality' to the Gay Maen's Community? *Journal of Advertising, 28*(1), 25–37.

Kates, S. (2000). Out of the Closet and Out on the Street! Gay Men and Their Brand Relationship. *Psychology and Marketing, 17*, 493–512.

Kirsch, M. H. (2000). *Queer Theory and Social Change*. London: Routledge.

MacKinnon, K. (2003). *Representing Men: Maleness and Masculinity in the Media*. London: Arnold.

Milani, T. (2014). Queering Masculinities. In S. Erlich, M. Meyerhoff, & J. Holmes (Eds.), *Handbook of Language, Gender and Sexuality* (2nd ed., pp. 260–278). Hoboken, NJ: John Wiley.

Oakenfull, G. W. (2013). What Matters: Factors Influencing Gay Consumers' Evaluation of 'Gay-Friendly' Corporate Activities. *Journal of Public Policy and Marketing, 32*, 79–89.

Penney, J. (2013). *After Queer Theory: The Limits of Sexual Politics*. New York: Pluto Press.

Poole, J. (2014). Queer Representations of Gay Males and Masculinities in the Media. *Sexuality and Culture, 18*(2), 279–290.

Semprini, A. (1996). *Analizzare la comunicazione: come analizzare la pubblicità, le immagini, i media*. Milano: Franco Angeli.

Stein, A. (1989). All Dressed Up, But No Place to Go? Style Wars and the New Lesbianism. *OUT/LOOK, 1*(4), 37.

Talbot, M. M. (2000). 'It's Good to Talk?' The Undermining of Feminism in a British Telecom Advertisement. *Journal of Sociolinguistics, 4*(1), 108–119.

Tsai Wan-Hsiu, S. (2004). Gay Advertising as Negotiations: Representations of Homosexual, Bisexual and Transgender People in Mainstream Commercials. In L. Scott & C. Thompson (Eds.), *GCB—Gender and Consumer Behaviour 7* (pp. 1–26). Madison: Association for Consumer Research.

Tuten, T. L. (2005). The Effect of Gay-Friendly and Non-Gay Friendly Cues on Brand Attitudes: A Comparison of Heterosexual and Gay/Lesbian Reactions. *Journal of Marketing Management, 21*, 441–461.

Whitehead, S. (2002). *Men and Masculinities: Key Themes and New Directions.* Cambridge: Polity Press.

Wiegman, R., & Wilson, E. (Eds.). (2015). *Queer Theory Without Antinormativity*, special issue of *Differences: A Journal of Feminist Cultural Studies, 26*(1), 192.

4

Come and Get Your Love: *Starsky & Hutch*, Disidentification, and US Masculinities in the 1970s

Vincenzo Bavaro

1 Introduction

Despite the ironic ambition of my title, this chapter will not talk primarily about the production and reception of "love," nor of the 1974 hit song by Native American band Redbone from which the quotation is borrowed. It instead focuses on the American television series *Starsky & Hutch*, originally aired on the ABC network between 1975 and 1979. This chapter addresses the way in which the series responded to and rearticulated the tensions and anxieties of its era, while envisioning a strategic reconfiguration of male identity.

In the first part of this chapter, I will attempt to outline features of the cultural and social context to the series, mentioning a few crucial issues at stake during the 1970s and suggesting ways in which a complex historical moment has had an impact on gender identity. I will then move to an

V. Bavaro (✉)
Dipartimento di Studi Letterari, Linguistici e Comparati,
Università degli Studi di Napoli "L'Orientale", Napoli, Italy

P. Baker, G. Balirano (eds.), *Queering Masculinities in Language and Culture*,
Palgrave Studies in Language, Gender and Sexuality,
https://doi.org/10.1057/978-1-349-95327-1_4

analysis of a few episodes from the first season of *Starsky & Hutch*. This series largely seems to reiterate and actualize a hegemonic vision of masculinity while justifying a traditionally conservative representation of state violence. However, *in spite of* these claims, I will propose a reading of the series as a fascinating experiment in progressive screenwriting and acting, as a somewhat new product on the American television screen that attempted to challenge old conventions in the representation of men's lives. I argue that *Starsky & Hutch* opens up a window of possibility for a new and more inclusive male identity, one that, in open conflict with traditional embodiments of hegemonic masculinity, thrives in collaborative efforts with the queer other while it articulates what I call a pragmatic egalitarianism. This "window of possibility" would arguably be shut down by the neoconservative backlash of the 1980s, the Reagan era.[1]

This interpretative endeavor originates, like quite often is the case, not only from my own critical standpoint but also from a personal, autobiographical positionality. As a young queer boy growing up in the late 1980s, I watched the series reruns on Italian television. My position, which I could only begin to assess and appreciate many years later, was akin to what José Muñoz termed "disidentification" in his groundbreaking work of 1999. The term refers to a multifaceted and heterogeneous survival strategy performed by the minoritarian subject in a repressive public sphere that marginalizes her/him or erases her/his very existence (Muñoz 1999: 4). It is an appropriative gesture that is neither an obedient identification nor a confrontational counter-identification, but rather an oblique, libidinal queer appropriation of a discourse that is potentially meant to exclude the subject; it marks the inhabitation of a hostile place that successfully transforms it into a playground of possibility.

Unlike most of the television that was available at the time, *Starsky & Hutch* provided me with a livable *space*. I could dwell in-between the lines of their script, amid the protagonists' acquaintances and friends, and thrive in their silent interaction. Despite the fact that there was no "me" there, and that I could not readily identify with any of the two detectives, the series seemed to me to produce a hospitable place where people like me could exist: "we" were not the abject to exorcize and destroy, the ghostly screen onto which the hero's rightful fury had to be directed. Queers were informants, teammates, and friends: they were equal citizens, albeit on the margin of the storyline, who were treated fairly and considered as full persons.

Muñoz argues that disidentification relies on a powerful "tactical misrecognition" (1999: 160) of the Althusserian's ideological interpellation, whereby the subject may defy the State apparatus's call "Hey you!" appropriating and inhabiting positions that were not meant for her/him. The performance of disidentification, for the late scholar, disassembles the majoritarian public sphere and "uses its part to build an alternative reality. Disidentification uses the majoritarian culture to make a new world" (Muñoz 1999: 196). As I will argue later, many of the discourses articulated by the series were, indeed, not meant primarily for me or people like me, but the history of mass media is as much a story of its production as it is the story of its appropriation and defiant reception. The ten-year old me sitting unsupervised in that living room could at once consume the cathartic parable of the detection narrative (meant to purify society from the "bad guys"), appropriate the sexualization of the male body on screen, and ultimately envision a collaborative queer constellation, a utopian vision of inclusivity and respect.

My own conflicting disidentification with the series, and my retrospective understanding of it today, inform my reading of *Starsky & Hutch* and give life to the following pages.

2 Hegemonic Masculinity, Persuasion, and Historical Change

Unlike the 1960s, with their grandeur, tragedy, and social-change movements, the 1970s, known as the "Me Decade" (Wolfe 1976), were an era of limited dreams, characterized by a dramatic economic restructuring. In the United States, the old national manufacturing model gave way to a new global service model, creating an explosive combination of high unemployment rate and so-called stagflation, where a stagnant economy is coupled with high inflation rate (see Bailey and Farber 2004: 1–8). Internationally, both the OPEC oil embargo (1973) and the "Fall of Saigon" (1975) eroded the nation's self-representation and confidence. On the other hand, in the domestic arena there was a colossal defining moment: the Watergate scandal in 1974 and the resignation of President Nixon. Some of the old certainties were crumbling, and at the same time, new social and cultural phenomena were becoming more established. In fact, it was a socially explosive decade when most of the cultural changes prompted in the 1960s finally "settled in": from the normalization of sex outside marriage to a peaking divorce rate, from the erosion of censorship laws to the rise of widespread contraception. In 1973, the Supreme Court ruled in *Roe V Wade* regulating abortion rights, and in 1978 the landmark decision of the Supreme Court, known as the "Bakke" decision, upheld affirmative action programs and declared *diversity* a "compelling state interest" (see Porter 2004: 50–52; Schulman 2001: 8–14).

Many of the conflicts that arose from these social transformations were reconciled in the consumer marketplace, and on television screens. Rebecca Feasey argues that the examination of masculinity in television "is crucial, not because such representations are an accurate reflection of reality, but rather, because they have the power and scope to foreground culturally accepted social relations, define sexual norms and provide 'common-sense' understandings about male identity for the contemporary audience" (2008: 79).

The concept of hegemonic masculinity has been one of the few landmarks in the field of masculinity studies. It was first coined in the mid-1980s by the sociologist R. W. Connell and an Australian-based research group in the article "Towards a New Sociology of Masculinity", which critiqued the "male sex role" approach to masculinity and advocated for a model that could acknowledge multiple masculinities and power positions (Carrigan et al. 1985). Put concisely, it provides a framework for understanding and analyzing the most desirable and rewarded ways of being a man in a given society. However, hegemonic masculinity does not represent a certain type of man, but rather "a way that men position themselves through discursive practices" (Connell and Messerschmidt 2005: 841).

The term "hegemony," borrowed from the early twentieth-century Italian intellectual Antonio Gramsci, originally referred to class struggle and the ideological stabilization of social classes, and the "dynamics of structural changes involving the demobilization and mobilization of whole classes" (Connell and Messerschmidt 2005: 831). In other words, Gramscian hegemony evokes a relentless struggle for dominance. For

Connell, the idea of a hierarchical relation between different masculinities was initially inspired by the experience of gay men, and the violence and marginalization they received from straight men (831). Another central research area developed around the idea of complicity with hegemonic masculinity, the complicity of those men who enjoy the benefits of patriarchy, of male privilege over women, without themselves articulating dominant practices of masculinity. In other words, these men enforce and support normative models of masculinity (even though they may perceive them as oppressive for themselves) precisely because they receive benefits over women in a male-dominated social environment.

In this sense, Connell continues, hegemony means "ascendency achieved through culture, institutions, and persuasion" (832), the ideological process whereby a subordinated class internalizes the condition of its very subjugation as natural and immutable, and therefore perpetuates it: the hegemony of "hegemonic masculinities" is therefore significantly *also* the hegemony of men over men. However, with its focus on historical change, Connell highlights, the concept of hegemony is far from being a simple model of cultural control: it is a means for comprehending social dynamics. It aims, in fact, at accounting for difference (and change across time, cultures, and geographies) and power imbalances, and at overcoming clear-cut dichotomies between dominant/dominated, and investigating social transformation and multiple and overlapping layers of complicity and resistance.

When we focus on the decade of the 1970s, we can highlight how its social and cultural context informed a reconfiguration of male identity. During this decade, what R. W. Connell would term "hegemonic masculinities" was challenged by a crossfire of cultural and social forces: second-wave feminism, sexual and gay liberation, a fierce intergenerational conflict, and an ensuing widespread attack on patriarchal society. On the one hand, these movements and the discourses they produced undermined the dominance of traditional performances of gender identity, denaturalizing them. On the other hand, the social reconfiguration called for unprecedented and potentially progressive embodiments of masculinity and femininity. These new representations developed and circulated widely in the arena of popular culture, whose market-driven, consumption-oriented nature often positions it at the forefront of cultural production when it comes to responding to new needs and satisfying new sensibilities. What the success of a Supreme Court decision like "Bakke" brought to the surface again at the end of the decade was the need for a renewed self-representation of the United States. Diversity had been a compelling interest of the United States long before, but it is in the 1970s that the media industry had to finally acknowledge the full significance of this statement. Television productions became more diverse, and social minorities that had hitherto had little visibility entered the American household: with them, a plethora of social constituencies that for the first time, and only gradually, started to acquire the complexity of real characters and to steer away from a tradition of one-dimensional degrading stereotypes (Bailey 107–128). Both as an inevitable response to a changed social context and in a conscious effort to please a growing number of young viewers, some of the character types that only a generation before were connoted positively as the heroes became the villains, and social patterns associated with normalcy and "righteousness" were discredited and ridiculed.

3 *Starsky & Hutch*, the TV "Cop Genre," and Its Discontents

In April 1975, the 90-minute pilot episode of *Starsky & Hutch* aired on ABC, directed by Barry Shear and written by William Blinn (the series creator). It starred Paul Michael Glaser as David Starsky and singer/actor David Soul as Kenneth "Hutch" Hutchinson, two plainclothes detectives riding a red 1974 Ford Gran Torino in an unnamed city resembling Los Angeles. Starsky was characterized as highly excitable: later in the following seasons, viewers learn that he is a Brooklyn native from a working-class background, and that his mother was herself a member of the police force who died on the job. Hutch was portrayed as the more thoughtful of the two and from a more economically advantaged background. He eats healthy organic food and has elegant taste for interior design. The show co-starred two African American actors: Bernie Hamilton as Captain Harold Dobey, their boss, and Antonio Fargas as Huggy Bear, a flamboyant pimp-turned-informant who owns a bar in town. The producers targeted a diverse audience made of younger viewers hooked in by the fast-paced action and the car chase scenes, as well as older males who could buy into the "buddy" dynamics (Snauffer 2006: 102). Finally, it addressed a vast section of the female audience, which could make or break many television products, the intended audience of the sexualization of the two protagonists who became instant sex symbols and were shown shirtless or half naked—in locker rooms, showers, saunas, laundry rooms—an incongruous number of times (see Fig. 4.1). The show premiered in September 1975, on Wednesday at 10 pm, safely outside of family viewing time.

Police and crime drama is possibly the most masculine of all television genres, having an emphasis on physical action, the public sphere, and professional roles. Through a very simple formula—crime/pursuit/capture—the genre traditionally functions as a mechanism of social control, asserting not only the paternal care (and sanctioned violence) of the State but also the inescapability and powerlessness of the criminal. In the 1950s and 1960s, most cop characters were seen to "uphold standards of decency, honesty and humanity" and possess a strong moral compass (Feasey 2008: 82). Starting from the late 1960s, but especially in the 1970s, police force transformed into specialized squads, and this resulted in a new representation of cops that were at once more aggressive, unorthodox in their methods, and gradually out of touch with their community (Feasey 2008: 80).

The cop genre, and by extension the detection narrative at large, re-inscribes social tensions and resolves cultural anxieties by containing them into a strictly repetitive format, that aims at reassuring the viewer on the good use of the State's violence over its subjects. To some extent, the genre repetitively stages the rise of murderous chaos and anarchy in order to reinforce and justify the triumph of authority and order (Ibarra 1998: 409–414). We may argue, indeed, that the popularity of the genre quite often rises in times of crisis and social turmoil.

The 1970s were the busiest in TV history for those involved in the production of crime television (Snauffer 2006: 73). Universal Studios production, as well as the ABC network, had a leading role in this phenomenon, together with one of the most powerful TV producers,

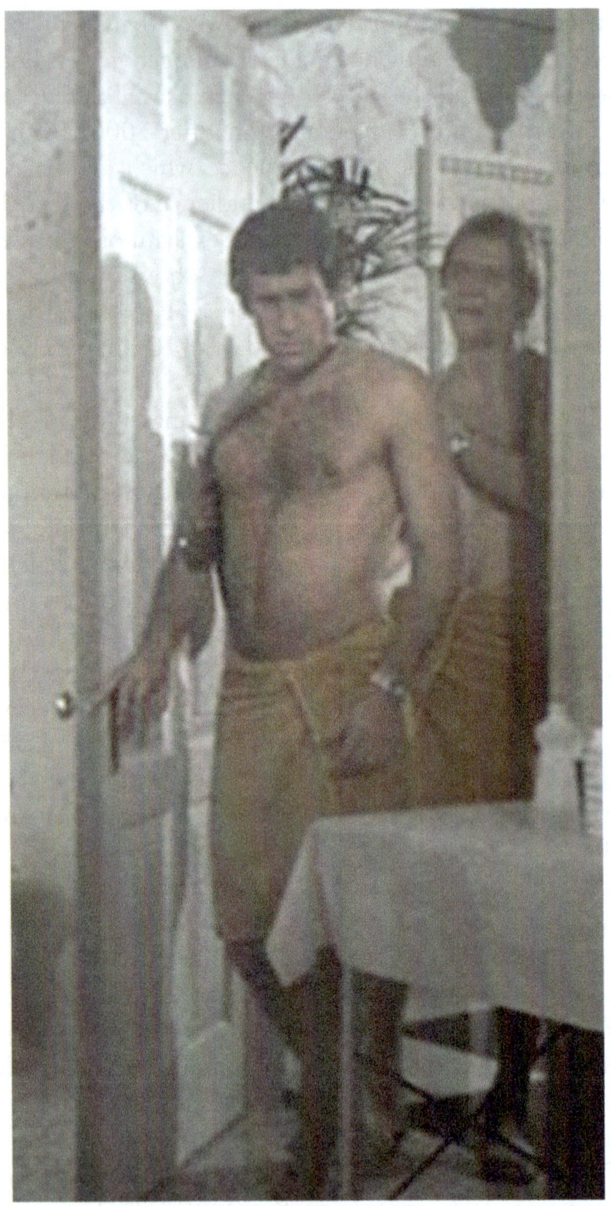

Fig. 4.1 Screenshots showing the sexualized representations of the lead actors in *Starsky & Hutch* (https://it.pinterest.com/pin/117656608994230584/; https://it.pinterest.com/pin/562457440940798439/; http://sara-merry99.livejournal.com/photo/album/1838/?mode=view&id=216389&page=1)

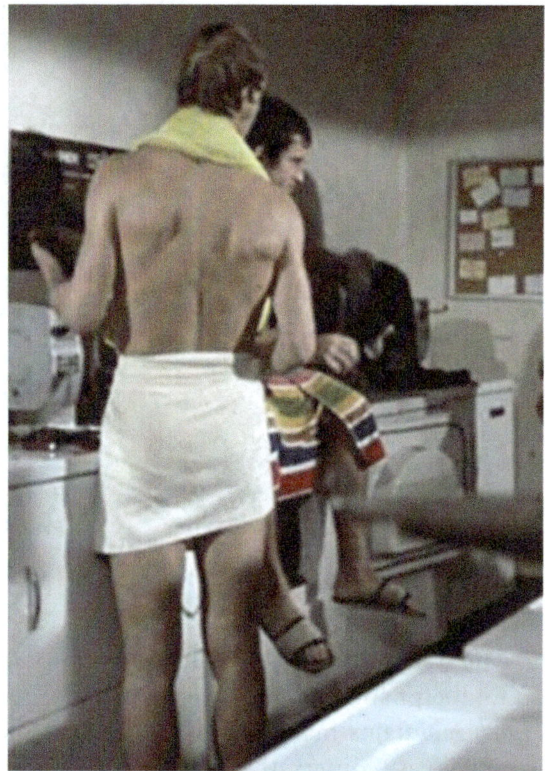

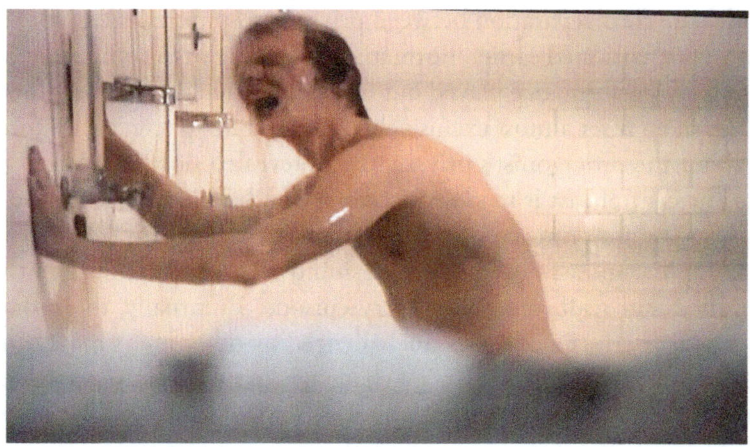

Fig. 4. 1 (Continued)

Fig. 4.1 (Continued)

Aaron Spelling, who was responsible for cult shows like *Starsky & Hutch* (with Leonard Goldberg) and *Charlie's Angels*.

Starsky & Hutch maintains many of the elements of the cop genre, most of which I define as "conservative," and consequently it also reinforces a somewhat traditional vision of hegemonic masculinity. Let us consider the clear separation between private and public sphere, for illustration. As mentioned earlier, normative masculinity is a competitive and compulsory performance played out in a public arena—for other men to see. The show is set almost exclusively in the public sphere, and information about the protagonist's private lives is revealed slowly and only partially. The central cast is made entirely of men, both in the office, on the streets, and on the crime scene. Their masculinity, leadership, self-reliance, and ability to figuratively stand above and dwarf other men is iteratively questioned and reaffirmed with every episode. Eventually, the protagonists' gender performance goes unchallenged by other men's masculinity: nowhere can we find another male character that may aspire to the leadership of the two detectives, or who can command a similar power of seduction, not even among the sympathetic co-protagonists.

Captain Dobey, despite his role as the "boss," often appears to be ineffective in his leadership, and the heroes frequently escape his authority—but after all, would they be heroes if they did not resist this hierarchy? The Captain mirrors a post-60s liberal father figure, who respects the two protagonists and is in turn respected by them, while displaying the flexible, eroded authority that often marks him as a colleague rather than a boss. On the other hand, Huggy Bear is outside of the "masculine contest," so to speak. This eccentric character, quite literally off-centered, dressed in flashy polyester suits, fedoras, bowties and jewelry, functions as a foil to the protagonists but almost always resists the simplification of a caricature, mostly by way of a powerfully (and paradoxically) nuanced acting. His performance of masculinity is outside the realm of sanctioned manhood: part pimp, part child, part queer, part womanizer—from today's perspective, his ungraspable personality makes him one of the most intriguing characters in the show. While he nominally utters his heterosexual desire from time to time, his performance of masculinity seems to subvert any expectation of normative heterosexual manhood.

Both African American co-stars, however, produce a non-threatening image of masculinity, in a time when African American cultural nationalism and political activism was circulating models of manhood and hypermasculinity that were highly visible and pervasively powerful: think Malcolm X, or the TV series *Shaft* (1973–1974), but also Huey Newton and the Black Panthers. In tune with the rise of neoliberal multiculturalism, which co-opts diversity and commoditizes it, depriving it of most of its disruptive political significance, this is an instance of increasing diversity on screen while maintaining a traditionally reassuring distribution of power for the white majoritarian audience. In truth, this practice displaces tensions and anxieties that are hardly manageable in the actual social arena. Mr. Dobey may well be the captain in the workplace, but the fictional realm of masculinity in the series is still securely in the hands of white men.

While the performance of masculinity that the heroes embody, in all its nuances and ambiguity, is presented as appealing and worthy of our admiring gaze, the male gender identity exemplified by the villains of each episode is disposed of as negative, "corrupted" and ultimately doomed to failure. In particular, most of the villains in the show are the stereotyped embodiment of popular pre-1960s hegemonic masculinities: cocky patriarchs, quite often in a suit and tie, who thrive in hierarchical relations with fellow men and subordination and objectification of women. They function as a screen onto which the new man of the 1970s can be projected, with his new understanding of sex, marriage and gender.

4 Eccentricity and Collaborative Visions

In the early examples of the "buddy cop" TV show, the two protagonists were just work "partners," however, in *Starsky & Hutch* they become best friends (Snauffer 2006: 100–102). In the pilot episode, after realizing that someone inside the police department is plotting to kill him, Starsky asks his partner "Who in the hell are we supposed to trust now?" Hutch replies "same people we always trust. Us." The two protagonists seem to have no family, or no close ties that are unrelated to their job, or that are even just unknown to the other half of the pair. Because the series begins *in media res* (not at the moment when, e.g., they first meet on the job), the audience has the impression that Starsky and Hutch have known each other for a long time, and the two reference their partner's private life, albeit seldom, in a tone that bespeaks an intimate relation. For instance, through a fleeting reference in the pilot episode, and again in the "Texas Longhorn" episode, we learn that Starsky has been dating someone for some time, and that Hutch used to be married to a certain Nancy.

Their friendship is certainly the strongest thematic core in the series, and the chemistry between the two actors articulates their relation through the scripts as well as through many sideway glances, silences, and a remarkably effusive body language. Their relationship at times resembles what we now call a *bromance* dynamics, and it is possibly one of the first representations of this kind to reach the television screens. In fact, the term was coined much later, in the late 1990s, likely within the skateboarding community, but it started to circulate widely in popular culture only in the early twenty-first century (see De Angelis). Unlike the traditional "buddy" male friendship, a *bromance* is a homosocial bond that crucially relies on a shared emotional and physical intimacy, and while it still steers away from overly sexual undertones, it effectively challenges traditional binaries of heterosexual masculinity. For example, Fig. 4.2 shows a series of screenshots (from Season 2 Episode 9), where Starsky teaches Hutch to dance, ending at a point where the pair look as if they are about to embrace.

Despite the enormous potential for a homoerotic "slash" fiction reading of the central relationship in the programme, I would argue that one of the central motifs of the series is based around mutual help and collaboration. Unlike the lonely hero of the hardboiled fiction and crime narratives of the early and mid-twentieth century (Feasey 2008: 80–93), these men crucially rely on each other and on a wide network of friends and collaborators to succeed.

Therefore, the self-reliance and independence that so strongly epitomize dominant images of masculinity are both maintained, as the cops defend their autonomy of action even from their own boss, yet also challenged, since they do not hesitate to ask for help from each other and from a vast network of eccentric collaborators. These include, for example,

Fig. 4.2 Screenshots showing Starsky teaching Hutch to dance (Season 2 Episode 9)

what seems to be a stereotypical lesbian tattoo artist, Ray, who is apparently an old friend, appearing for the first time in "Texas Longhorn," the third episode of the first season. In this episode, written by Michael Mann (who later became the award-winning director of *Collateral*, *The Insider*, *Ali*, *Heat*, among others), two criminals rob, rape, and murder the wife of a Texan car dealer, and then disappear. According to the established pattern, the two detectives have to rely first on their network of friends and acquaintances to find the criminals. When they find out that one of the aggressors had a particular tattoo on his forearm, they go to a tattoo parlor and ask their friend and tattoo artist Ray.

HUTCH: *(enters)* Ray?

RAY: *(with a cigarette between her lips, without interrupting her tattooing of a young woman's leg)* Back here! *Starsky and Hutch* … what's this?

STARSKY: Looking just fine, sweetheart *(He is standing behind Ray, facing the client. It is unclear whether he is referring to Ray or to her client).*

RAY: *(turning her head around to face Starsky)* What about me?

HUTCH: Well, you're special. We brought you something. *(showing her the photo of a full body traditional Japanese tattoo).*

RAY: That's really nice!

HUTCH: *(looking around her tattoo studio, whose walls are covered with drawings and photos of tattoos)* Where do you want me to tuck it up?

RAY: Anywhere gorgeous. (*to Starsky*) Thoughtful of you boys. *(Hutch is behind the client, and he is gesturing toward Ray to dismiss her)* … Well, that'll be 15 bucks. *(the client pays and leaves)*

STARSKY: That's a lot of lady.

HUTCH: *(now sitting in front of Ray, where the client was before. He looks in the direction of the door and then towards Ray)* Well, she was distracting. Ray you can do something for us.[2]

We understand that they are friends with her from the way they greet each other, and from the fact that Hutch brings her a gift, a photo of a

Japanese full body tattoo, which she seems delighted to receive. Ray is a short-haired, butch woman, who sports a lit cigarette in her lips and is intent on tattooing the upper leg of a young woman in a skimpy dress. As soon as the client is dismissed, Hutch exclaims, while taking a seat in front of Ray, "well, she was distracting" and glances toward the tattoo artist. Even these minor details reveal that for the protagonists Ray is a part of the team, "one of us," so to speak, not only as an acquaintance close enough for Hutch to express his implied sexual interest toward another woman, but possibly as someone who could share the same interest toward that client (distracting for whom? whose attention was required, in this scene?). With regard to this last aspect, however, the entire dynamic is so understated that we are left with mere conjectures. The way Ray addresses the two detectives, "gorgeous," and "boys," at once echoes the affectionate or seducing "sweetheart" pronounced by Starsky, and on the other, it reverses the typical masculine attitude of using nicknames to praise a woman's physical appearance and beauty, interestingly and subversively infantilizing the two detectives in the process. This scene presents the viewer with the possibility of diverging interpretations: even for just a few seconds, it displays a rather conservative imagery of two predatory men intent on seducing and visually consuming a woman's partly exposed body. Conversely, it stages a seemingly independent (and unaccompanied) young woman who is getting her skin tattooed with a traditionally rebellious mark, but also, in the character of Ray, an affirmative queer female professional who relates to the heroes in a loving and egalitarian way. The queer window that may open with Hutch's glance toward Ray and his "she was distracting" may produce a vision of inclusivity, whereby Ray's sexual desire and identification are known to the protagonists and do not constitute a hurdle to their friendship and to the apparent affective connection between them.

What is not simply conjectural, on the other hand, is the overall respectful attitude toward a cultural phenomenon and a profession like tattooing that certainly did not share the degree of popularity and respectability it has today. In fact, her response regarding who can tattoo "those kind of fish" in town ("Macao is the only place"), Ray acts as an expert professional, who knows the schools and trends in tattooing, and points the men in the right direction for solving the case. The tattoo artist, like many other analogous eccentric informants in the series, is represented as someone with whom the detectives relate respectfully and have a friendly dialogue—these are significant changes for a television genre where cops traditionally demanded obedience, or extorted information by threat (or actual use) of force, and looked down on any unorthodox lifestyles. Here instead, the two detectives courteously wave goodbye to Ray at the end of the scene, with an affectionate "See you Ray!" which sounds surprisingly chivalrous for two characters that otherwise tend to rush outside of a room heading somewhere else and interrupting whoever is in the process of talking to them. Additionally, the tattoo parlor and the tattoo artist, and even the single female client, are portrayed matter-of-factly, avoiding any charged characterization of the tattoo profession as a dirty business (and counterbalancing the fact that the murder/rapist himself had a tattoo on his forearm).

These interactions reinforce the perception that Starsky and Hutch (unlike the traditionally conservative TV cops of the previous decade, as well as most pairs of the same era) are perfectly in tune with their social environment, their narrative time and place. Not only do they withhold judgment of "eccentric subjects," in a pluralist/multicultural fashion, but they also establish synergies with them, egalitarian relations, and they treat traditionally marginalized subjects as peers, with dignity and respect. Because of their position as television role models and exemplars of masculinity, the identity they embody becomes a powerful new vision of collaborative, non-hierarchical masculinity.

5 The Caring Man

I would like to conclude with a discussion of an episode titled "The Fix" (Season 1 Episode 4), in which the progressive gender performance I highlighted above is further complicated by the representation of the "good" man as a caring man, a man who is not afraid to display physical affection to his fellow man.

In this episode (which was banned from British television in the 1970s due to the topic of heroin use), Hutch is dating a young woman named Jeanie, and judging from a photo of the couple in his bedroom, we understand that this must have been a long relationship. For the audience it may nonetheless be perceived as a surprise, an abrupt opening in the private life of a character that they had been following for a few episodes. As I mentioned above, the erasure of their private life from the narrative is a traditional move in the genre, and it is functional to the representation of their normative masculinity. In "The Fix" Hutch is kidnapped and drugged because an older mobster (played by Robert Loggia), Jeanie's former partner, wants her back. Immediately we see the obviously marked difference between the villains' masculinity, hierarchical and objectifying, and Hutch's, who protectively refuses to reveal Jeanie's location under torture, and needs to be nearly overdosed with heroin to do so. At the same time, Starsky first gives his partner a long leash for a week of absence because, as he says justifying Hutch to their boss, "Captain, he is in love!," but then he realizes that something must be wrong and finds out that *his man* is missing.

The pursuit and rescue here have an unparalleled emotional intensity: Hutch's helplessness is counterbalanced by Starsky's determination and urgency. Hutch is finally rescued, still hooked to heroin and "weak as a kitten" (in Starsky's words), and for the next two days he is kept hidden in Huggy Bear's place. Starsky is invested in finding the men responsible for Hutch's abduction and is motivated by what seems to be personal revenge: "[this case] is mine!" is what he tells Dobey, who immediately understands that the case and all the information related to it must be given to no one but Starsky. Meanwhile, at Huggy Bear's, Starsky takes care of his partner, with the help of Huggy, and the dynamic between the three is remarkably affectionate: from Huggy who does anything from untying Hutch's shoes to bringing them hot coffee, food, and towels, to Starsky who literally holds and lulls a sweating and trembling Hutch to sleep (see Fig. 4.3). In a phone call, Captain Dobey calls Huggy and in a heartfelt way says "Huggy, I appreciate what you're doing for my boys." The entire male cast embraces a motherly concern, and masculinity becomes visibly the ability to take care of your "weak other," displaying physical affection and intimacy.

The larger plot of the episode is nonetheless both classic and conservative, and reminds us of Eve K. Sedgwick's influential work on homosocial bonding in British literature (1985): in this quintessential paradigm, a

Fig. 4.3 Starsky and Huggy Bear hold Hutch as he recovers from heroin addiction

woman/outsider interferes with the intense relationship between two men causing chaos and disruption. In order for harmony to be restored, the female character must eventually disappear. "The Fix" episode inaugurates the use of Starsky and Hutch's various girlfriends, almost exclusively seen at the beginning or the end of each episode, as counterpoint to their "manly" adventures, and possibly as a guarantee of their inherent heterosexuality. Not incidentally, the absence of female characters from the visual horizon of the series also functions to reveal the two male sex objects as available to the visual consumption of the audience—an audience traditionally understood by television studies scholars as predominantly female (Joyrich 1996: 11).

6 Conclusion: The Matter with Representation

Certainly, any hegemony creates its own counter-hegemony, and any institution of power aims at maintaining its power. Therefore, we could justly ask ourselves, with the scholar MacKinnon, whether these figures of masculinity are choosing "to become less hegemonic precisely in order to stay hegemonic" (2003: 73). We must remember that we are discussing cultural products that are entangled with the dynamics of late capitalism and neoliberal cultural politics, whereby inclusivity and multiculturalism are co-opted by the forces of the marketplace, and are at the service of an increased productivity and profit making. Therefore, on the one hand, the inclusion of complex and sympathetic African American characters, as well as that of strong and independent female characters (although in both cases more peripheral to the storyline), may be suspect, because in order to appeal to a wider audience it simulates the resolution of a social conflict in the realm of representation. On the other hand, representation matters precisely *as representation*, since cultural work impacts the way in which we understand ourselves, it can give us awareness of our marginalization, as well as shape our dreams and visions of empowerment. Similarly, circulating images of counter-hegemonic masculinities, may be both a strategy for maintaining men in control (by giving them a friendlier face), or instead, as I prefer to believe, a way to envision new possibilities of masculinity, and providing powerfully appealing models that refuse hierarchy, value diversity, and embrace collaboration across difference as a strategic resource.

I intentionally resist promoting a gay reading of the relationship between the protagonists (these readings abound, as you can guess, both by the gay community and by homophobic viewers) not only because at this point in critical history they are relatively easy to make, but also, and more precisely, because I am fascinated by the cultural significance of these two men being, after all, embodiments of a "new" heterosexual man (see also De Angelis 2014). The performance of gender they endorse is therefore, or strives to be, an innovative "mainstream" embodiment of masculinity: to envision any variation from a dominant, traditional representation of manhood as a "gay" variation is clearly reductive, and it jeopardizes the very transformation and struggle that concepts like "hegemony" evoke. If they were gay, anything they say or do would always already be outside of the sanctioned masculine behavior: this rhetorical move would do nothing but stabilize a monolithic and oppressive understanding of heterosexual masculinity, rather than questioning its inherently exclusionary construction. This would actually be in line with the most oppressively bigoted ideas that define physical displays of affection between men, as well as emotionality, caring and empathy across diversity, as less-than-masculine, or other-than-masculine.

In other words, it is precisely because this television series is expanding the realm of alluring "straight" masculinity, embracing egalitarianism, cooperation, and the display of affection as its main features, that I argued for its potentially progressive message.

The title of this chapter aims at highlighting, somewhat ironically, precisely this libidinal traffic, this circulation of affect and attachment, both within the show and between the series and its audience. The direct interpellation of the Redbone's hit song, *Come and Get Your Love*, then may signal at once the ideological power of the media, imperatively addressing the individual viewer to "join" its product, but simultaneously it marks its own powerlessness in the face of that viewer's agency. It is *your* love, after all, that you are going to *get*, and the act of viewing, of consuming the media product becomes in itself an active, and potentially subversive, appropriation: one that I evoked at the beginning of this chapter by borrowing the notion of "disidentification" by the late scholar Muñoz.

The massive circulation of these images of care, collaboration, and egalitarianism becomes a trademark of the series and the performance of masculinity it endorses and even encourages. It creates a productive, counter-hegemonic space of possibility for a queer utopian community, which is less a revolutionary rewriting of gender identity and structural power imbalance as it is a strategic egalitarianism aimed at producing a functioning and successful new society, and it is therefore uniquely entangled in a historical time of reconfiguration of gender and national identity.

Notes

1. A satisfactory outline of the extent of the 1980s backlash clearly exceeds the scope of this chapter. Let me just mention here the heating of the Cold War by the Reagan administration following several operations in Latin America and Africa, as well as the erosion of policies supporting social justice and the aggressive pursuit of a neoliberal economic agenda, and finally the systematic attempt to justify through religious language a conservative political agenda. Many of these issues converged in the AIDS crisis and Reagan's responsibility and disastrous (in)actions in response to it.
2. The transcript of this scene is mine, from *Starsky & Hutch: Season 1.* (2014) DVD version.

References

Bailey, B., & Farber, D. (Eds.). (2004). *America in the Seventies*. Lawrence, KS: University of Kansas Press.

Carrigan, T., Connell, R. W., & Lee, J. (1985). Towards a New Sociology of Masculinity. *Theory and Society, 14*(5), 551–604.

Connell, R. W., & Messerschmidt, J. W. (2005). Hegemonic Masculinity: Rethinking the Concept. *Gender & Society, 19*(6), 829–859.

De Angelis, M. (Ed.). (2014). *Reading the Bromance. Homosocial Relationships in Film and Television*. Detroit: Wayne State University Press.

Feasey, R. (2008). *Masculinity and Popular Television*. Edinburg: Edinburgh University Press.

Ibarra, P. R. (1998). Dislocating Moral Order and Social Identity in Cinematic Space: The Inverted Detective Figure in *Tightrope* and *Cruising*. *The Sociological Quarterly, 39*(3), 409–433.

Joyrich, L. (1996). *Reviewing Reception, Television, Gender and Postmodern Culture*. Bloomington: Indiana University Press.

MacKinnon, K. (2003). *Representing Men: Maleness and Masculinity in the Media*. London: Arnold.

Muñoz, J. E. (1999). *Disidentifications. Queers of Color and the Performance of Politics*. Minneapolis: University of Minnesota Press.

Porter, E. (2004). Affirming and Disaffirming Actions. Remaking Race in the 1970s. In B. Bailey & D. Farber (Eds.), *America in the Seventies* (pp. 50–74). Lawrence, KS: University of Kansas Press.

Schulman, B. J. (2001). The Seventies. In *The Great Shift in American Culture, Society and Politics*. Cambridge, MA: Da Capo Press.

Sedgwick, E. K. (1985). *Between Men: English Literature and Male Homosocial Desire*. New York: Columbia University Press.

Snauffer, D. (2006). *Crime Television*. Westport, CT: Praeger.

Wolfe, T. (1976, August 23). The 'Me' Decade and the Third Great Awakening. *New York Magazine*.

References

5

The Televisual Representation of Ageing Gay Males: The Case of *Vicious*

Laura Tommaso

1 Introduction

Over time it has become commonplace for Lesbian, Gay, Bisexual, or Transgender (LGBT) people to be included in popular culture. Clear examples of this are TV shows like *Ellen* which paved the way for *Queer as Folk* and *Will & Grace* and later *Sex and the City*, *True Blood*, *Buffy the Vampire Slayer*, *Ugly Betty*, *Six Feet Under*, *Gray's Anatomy*, *ER*, *Brothers & Sisters*, *Pretty Little Liars*, *Orphan Black*, *Orange is the New Black*, *Modern Family*, and *Glee*—to name just a few—where LGBT characters appear, though more often than not, in supporting roles. TV shows solely based on the lives of gay men and lesbians, such as *The L Word*, the drama series about a group of lesbian friends struggling with romance and careers in Los Angeles, are still relatively rare. But such growing visibility is not always unproblematic. Media representations are not simply a mirror of society but rather are highly selective and constructed portrayals. There is

L. Tommaso (✉)
Department of Humanities, Social Sciences and Education,
University of Molise, Campobasso, Italy

P. Baker, G. Balirano (eds.), *Queering Masculinities in Language and Culture*,
Palgrave Studies in Language, Gender and Sexuality,
https://doi.org/10.1057/978-1-349-95327-1_5

consensus within the field of media and cultural studies that the depictions of different gender identities in film and television affect perceptions of the LGBT community and have been important in pushing the public to a more tolerant position (Seba 2014). Such portrayals are highly instrumental in the formulation of stereotypical and heteronormative conceptions of LGBT experiences, resulting in representations that are often simplified for ease of consumption or tied to commercial interests (Gross 2001; and see earlier chapters in this book).

However, it is also notable how these depictions have changed over the years, gradually becoming more inclusive and complex. In particular, gay characters have been presented in ways that increasingly depart from the stereotypical formulation of the perverse, flamboyant, and hypersexual figure (Becker 2006; Steiner et al. 1993; Netzley 2010) that has never been portrayed in the community or in a romantic relationship (Dow 2001). More recently, they are shown as neighbours, best friends, and family members, people who are part of everyday life and happen to be gay.

Despite this encouraging scenario, gay individuals aged 50 or above who look to the screen for characters to identify with are unlikely to encounter much success. The media under-representation of this cohort may be attributed to the fact that all elderly people remain a largely invisible minority in contemporary society, regardless of their sexual orientation. Not only do we live in an ageist world, "one in which the predominant attitude towards older people is coloured by a negative mixture of pity, fear, disgust, condescension and neglect" (Featherstone and Hepworth 1995: 30), but elderly LGBT individuals are, furthermore, disregarded due to the commonly held belief that old people are asexual (Bouman 2005: 144). LGBT older adults have a distinct experience of ageing, stemming from their unique historic position as witnesses to dramatic, rapid, and ongoing social changes in the construction of minority sexual and gender identity. Many among them have lived their identities secretly in part due to social and legal repression. As a result, much like other contemporary LGBT people, elderly gay men remain invisible not only due to media silencing of their voices, but also because they may "closet" themselves (Brown 1997: 41) and, whether more or less voluntarily, engage in several forms of denial (Glenn 2004: 15; Brown 2009) to avoid social condemnation. Like other exclusionary processes, this age discrimination draws its origin from several factors. It not only results from the widespread ageism that pervades Western cultures and the stigma elderly gay men have historically faced, but of equal significance in their effect upon older gay male lives are the dominant cultural constructions of masculinity, which older gay males cannot align with due to both their age and their sexuality. Despite some progress, ageing is still seen as a negation of masculinity, where older men are portrayed as effeminate or not men at all (Thompson 1994: 13). As sociologists and anthropologists have argued, this belief is even more widespread among elderly gay men since "[t]he hegemonic form of masculinity is youthful *and* heterosexual" (original emphasis) (Slevin and Linneman 2010: 486). In this way, elderly gay men are further marginalized by the dominant gender order which is socially and culturally legitimized through the production of "exemplars of masculinity [...], symbols that have authority despite the fact that most men and boys do not fully live up to them" (Connell and Messerschmidt 2005: 846). Mainstream society, therefore, contributes to the disempowerment of elderly gay men from different perspectives, brushing them aside while also construing them as a demasculinized, vaguely threatening "other". In addition, elderly gay men may face judgement from within their own community (Brown 2009: 69) due to the fact that "[g]ay male culture, in many of its commodified forms, holds up as its masculine ideal the young, muscular man, even more so than in heterosexual culture" (Slevin and Linneman 2010: 488). Baker (2008: 195) notes that when queer is cast as anything that is against the normal, we need to consider what constitutes the normal. If gay male culture is sufficiently accepted as one type of "new normal," and if a person spends most of their time in that particular subcultural context, then elderly gay men will be queer when measured against it.

Moreover, some scholars thus suggest that older gay men, like heterosexual women, are subject to the "male gaze" because their sexual partners are men who put more focus on physical appearance (Drummond 2006: 60). The cult of physical perfection often leads mature gay men not only to feel excluded within their own community, but also to feel old sooner than their heterosexual counterparts (Berger 1996; Bennett and Thompson 1991), a notion of ageing which subsequently impacts on identity and self-esteem. This sort of (visual) discriminatory, and potentially detrimental, behaviour of younger cohorts towards ageing gay males can also be ascribed to the fact that, as Brown (69) stresses, LGBT communities "have traditionally been less intergenerational in structure."

It gradually becomes clearer that the scant attention that gay elders have received from both mainstream and LGBT cultures mirrors their societal situation at large. In fact, in a variety of cultural media, older gay men tend to be stereotypically represented as more passive and feminine than their younger counterparts (Lescure and Yep 2015). When dealing with the theme of gay representation in popular media, the already mentioned series created by Russell T. Davies, *Queer as Folk*, is the most popular example that comes to our mind as being the first hour-long drama on Western television to portray the lives of gay men and women. The ageing dilemma is an ongoing theme throughout the series where age fear, age mockery, and youth worship are central to most episodes. For instance, Episode 11 from the American version is centred on Mike who is turning 30 and opens with these two scenes:

> [The boys stroll down Liberty Avenue after work. Brian has an arm slung around Mike's shoulder, and he points to an old bug-eyed leather queen walking towards them.]
>
> *Brian:* See that guy? *He just turned thirty*. That's what you will look in a couple of days, Mike.
>
> *Emmett:* Oh, don't listen to him. *You look like you're ten.*
>
> *Brian*: Yeah, but this strange thing happens on your thirtieth. You look great the night before and when you wake up the next morning *your ass falls down to here* and *your dick disappears.* [...]
>
> [Steam room. Brian and Mike are in towels]
>
> *Mike:* They threw a party for me at work today.
>
> *Brian:* Aw, that's cute.
>
> *Mike:* Right, like that's supposed to make me happy, knowing that *all my best years are behind me.* You are not planning some hideous birthday surprise are you?
>
> *Brian:* Why would I want to celebrate a *tragic event* like that?
>
> *Mike:* Good, because I want that day to pass without a single reminder that *I'll never be young and cute again.*[1]

As the dialogues clearly show, the characters talk about turning 30 and how dreadful this event is or might be, associating the process of ageing with corporeal deterioration and diminished masculinity. Not only is the old gay man *othered* as sexually dysfunctional but, as Goltz writes, he also "represents the tragic punishment of gay ageing, a sacrifice in the reification of youth dominance and a ghostly reminder [...] of the punishment that awaits the boys in the future" (2010: 62; see also 2016: 197).

More recently, whilst still rare, manifestations of gay ageing in TV series are forging new paths that can promisingly lead to a reformulation of queer temporalities. For example, *Old Dogs & New Tricks* (2011–2014), a comedic, fast-paced, and serialized web series, created by Leon Acord, follows the sex lives of four diverse and otherwise successful West Hollywood gay men as they approach 50. Hollywood as the land of the perpetually young and beautiful adds a strong flavour to *Old Dogs & New Tricks*, with its traffic, earthquakes, plastic surgery, and strongly youth-obsessed culture. But the focus remains on how these four different gay men react (or overreact) and adjust (or not) to getting older. The HBO series *Looking* (2014–2015), written by Michael Lannan, offers a multi-generational perspective of gay experience set in the most iconic gay place: San Francisco. The title is a double entendre, whereby "looking?" is a one-word question that some gay men use in online dating apps when willing to have sex, but it also suggests a search in progress. The story revolves around a group of three gay friends between the ages of 29 and 39 who are looking for something in life that they just cannot find, and might not even be able to define. Patrick (Jonathan Groff) seeks love, and a roadmap to being gay, Agustín (Frankie J. Alvarez) is an artist who has not found his muse, and Dom (Murray Bartlett) is trying to have a fulfilling life after 40. In particular, the ageing theme is embodied in this last character who is at a crossroads as his traumatic 40th birthday approaches: "You know, at 40, Grindr emails you a death certificate, [...] It'll be like the ghost of Christmas past walking through gay beach tomorrow".[2] However, in this series, the cultural anxiety surrounding the ageing gay body and its declining attractiveness is balanced by the introduction of a much older character. Lynn (played by Scott Bakula) not only is "liberated from confining myths of the older, sad, and sexually desperate gay male" but, more importantly, provides a positive articulation of gay temporality to look at with "envy and hope"

(Goltz 2016: 198–199). Russell T. Davies has brought new gay voices to TV through his three interrelated series called *Cucumber*, *Banana*, and *Tofu* (2015). They take their titles from the various stages of the male erection—as the protagonist in *Cucumber* explains in an opening sequence in which he eyes up other men in a supermarket. The main show *Cucumber* follows middle-aged, middle manager Henry as he trades his suburban Manchester life and comfortable long-term relationship to live in a city-centre warehouse with two young gay men. *Banana* is a shorter spin-off series that focuses on the younger character's perspectives, while *Tofu* is an online special featuring real people talking about their sex lives. Where *Queer as Folk* looked at the young, sexy side of the gay scene, *Cucumber* turns its attention to middle-aged gay men in a world where only young, attractive gay people are visible in the media. As Davies said in an interview, the televisual representation of ageing gay identities is an uncharted territory that calls for careful exploration (emphasis added):

> I'm getting older—I was once that beautiful, dancing young man, believe it or not, and I've had 20 years to kind of look at life and reflect and become that older man. But I think, again, as a writer, you kind of want to go those *open prairies* where no one else is writing, where stuff is *untouched*, and actually the *lives of middle-aged men are comparatively unexplored.* I think there's a tendency for gay characters who are now brilliantly, marvellously cropping up in more and more numbers and more and more shows and becoming more and more *visible*—I think we're culturally at a stage where those characters are pretty and sexy. I love my middle-aged cast, I'm not saying they're not sexy, but actually…they're not the most beautiful people in the world, and neither am I, so that's fair enough. There are essays to be written about the fact that our culture is seen as pretty; our culture is seen as handsome; our culture is seen as fit and beautiful…. But I think in gay terms, [my shows cover] *new territory.*[3]

With television being as ubiquitous as it is in Western world and the medium in which society's values and visions of reality are formed, reinforced, and circulated, understanding why and how ageing gay males are or are not depicted on television as well as what messages and/or beliefs are conveyed about them within these characterizations is crucial to all viewers of the content, particularly today's youth who come out in a climate more accepting of same-sex coupling, but still very much phobic and censorious of (gay) ageing.

These considerations set the stage for the present chapter, which will present a textual analysis of *Vicious* with the aim of investigating how ageing masculinity is represented in the series. The choice of analysing this British sitcom is based on its brave specificity: *Vicious* is the first TV series to deal primarily with elderly gay men. In other words, what makes it such a bold undertaking is not that the main characters played by Ian McKellen and Derek Jacobi are gay, it is that they fall far outside the 18–49 demo. In this regard, McKellen comments, "[Vicious] in a sense, is a little bit radical. It just takes for granted that an audience will find a couple of this age who are also gay to be as worthy of their own sitcom as any other couple might be."[4] Moreover, it tells us that gay people of that age still have sex, as Gary Janetti said:

> Nobody's desexualized, you know? Violet, [played by] Frances de la Tour, is always looking for somebody and trying to connect and always having horrible failed romances. In a very early conversation with Ian, he asked me, when we were talking about these characters, "Do they still have sex?" And that was such a good question because I just recently had asked that question of myself about them and the answer is yes. So much more interesting, obviously. Yes. They love each other. Yes. That part of their lives is still alive. They're very completely vital people.[5]

In the present chapter it will be argued that, although the two main characters make a considerable use of ageist remarks and jokes about older gay sexuality and physicality, they also reframe old age as a time of enduring love, sexual drive, and positivity. Accordingly, the rest of the chapter is developed as follows. Section 2 provides a brief account of the show in terms of storyline, characters, and aesthetics. Section 3 surveys the reviewers' responses that have been published in the major online newspapers which vary in nature but have, in part, been concerned with the stereotypical depiction of gay characters. These debates serve to establish the range of socio-cultural meanings and interpretations that coalesce around ideas of televisual representation of LGBT identities more generally. Section 4 describes the research questions while Sect. 5 outlines the specific methodology adopted in this study that, due to the limited number of episodes to date (13 including Seasons 1 and 2, and the Christmas Special episode), is exclusively based on a qualitative linguistic analysis and incorporates theoretical insights from pragmatics and stylistics. Section 6 provides an in-depth analysis of the textual construal of the character identities and attitudes towards gay male ageing by using several excerpts of the show to exemplify some of these traits. Finally, Sect. 7 concludes the chapter with some final remarks.

2 Storyline, Characters, and Format

Set in England, *Vicious* (2013–2015) is an ITV sitcom created by Gary Janetti (*Will & Grace*, *Family Guy*) and Mark Ravenhill, the playwright whose works include *Shopping and Fucking* and *Mother Clap's Molly House*, written by Janetti himself and directed by Ed Bye (*Red Dwarf*, *The Detectives*). It is loosely inspired by the film *Staircase* (1969) which starred Rex Harrison and Richard Burton as an ageing gay couple, exactly like Freddie Thornhill (Ian McKellen) and Stuart Bixby (Derek Jacobi) in the series—who have lived together in a small London flat for nearly 50 years. Freddie is an actor with a small, sad set of career highlights and a vast ego, who enters most episodes by swanning down the small flat's oddly grand staircase. Stuart is his long-suffering partner, bustling about, fretting that he is losing his looks and worrying over the couple's apparently comatose dog, Balthazar. Much of their dialogue consists of startlingly bald insults directed at "the other's age, appearance and flaws," as with many couples who have fallen into the habit of being rude to each other. That is where the "vicious" title comes from. However, viewers get a sense that there is also love beneath all the viciousness. Throughout the series, Freddie and Stuart are accompanied by their long-time friends Violet (Frances de la Tour), Mason (Philip Voss), and Penelope (Marcia Warren), and their new upstairs neighbour, 22-year-old Ash (Iwan Rheon).

As has been discussed elsewhere and at length (Buscombe 2000; Dalton and Linder 2005; Mills 2005), the multi-camera sitcom is an old-fashioned TV genre which employs a few characters interacting in an enclosed, theatre-like space and a live or recorded audience laughing after every joke. A meaningful yet concise definition of this distinctive filmic format has been provided by Chuck Lorre, a writer, director, and producer of widely acclaimed shows: "It's a very intimate genre. There's no music. There's no camera magic. There are no editing tricks. It's not a visual medium. It's about people and words" (quoted in Bissell 2012: 232). *Vicious* certainly is an exemplary execution of this genre which follows the tradition of British sitcoms known for their broad, boisterous humour (Kamm and Neumann 2016). Its deliberate retro format is part of the joke and has been compared to such classics as *I Love Lucy* and *The Odd Couple*. Much like in the American classics, Freddie and Stuart constantly make use of sharp-tongued talk and embark on hideous break-ups and heart-warming make-ups that keep alive this particular style of comedy.

3 Reception: The Marmite Comedy[6]

However, Anglo-American reviewers have had divided opinion about *Vicious* as to whether its portrayal of two quintessentially old gay males is televisually progressive or regressive. For example, *The Stage* said that its "gay characters are nothing more than camp stereotypes" and that the scenarios "bear no resemblance to the lives of the viewers at home," while *The Guardian* wrote that the series "cheerfully trades in clichés of homosexuality." Benjamin Secher for *The Telegraph* called it the "least funny new comedy in recent memory." "There was the odd glimpse of how *Vicious* might have amounted to something sharper," he said. "But for the most part, the script fell disastrously flat." Tom Sutcliffe, writing for *The Independent*, also criticized the script saying the writer Gary Janetti was writing a "depleted" version of his American hit *Will & Grace*. "It's delivered by McKellen and Jacobi as if they're playing in Wembley Stadium and only the upper tiers are occupied, with a heavily semaphored effeminacy that seems to belong to an entirely different era," he said. Alex Hardy, writing for *The Times*, found the comedy not to his taste, but said the script was "packed with zingers" but conversely, Ben Summerskill, the chief executive of gay rights charity Stonewall, praised the show. He said, "A mainstream audience is now laughing with, rather than at, two grand dames of British theatre, Ian McKellen and Derek Jacobi." Gay actor Christopher Biggins wondered whether the show would appeal more to a heterosexual audience than a gay one.[7] Speaking on BBC's Radio 4, he said, "I think that gay people might find it rather offensive that they're being portrayed in this way, but I think the general public, the heterosexual public, will absolutely adore it."[8] As *Vicious* arrived in the United States, the debate over its depictions of gay men has reopened an argument that has confronted American comedies like *Will & Grace*, *Glee*, *Modern Family*, and other shows with gay characters. To pick one example, Matthew Gilbert's *Boston Globe* headline suggested that *Vicious* was little more than "a vicious circle of gay stereotypes." As we have seen from this brief overview, the sitcom's camp-infused sensibility and old-fashioned aesthetics have received much attention and criticism, despite its groundbreaking significance as a mainstream show dealing with such an underrepresented cohort. In my view, rather than offer a negative, stereotyped image of elderly gay men, *Vicious* draws on camp codes and values to celebrate a means of expression that represents a constitutive factor of gay identity and, as will be discussed, reinforces a positive representation of old gay masculinity as a time of love, vitality, and pride.

4 Research Questions

This chapter considers televisual discourse as a source that shapes knowledge in relation to late life and the contemporary challenges of ageing. In this perspective, the Foucaultian concept of discourse has been used to explore how *Vicious* positions ageing gay men while also functioning as site of contestation and potential release. In particular, attention has been devoted to the matured gay characters' dialogues in Seasons 1 and 2 as a form of self-representation addressing the following questions:

1. How are the elderly gay characters portrayed in *Vicious*, specifically looking at what they say?
2. How is ageing gay masculinity constructed?

5 Methodology

As the introduction emphasizes, this chapter builds on social research related to LGBT ageing and adopts a qualitative linguistic approach to investigate the representation of older gay males and masculinity in *Vicious*. The proposed methodological framework will help to extend previous research (Goltz 2016; Betancor, Esteban 2015) exploring the linguistic strategies that have been used in *Vicious* to construct old age identity. Although the analysis of the scripted television linguistic phenomena in the sitcom under investigation was complemented by an exploration of its visual articulation, due to space constraints the focus is restricted to the verbal communication. In particular, it takes into account both explicit and implicit *textual cues* (Culpeper 2001; Bednarek 2010) in the two leading protagonists' dialogues. The character-based approach has been used in order to anchor analysis to characters and the linguistic choices they are allocated. The analysis is complemented by more in-depth investigations that focus on particular distinctive aspects of "camp talk," which is based on hyperbole, artifice, wit, mocking, and self-mocking humour (Baker 2003, 2005). An analysis of informal language, such as slang and expletives (Quaglio 2009; Bednarek 2010), will be also included.

For data collection procedure, I took advantage of an online database offering transcripts—not scripts—of the individual episodes in html format (http://www.springfieldspringfield.co.uk, last accessed June 30, 2016). However, it is crucial to note that the transcriptions on these internet platforms are written by fans of the shows, who are usually non-linguists. They transcribe their favourite shows only for their personal fun and entertainment and then share their work with other fans of the shows on these websites. Since the inconsistencies, omissions, and inaccuracies by the lay transcribers may have affected the analysis, it was necessary to proofread the transcripts and add relevant information, including the characters' names. Then, a close reading of the dialogues allowed me to identify the linguistic features pertaining to the two main characters which will be analysed and discussed in the following section.

6 Analysis and Discussion

The repertoires of the individual characters do not differ by narrative importance (both are the sitcom protagonists) as well as by gender and generation. Both Freddie and Stuart's character traits are repeated throughout the series and are established through their own and others' dialogue, a process that Bal (1997: 126) calls *accumulation* (of character traits). The characterizing effect of these textual cues is reinforced through narrative repetition (Lothe 2000: 84), as they are intensified through self- and other-presentation. To do full justice to the generated results is not possible within the scope of this chapter. Instead, observations are limited to some significant results that are particularly relevant to the issues raised in the preceding sections.

From a rapid look at the scripts it emerges that Stuart is the most effete of the pair, delivering his bons mots with fruitier notes, while Freddie is bone dry. It becomes apparent that the couple is represented as adhering to an almost heteronormative model where "one is the man and the other is the woman." Their constant bickering over the most meaningless matters echoes that of seasoned comedy married couples like the Duckworths or the Odgens in *Coronation Street*, for example. Freddie is the more aggressive of the two: "I never know when I'm going too far," he says with a smirk after delivering an especially harsh zinger, "but I'm always glad when I do" (episode 1, Season 1). He often uses the so-called bad language as in the following interjections of annoyance, surprise, and frustration: *Christ's sake* (5), *Oh, for Christ sake* (2), *Jesus Christ!* (2), *For God's sake* (3), *bollocks* (3), *damn it!* (1), *who the (bloody) hell* (3), *what the (bloody) hell* (4), *where the (bloody) hell* (2), *shit* (6), *what the fuck* (1), *bugger* (3). In contrast to Stuart, Freddie's interjections seem more aggressive, and perhaps pertaining to a more "male" speech (McEnery 2006). On the other hand, Stuart's effeminacy is emphasized by his frequent interjections of surprise and disdain: *Oh* (57), *Oh God* (9), *Oh my God* (3). Both characters are frequently sarcastic to each other by using fairly disparate realizations of insults. Freddie's mockery usually refers to Stuart's appearance, idleness, and speech, and employs a variety of animal terms that carry feminized connotations. For example, Stuart's utterances are often described by Freddie as gossipy and irritating: "Who were you *squawking* at on the phone just now?" (episode 1, Season 1, emphasis added), where the verb "to squawk" conveys the idea of a "loud, harsh cry, as a duck or other fowl when frightened," as the *Oxford English Dictionary* suggests. In the same episode, he again dismisses Stuart's high voice as if "*high-pitched, piercing shrieks* were coming from a *gaggle of schoolgirls,*" resembling the noise that a group of geese makes. To Freddie, Stuart's tone also sounds as a rusty hinge opened, emitting "squeaks" which obliquely evoke a sort of "dolphin talk": "After 50 years of Stuart's *high-pitched, octave-defying squeaks,* it's so refreshing to finally be summoned to tea by a man's voice" (episode 5, Season 2, emphasis added). As other examples from Freddie's dialogue imply, he is not merely feminizing Stuart (emphasis added):

1. Don't rush me, you *cheating slut*! (episode 2, Season 1)
2. "Where are you going, all *tarted up*?" (episode 2, Season 1)
3. Horrible, old *cow*! (episode 2, Season 1)
4. Watching you behave like a *whore* entertaining sailors on leave is not my idea of a good time. (episode 3, Season 2)
5. Well, I suppose I haven't heard your constant *mewling* for so long, I'd forgotten what it sounded like. (episode 3, Season 2)

Here, Freddie makes reference to a *certain* type of feminine identity. In other words, Stuart receives lexical treatment comparable with that of revolting, promiscuous, loquacious woman, falling to the status of animal, who may prefer a male partner who "spoils" her: "I've provided you with everything you could ever want since the moment we met" he retorts (episode 1, Season 1). More generally, Freddie is implying that it is bad to be like a woman, expressing, in this way, a male double standard. Moreover, Freddie asserts his masculinity by ordering Stuart around: "So why don't you get us some drinks and stop standing there with your mouth gaping open like a cheap Italian fountain?" (episode 4, Season 1). As the home-maker, Stuart exhibits more stereotypically effeminate behaviour: "Well, I should start dinner and check on Balthazar" (episode 2, Season 2). However, in Freddie's eyes, he is not even very good at a domestic feminine role: "Tell us, what crime against nature will you be serving this evening?" (episode 2, Season 1).

Stuart's sarcastic remarks are mainly directed at Freddie's mediocre acting career—"How could I forget? Didn't your arm get nominated for a BAFTA?" (*Christmas Special,* Season 2)—and declining attractiveness. Freddie is perpetually obsessed with the idea of looking younger while struggling to perform as a seasoned actor. If it is better to *look* younger, then the implication is that it must be better to *be* younger as the following interaction, retrieved from episode 3, Season one, seems to point out:

Freddie: Now, I want you to be brutally honest. I have an audition tomorrow.
Do you think I can pass for 50?
Stuart: I'm not even sure you can pass for alive. [...]
Freddie: I've got this fan club screening of my *Doctor Who* episode, this week.
What can I do to look younger?
Stuart: Not go?

In the scenes featuring the ageing theme, *Vicious* is permeated by explicit, and in part also implicit, stereotypes of (gay) ageing, and thereby constructs shared common ground with the audience. In the sitcom, references to the decaying male body and the deterioration of mental functioning, as well as blatant lies about age and vain attempts to look younger, are played for laughs, as these examples, retrieved from both seasons, clearly show (emphasis added):

1. *Freddie*: What's wrong with you? Aside from that *visual horror show* your *body* has become.
2. *Freddie:* Bollocks! You look like a *rotting* pumpkin!
3. *Freddie*: You remember him? *Shrunken, old gnome*?
4. *Freddie*: Is that why *you look a thousand*? You're practically *melting* onto the rug!
5. *Freddie*: I'm surprised you could see it through the *milky film that coats your cataracts.*
6. *Freddie*: I see you're wearing an *extra chin* for the occasion.
7. *Freddie*: Just so you know, he runs like a girl ... An *old, fat, stupid girl.*

8. Stuart: I only hope his [Ash] *flesh* didn't *rot off* where you touched him.
9. Stuart: I think one of your *teeth* just *fell out*.
10. Stuart: His *breath* is nothing to be alarmed about, Ash, it's just his *insides decaying*.
11. Stuart: I'm right here, you *walking corpse*.
12. Stuart: Have you been to a doctor? Do they know why your *hair* is *falling out in clumps*?

Throughout the series, the old gay couple display difficulty in accepting their age, revealing a fixation on youth, smell, hair, and male vigour:

Freddie: We just want to thank you for working out with us, these past few days. Yeah, I've become so *strong*. And *I've never looked better*. I could probably go up for leading man roles. I'd even be open to doing a nude scene, if the part required it.
Stuart: The only way you'll be required to be nude again is if you're donating your organs.
Freddie: *At least I have a penis.* (episode 2, Season 2, emphasis added)

In the exchange below, significantly entitled "Clubbing"[9] (episode 4, Season 1, emphasis added), a detailed account of the degeneration of the gay male ageing body is followed by other expressions denoting a reaction to a diminishing bodily and mental process and, implicitly, a response to an acknowledged decline of physical strength and vitality with ageing.[10] We again see how ageist discourses within the gay community form a background to the character's representations which recycle assumptions about gay later life, rather than fighting them:

Freddie: Christ! Every morning I wake up to some new *abomination with my body*. All *my toes are now sticking out* in different directions. It's like someone yelled 'Fire!' in a crowded theatre.

Stuart: Yes, your *back was cracking* so much last night, I thought you were making popcorn in bed.
Freddie: That's because I have to contort myself into ridiculous positions to get as far away from you as possible!
Stuart: Oh! Believe me, I don't want you anywhere near me either. It takes all my willpower every night not to roll you onto the floor.
Freddie: *My entire body is creaking*. I sound like a haunted house. *When did this happen to us?*
Stuart: Us?! *I feel perfectly spry. I've never felt younger*. In fact, I was thinking of going running today.
Freddie: Good. Just so long as you keep going in the one direction!
Stuart: At least *I still have my looks*. You haven't held onto them nearly as well as I have. But, of course, everybody knows that.
Freddie: Bollocks! *You look like a rotting pumpkin*! How could anyone find you more *attractive* than me?
Stuart: I don't know. But they do.

But is this recurring, sometimes crude, mockery really insulting or troublesome? Where is it coming from? The issue of male homosexuality as a cultural practice cannot be fully discussed in the current chapter. However, what the sexuality studies scholar David M. Halperin writes about on the ironic perspective on love that male gay culture supplies, resonates with the two *Vicious* protagonists whose love for one another is deep, even if their way of expressing is unconventional:

> Gay male culture has in fact elaborated a distinctive, dissident perspective on romantic love, a camp perspective, which straight people often regard as cynical, precisely because its irony—which emphasizes the performativity of romantic roles—seems to them to undermine the seriousness and sincerity of love, and thereby to demean it … [But] Gay male culture's vision of love is not a cynical one. Rather … [it encourages] an outlook on love that is disabused, but not disenchanted. (2012: 293)

Many interactions revolve around exchanges of insults and teasing[11] between the couple, yet we are ultimately reminded that, despite their differences, their bond is essentially one of love nurtured by their shared history of secrecy and discrimination, as Freddie reminds Stuart's mother:

> The man you are talking so disrespectfully to is not only your son, but my partner of 49 years. [...] And I'll have you know he's the most wonderful man in the world and I'm proud to call him my lover. [...] Yes, we've had a few major differences over the years but I can't imagine my life without him. So when you talk to him, you talk to him with respect. [...] He cares very deeply about you, but unless you can accept him and our relationship, you are not welcome here. (episode 6, Season 1)

A more positive reading of *Vicious*, then, is that although Freddie and Stuart's interactions largely involve insults about ageing and gender, they are ultimately comfortable with their ageing gay identities and one another, and live their lives proudly in the face of repression and youth-obsessed (gay) culture.

7 Conclusion

In the present chapter, a brief overview of selected TV series depicting mature gay characters has been provided with the aim of shedding light on an emerging cultural trend in Anglo-American popular culture. In particular, a character-based analysis of Freddie and Stuart in *Vicious* has been conducted to examine the discourses that shape gay male ageing and masculinity and to determine how old gay men are portrayed in the chosen sitcom. Findings indicate that in *Vicious*, traditional and counter narratives of ageing gay identities coexist. Although the ageist discourses typical of the gay scene are reproduced through the employment of camp putdowns and zingers, this British sitcom might be praised for presenting, at the centre of a story, elderly gay males who can lead fulfilling social, intimate, and passionate lives and relationships long after the age of 30. Bringing old age into view in popular media, humorously or otherwise, at least breaks the silence about old age, revealing an emerging cultural shift within and outside the gay scene. The examples given here do not provide an exhaustive list and represent just a slice of the LGBT world that is unfolding in television. However, the growing number of these portrayals circulating also indicates the emergence of a wider vision of ageing and old age in LGBT representations. By depicting mature LGBT characters as in-depth, multi-faceted human beings, no different from their younger counterparts, media has certainly a positive impact on attitudes and perceptions towards LGBT ageing. In particular, these various examples offer hope and validation for members of all ages within and outside the LGBT community producing new timelines of transition, maturation, and growth.

Acknowledgements The author would like to thank the editors for their valuable insights that greatly contributed to the development of this chapter.

Notes

1. *Queer as Folk*, 1.11, 2001.
2. *Looking*, 1.6, 2014.
3. In "From 'Banana' To 'Cucumber,' New Series Spans The Spectrum Of Sex," *NPR*, April 1, 2015.
4. In Lanford Beard, "Ian McKellen teases his 'Vicious' chemistry with costar Derek Jacobi, a 'Downtown Abbey' audition," *Entertainment Weekly*, June 29, 2014, accessed May 3, 2015, http://www.ew.com/article/2014/06/29/ian-mckellen-vicious.
5. Jim Halterman, "Gary Janetti Talks Shaping 'Vicious' With Iconic Stars Ian McKellen and Derek Jacobi," *Xfinity*, July 11, 2014.
6. Itzkoff (2014) writing in the *New York Times* comments: "Marmite is a spread in England that you either love or loathe," Mr. Jacoby explained, "and 'Vicious' brought with it a touch of the Marmite."
7. A new and comprehensive research from BBC Audiences into LGB viewing habits has revealed that *Vicious* has been watched by nearly 37% of the 16–34 age group gay/bisexual audience. Significantly, the youth of the *Vicious* fans is a good rebuttal of presumptions of ageism. The survey also reveals that the sitcom was appreciated by 23% of the 35–54 and only 8% of the 55+ age groups. The data comes from 1000 people who identified themselves as gay, lesbian, or bisexual on the BBC's Pulse panel, an independent audience reaction group that numbers approximately

20,000. See the LGB audience research charts at http://www.bbc.co.uk/programmes/p01k8rjg/p01k8v66.

8. Quoted in Joe Morgan, "What did the critics think of Ian McKellen, Derek Jacobi's gay sitcom Vicious?" *Gay Star News*, April 30, 2013.
9. In *Vicious*, the shift in later life is paralleled by a move away from the youth-coded club scene towards more domestically staged spaces. This shift in relational practice is narrated largely as a response to loss of bodily value (sexual/physical) on the gay scene where older gay men could feel marginalized by age. In other words, the transition from public to domestic spaces is typically represented as a natural development of the ageing process.
10. A similar situation is displayed in the second episode of Season 2 entitled "Gym." Here, feeling unfit, Freddie and Stuart join Ash at the gym, where they are persuaded by handsome young trainer Theo to sign up for a three-month "special" course.
11. It is important to stress that Freddie and Stuart insult everyone, especially their friends: horny Violet, in-and-out-of-it Penelope, and stingy Mason.

References

Primary Sources

Cucumber. Writ. R. T. Davies. Dir. D. Evans, A. Troughton and E. Lyn. Channel 4. 22 January 2015–12 March 2015. Television.

Looking: The complete series + movie. Writ. M. Lannan et al. Dir. Various. HBO studios. DVD. 2015.

Old Dogs & New Tricks: *Complete Seasons 1 & 2.* Written and directed by L. Acord. Wolfe video. 2013. DVD.

Staircase. Writ. C. Dyer. Dir. Stanley Donen. Twentieth century fox film corporation. 1969.

"Surprise". In *Queer As Folk: Series 1.* Writ. J. Schafer and J. Tolins. Dir. M. DeCarlo. 25 February 2001. Television.

The New Normal: The complete series. Writ. A. Adler and R. Murphy. Dir. R. Murphy. Twentieth Century Fox Film Corporation. 2014. DVD.

Vicious: *Season One*. Writ. G. Janetti. Dir. E. Bye. Channel 4, 2013. DVD.

Vicious: *Season Two*. Writ. G. Janetti. Dir. E. Bye. Channel 4, 2015. DVD.

Secondary Sources

"From 'Banana' To 'Cucumber,' New Series Spans The Spectrum of Sex". (2015, April 1). *NPR*. Retrieved May 4, 2015, from http://www.npr.org/2015/04/01/396809966/from-banana-to-cucumber-new-series-spans-the-spectrum-of-sex

Baker, P. (2003). *Polari-The Lost Language of Gay Men*. London: Routledge.

Baker, P. (2005). *Public Discourses of Gay Men*. London: Routledge.

Baker, P. (2008). *Sexed Texts*. London: Equinox.

Bal, M. (1997). *Narratology. Introduction to the Theory of Narrative*. Toronto: University of Toronto Press.

Becker, R. (2006). *Gay TV and Straight America*. New Brunswick, NJ: Rutgers University Press.

Bednarek, M. (2010). *The Language of Fictional Television: Drama and Identity*. London: Bloomsbury.

Bednarek, M. (2012). Constructing "Nerdiness": Characterisation in *The Big Bang Theory*. *Multilingua, 31*, 199–229.

Bennett, K. C., & Thompson, N. L. (1991). Accelerated Aging and Male Homosexuality: Australian Evidence in a Continuing Debate. *Journal of Homosexuality, 20*(3–4), 65–76.

Berger, R. M. (1996). *Gay and Gray: The Older Homosexual Man*. New York: Harrington Park Press.

Bissell, T. (2012). *Magic Hours: Essays on Creators and Creation*. San Francisco, CA: McSweeney's.

Booker, M. K. (2006). *Drawn to Television: Prime-Time Animation from the Flintstones to Family Guy*. Santa Barbara: Greenwood Publishing Group.

Bouman, W. P. (2005). Review of Reeling in the Years: Gay Men's Perspectives on Age and Ageism. *International Psychogeriatrics, 17*(1), 14.

Brown, L. B. (1997). *Gay Men and Aging*. New York: Taylor & Francis.

Brown, M. T. (2009). LGBT Aging and Rhetorical Silence. *Sexuality Research & Social Policy: Journal of NSRC, 6*(4), 65–78.

Buscombe, E. (Ed.). (2000). *British Television: A Reader*. Oxford: Clarendon Press.

Connell, R. W., & Messerschmidt, J. W. (2005). Hegemonic Masculinity: Rethinking the Concept. *Gender & Society, 19*(6), 829–859.

Culpeper, J. (2001). *Language and Characterization. People in Plays and Other Texts*. London: Longman.

Dalton, M. M., & Linder, L. R. (2005). *The Sitcom Reader: America Viewed and Skewed*. New York: SUNY Press.

Dow, B. E. (2001). Television, and the Politics of Gay and Lesbian Visibility. *Critical Studies in Media Communication, 18*(2), 123–140.

Drummond, M. (2006). Ageing Gay Men's Bodies. *Gay & Lesbian Issues and Psychology Review, 2*(2), 60–66.

Fejes, F., & Petrich, K. (1993). Invisibility, Homophobia and Heterosexism: Lesbians, Gays and the Media. *Critical Studies in Mass Communication, 10*(4), 396.

Foucault, M. (1972). *The Archeology of Knowledge*. London: Tavistock.

Gilbert, M. (2014, June 27). A "Vicious" Circle of Gay Stereotypes, *The Boston Globe*. Retrieved October 3, 2015, from https://www.bostonglobe.com/arts/television/2014/06/26/vicious-circle-gay-stereotypes/51nUSgFec6k5tPdQXuFG4J/story.html

Glenn, C. (2004). *Unspoken: A Rhetoric of Silence*. Chicago: SIU Press.

Goltz, D. B. (2010). *Queer Temporalities in Gay Male Representation: Tragedy, Normativity, and Futurity*. London: Routledge.

Goltz, D. B. (2016). Still Looking: Temporality and Gay Ageing in US Television. In M. Oró-Piqueras & A. Wohlmann (Eds.), *Serializing Age: Aging and Old Age in TV Series* (pp. 187–206). Bielefeld: Verlag.

Gross, L. (2001). *Up from Invisibility: Lesbians, Gay Men, and the Media in America*. New York: Columbia University Press.

Gust, A. Y., Lescure, R., & Allen, J. (2015). Queering Aging? Representations of Liberace's Intimate Life in HBO's Behind the Candelabra. In N. Jones & B. Batchelor (Eds.), *Aging Heroes. Growing Old in Popular Culture* (pp. 65–76). London: Rowman & Littlefield.

Halperin, D. M. (2012). *How to Be Gay*. Cambridge, MA: Harvard University Press.

Halterman, J. (2015a). 10 "Vicious" Things We Know About Sir Ian McKellen and Derek Jacobi, *Xfinity*, June 26, 2014. Retrieved October 4, 2015, from http://my.xfinity.com/blogs/tv/2014/06/26/10-vicious-things-we-know-about-sir-ian-mckellen-and-derek-jacobi/

Halterman, J. (2015b). Gary Janetti Talks Shaping "Vicious" with Iconic Stars Ian McKellen and Derek Jacobi, *Xfinity*, July 11, 2014. Retrieved May 3, 2015, from http://my.xfinity.com/blogs/tv/2014/07/11/gary-janetti-talks-shaping-vicious-with-iconic-actors-ian-mckellen-and-derek-jacobi/

Hardy, A. (2013, April 30). Last Night's TV: Vicious, *The Times*, Retrieved May 3, 2015, from http://www.thetimes.co.uk/tto/arts/tv-radio/reviews/article3752082.ece

Harrington, C. L., Bielby, D. D., & Bardo, A. R. (Eds.). (2014). *Aging, Media, and Culture*. Lanham, MD: Lexington Books.

Hemley, M. (2013, May 9). ITV's Vicious—The Sitcom Even Ian McKellen Can't Save, *The Stage*. Retrieved April 30, 2015, from https://www.thestage.co.uk/opinion/2013/itvs-vicious-the-sitcom-even-ian-mckellen-cant-save/

Itzkoff, D. (2014, June 27). Oh You Silly Thing, of Course He's Gay "Vicious" on PBS Follows Two Gay Characters, *The New York Times*. Retrieved October 4, 2015, from http://www.Nytimes.Com/2014/06/29/arts/television/vicious-on-pbs-follows-two-gaycharacters.Html?_r=0

Jones, N., & Batchelor, B. (2015). *Aging Heroes: Growing Old in Popular Culture*. Lanham, MD: Rowman & Littlefield.

Kamm, J., & Neumann, B. (Eds.). (2016). *British TV Comedies. Cultural Concepts, Contexts and Controversies*. Basingstoke: Palgrave Macmillan.

Lawson, M. (2013, October 31). Revelation that Gay Audiences Like Vicious, Bake Off and Splash! Risks Perpetuating Gay Stereotypes, *The Guardian*. Retrieved May 3, 2015, from http://www.theguardian.com/tv-and-radio/tvandradioblog/2013/oct/31/gay-audiences-vicious-bake-off-splash

Leonard, W., Duncan, D., & Barrett, C. (2013). What a Difference a Gay Makes. The Constitution of the "Older Gay Man". In A. Kampf, B. Marshall, & A. Petersen (Eds.), *Aging Men, Masculinities and Modern Medicine* (pp. 105–120). New York: Routledge.

Lothe, J. (2000). *Narrative in Fiction and Film. An Introduction*. Oxford: Oxford University Press.

McEnery, T. (2006). *Swearing in English: Bad Language, Purity and Power from 1586 to the Present*. London: Routledge.

Mills, B. (2005). *Television Sitcom*. London: British Film Institute.

Morgan, J. (2013, April 30). What Did the Critics Think of Ian McKellen, Derek Jacobi's Gay Sitcom Vicious? *Gay Star News*. Retrieved May 3, 2015, from http://www.gaystarnews.com/article/what-did-critics-think-ian-mckellen-derek-jacobi's-gay-sitcom-vicious300413/#gs.CzcoCus

Netzley, S. (2010). Visibility That Demystifies: Gays, Gender, and Sex on Television. *Journal of Homosexuality, 57*(8), 968–986.

Ramirez-Valles, J. (2016). *Queer Aging: The Gayby Boomers and a New Frontier for Gerontology*. Oxford: Oxford University Press.

Reid, K. (2015). Lifeline or Leisure?: TV's Role in the Lives of the Elderly. *Center for Media Literacy*. Retrieved October 5, 2015, from http://www.medialit.org/reading-room/lifeline-or-leisure-tvs-role-lives-elderly

Seba, J. A. (2014). *Gay Characters in Theater, Movies, and Television: New Roles, New Attitudes*. Philadelphia: Mason Crest.

Secher, B. (2015). Vicious (ITV): The Least Funny New Comedy in Recent Memory, Review. *The Telegraph*, April 27, 2013. Retrieved May 3, 2015, from http://www.telegraph.co.uk/culture/tvandradio/10026311/Vicious-ITV-the-least-funny-new-comedy-in-recent-memory-review.html

Slevin, K. F., & Linneman, T. J. (2010). Old Gay Men's Bodies and Masculinities. *Men and Masculinities, 12*(4), 483–507.

Steiner, L., Fejes, F., & Petrich, K. (1993). Invisibility, Homophobia and Heterosexism: Lesbians, Gays and the Media. *Critical Studies in Mass Communication, 10*(4), 395–422.

Summerskill, B. (2015, April 29). Does Vicious Mark the End of Gay TV Characters Being Invisible?, *The Guardian*. Retrieved May 3, 2015, from http://www.theguardian.com/tv-and-radio/tvandradioblog/2013/apr/29/vicious-end-gay-tv-characters-invisible

Sutcliffe, T. (2013, April 30). Vicious (ITV) Starring Sirs Ian McKellen and Derek Jacobi—The Only Laughter It Provokes Is Canned, *The Independent*. Retrieved May 3, 2015, from http://www.independent.co.uk/arts-entertainment/tv/reviews/tv-review-vicious-itv-starring-sirs-ian-mckellen-and-derek-jacobi-the-only-laughter-it-provokes-is-8595474.html

Thompson, E. H. (1994). Older Men as Invisible Men in Contemporary Society. In E. H. Thompson (Ed.), *Older Men's Lives* (pp. 1–21). Thousand Oaks, CA: Sage Publications.

Viera, B., & Esteban, J. (2015). *Striving for Visibility: Representations of Elderly Gay Men in Christopher Bram's 'Father of Frankenstein' and ITV's 'Vicious'*. Universitat Autònoma de Barcelona. Departament de Filologia Anglesa i de Germanística. Retrieved September 2015, from http://ddd.uab.cat/record/138014

6

The Queer Peer: Masculinity and Brotherhood in Cain and Abel Literature and Imagination

Paola Di Gennaro

1 Introduction

Biblical rewritings often imply literary archetypes or, to use Jean-François Lyotard's words, grand narratives, the universalising discourses that govern a particular culture at a particular time.[1] The story of Cain and Abel, as a grand narrative, has a certain level of invariableness, although it also offers a certain level of indefiniteness as it is intrinsically ambiguous. The aim of this chapter is to outline the variations assumed in the literature and, more generally, in collective imagination, of this story—in particular, the story of a specific biblical figure, one of the founding characters of all Western literary and mythological traditions, Cain, in his relationship with his peer, his brother Abel. From a queer perspective this means studying an interesting, archetypal case of a relationship between males, thus concerning the representation of masculinity in pairs of men who

P. Di Gennaro (✉)
Università degli Studi Suor Orsola Benincasa, Napoli, Italia

P. Baker, G. Balirano (eds.), *Queering Masculinities in Language and Culture*, Palgrave Studies in Language, Gender and Sexuality,
https://doi.org/10.1057/978-1-349-95327-1_6

share a bond of blood, responsibility, crime, and guilt. Analysing what is stable and similar in the different literary and artistic representations of Cain and Abel over time and across different cultures, or the "evolution" in their representation, can lead to a reflection on the changes in culture and society regarding masculinity and otherness. Cain is always the "other", the marginalised, the "queer" one, who must be expelled from the community. In contrast, Abel embodies the outraged one, the victim counterpart, and, interestingly enough, a different kind of "queer", the feminine part of the pair. Additionally, Abel's voice has been muted—not marginalised, ignored, laughed at, but destroyed from the Earth's surface.

Since the term "queer", as theoretically conceived, implies the abolition of any hierarchies, Cain and Abel, a pair of brothers—who are not twins and hence include difference in age and appearance—become an interesting expression of gender and masculinity issues in specific cultures and societies. Although biblical rewriting is always a sensitive topic in literary criticism, in this case the topic is even more thorny as it refers to issues that relate to both matters of gender and religious assumptions. The topic implies a concern with revealing that the way we represent sexuality and gender is problematic and extremely susceptible to changes according to time and space, moving from orthodoxy to queer, which is by definition "whatever is at odds with the normal, the legitimate, the dominant".[2] Cain is the murderer, the dominant one who will found civilisation; Abel is the murdered, the gentle, passive one, whose semen is to be lost in myth.

The critical frameworks used in this analysis are based on a "middle-distance reading"—following Northrop Frye and Franco Moretti in rejecting barriers between different methods of analysis and fostering the cooperation of plural critical approaches, from close reading to archetypal criticism. Drawing on examples from contemporary Anglophone fiction, the story of Cain and Abel will be analysed in connection with the original myth and the social conflicts under which it has developed into new forms. In particular, I will take into account existing monographs on the topic: Ricardo Quinones' *The Changes of Cain: Violence and the Lost Brother in Cain and Abel Literature* (1991), and the two books by Véronique Léonard-Roques, *Caïn, figure de la modernité* (2003), and

Caïn et Abel. Rivalité et responsabilité (2007), and also my *Wandering through Guilt: The Cain Archetype in the Twentieth-Century Novel* (2015). In addition, Nikki Sullivan's and Steven Seidman's studies on gay identity and queer theory have been used as a more general framework. In the following sections I will focus on the original archetype and its interpretations, and then I will examine some of the new versions of the story in contemporary literature. Finally, the conclusion section will deal with the permeability of the archetype to queering perspectives and rewritings.

2 The Biblical Archetype

Let us start from the short story of Cain we find in the Bible. It consists of only 26 verses in the Book of Genesis (4:1–26) that describe the character's basic actions and attitudes. Adam and Eve have two sons, Cain and Abel. Cain is described as being a crop farmer and his younger brother, Abel, is a shepherd. Cain takes his brother Abel out to the fields, and kills him, possibly with a stone or a jawbone. There are two possible reasons for this apparently groundless action: firstly, Cain and Abel had offered God the produce of their work—respectively, the firstlings of the flock and of the ground, meat and grass—and Cain is possessed by jealousy at God's arbitrary preference for his brother's offerings; God had replied: "Why are you angry? Why is your face downcast? If you do what is right, will you not be accepted? But if you do not do what is right, sin is crouching at your door; it desires to have you, but you must master it"[3]; secondly—and this is a far less common interpretation—Cain's jealousy was caused by the obligation not to marry his twin sister, but to marry Abel's twin sister (according to this tradition, Cain and Abel have a twin sister each), as Cain's sister was the most beautiful.

Both interpretations are extremely rich in significance. Whatever the reason, Cain is sentenced by God to be "a fugitive and a wanderer on the earth" so as to atone for the murder of his brother, in some of the most powerful lines in literary history: "Now you are under a curse and driven from the ground, which opened its mouth to receive your brother's blood from your hand. When you work the ground, it will no longer yield its crops for you. You will be a restless wanderer on the earth"; to which Cain replies: "My punishment is greater than I can bear […]; I will be hidden from your presence; […] I will be a restless wanderer on the earth, and whoever finds me will kill me". Consequently, Cain is destined to bear a mark on his forehead, a mark that should protect him but also brands him in the eyes of the world. A mark that will be one of the most common features to be represented in retellings of the story, from the Bible to Harry Potter.

Nevertheless, paradoxically, and controversially, Cain would become the founder of the first city in the history of man, named Enoch, after his firstborn.

Cain, who, in his own words, is not his brother's keeper, is the first murderer in Western history. Let us not forget, though, that he is also the first human being to be born, while his brother is the first human to die. We have the ancestor of evil and the first martyr, the one who will be often paralleled with Christ in later literature.

It is noteworthy to mention that numerous important issues concerning masculinity and gender representation are at stake with this story. Traditionally, a set of oppositions have been unveiled in it: from an anthropological point of view, the change from a society based on nomadic shepherds to one of settled farmers; Cain's progeny, that of the Cainites, is the evil one, fighting with that of his brother's, the Abelites.

Cain's image in the Bible—the book considered, together with Homer's epics, the model of all future literary productions of the West by Erich Auerbach (Auerbach 1991)—is therefore ambiguous and polysemic. Cain is the remorseless killer of Abel, who, interrogated by God about the disappearance of his brother, merely replies: "Am I my brother's keeper?". Cain is the symbol of the division between the two main agricultural tasks and of a father's unjust discrimination. Cain is also the derelict wanderer in a hostile world, condemned by God to bear his mark. Commentators have conjectured a great deal on the possible nature of the mark, and of course literature has used it as one of the most fertile symbols when rewriting the story. Ruth Mellinkoff has published a rich volume on the various possible interpretations of the mark of Cain, which can be a mark on Cain's body, a movement of Cain's body, or a blemish associated with Cain's body (Mellinkoff 1981). In Mormon folklore, Cain is a black man who wanders the earth begging people to kill him and take his curse upon themselves.[4] His mark seems to be the possession of physical traits or attitudes that are typical of the "other", which very often also become assimilated to masculine features.

3 Cain and His Kind

Mainly through the metaphoric and allusive concision of this archetypal story, numerous evocative patterns emerge in the collective consciousness of Western society, and today on a global basis. If we consider all the patterns that originate from this story, we can gather many interesting ideas concerning queerness and masculinity in the representations of Cain in literature and other genres—films, TV series, comics, and so on.

An initial, and more evident pattern, is brotherhood marked by fraternal hate. As with all pairs in mythology, fraternal bonds can be the deepest relationships existing between human beings or, on the contrary, the mirror of the fiercest hate and competition—as often happens with twins, who can be two halves of the same whole, one representing the "other", the doppelganger, or the shadow. Twins are considered as representing the dualistic nature of the cosmos; in mythology we often find the figure of the "evil twin", that is, the villain necessary for every respectable hero who must engage in battle.

Cain and Abel are not twins, and this is perhaps the interesting part of the story. For some reason, it seems that in pairs of brothers who are not twins—and therefore the hypothesis of more closeness or even total equality can no longer be assumed—the older sibling is almost always the villainous one. The younger brother is often represented as the most "naïve", the one who is less experienced, the "underdog", whom we are supposed to support. And, as a matter of fact, this is what happens in the Bible: God the father stands on Abel's side, roots for him, and chastises the eldest, who, somehow, always seems to be wrong. In fact, he becomes even more wrong when he becomes the first murderer, and the first human being to fall under a curse.

So how have Cain and Abel been depicted in history? Which of the two brothers is the "queer" one, the strange(r), the one who posits himself outside the mainstream? As a matter of fact, Cain is the manly sinner or the other, the monster. For example, especially in medieval Christian art, Cain is sometimes represented as the stereotypical ringleted, bearded Jew, whereas Abel is the blonde, European gentile. In Western tradition, Cain has physically taken up all the most "oppositive" and even repulsive connotations—in some medieval traditions, after God's curse, Cain is portrayed as distinctly animalistic: hairy, horny, and with shiny eyes[5]—and in some ancient texts, Cain's descendants have monstrous features, a lonely and violent race, encompassing both man and monster, for whom even music is conceived as a weapon.[6] The same happens in *Beowulf*, where in all of Beowulf's encounters with Grendel and Grendel's mother, he is forced to take on Cainite weapons and a Cainite identity in order to win the fight.[7] More interestingly, Cain's crime has also been seen as the *original* of original sins: the act of kin slaying would be much greater than the eating of the forbidden apple by Adam and Eve.[8]

Fratricide versus knowledge: the killing of kinsmen requires diversity within equality. Even when not represented by the stereotypical opposites—dark/fair, tall/short, strong/delicate—Cain and Abel are made of a *younger* and an *older* brother. Differences that are necessary in order to make the arbitrariness of the father's choice—and the subsequent guilt—aggravated by a starting equality of terms. Cain and Abel are not Adam and Eve—Edenic heterosexuality—nor God and Adam—Fatherly love/punishment. They are peers, and hence they sometimes admit queering in representation, disordering hierarchies and history, putting brotherhood out of order.

Cain, the firstborn male, starts the progeny of assassins, of those who physically destroy and act irrationally because of testosteronic impulses—envy, rage, and fury. Heroism must be virile, be it positive or negative. Interestingly enough, the necessity of exclusiveness of masculine bonds eliminated Cain and Abel's twin sisters from the most common version of their story. And Eve, their mother, remains the ancient temptress, or the new weeping mother.

Let us see things from a different perspective now. In the Bible, how did evil enter the world? Evil entered the world through Lucifer's envy—again a male—but we must be careful, because Lucifer was an angel, and therefore less sexualised than other biblical figures (according to some texts Cain could have been borne by Eve after her rape by the serpent, and thus Cain would be half-human and half-angelic). Also, God and Satan are the opposing, fighting pair par excellence, and—leaving psychoanalysis and Lacan aside—we can see the Devil as dual, the image of God in the mirror. Unless we imagine a Western god as feminine,[9] as it appears very rarely in fiction,[10] from this perspective evil, and therefore Cain, cannot be but masculine. Gnostics associated the name Cain with the sun, the typical masculine deity, while, according to some scholars, in Hebrew Abel's name is composed by the same three consonants of the word for "breath": fire and air, pragmatism versus volatility.

Another archetype represented by the Cain and Abel story is the image of a wanderer, who, marked with guilt (or a sense of guilt) makes a journey of atonement in physical or psychological wastelands, to greater or lesser success. Cain's wandering is impelled by the first vendetta by the God of the Old Testament. Abel's blood demands vengeance—we have a curse *and* a mark—a thing that will be later eliminated with the coming of Christ.

4 The Archetype Rewritten

The Cain archetype has appeared in endless references, retellings, and less explicit rewritings, where we find characters who follow Cain's attitudes and actions in more suffused ways. Clear references were especially common in medieval art and in Shakespearean plays, as well as in present day fiction, comics, and films, as we are going to see shortly. It is extremely interesting to see how the two characters have been portrayed with "queered" features, sometimes marking characters by "deforming" Cain, thanks to villainous, murderous, ambiguous traits, sometimes deforming Abel, making him feminine, if not effeminate, delicate, passive. This is a process that is evidently more common as we approach contemporary literature and art. And the process itself is an exemplification of the extent of orthodoxy that a culture is ready to sacrifice for destabilisation. As Nikki Sullivan (2003) explains, "[q]ueering popular culture [...] involves critically engaging with cultural artefacts in order to explore the ways in which meaning and identity is (inter)textually (re)produced".[11]

Put simply, Cain has been used to "villainise" characters, whereas Abel to "queer" them. We have seen how Beowulf, Grendel, and his mother are believed to have descended from Cain. In Byron's play (*Cain*, 1821), Cain represents the rebel against injustice, the romantic hero who struggles for (masculine) emancipation from his family's bigotry. In Shakespeare's *The Merry Wives of Windsor* (1999) there is the expression "Cain-coloured beard"—in some traditions Cain was believed to have had red hair, although most commonly it was dark, in any case, unusual or not-fair. We can also find classic rewritings of Cain in other European literature—Unamuno's *Abel Sanchez* (1917), Hermann Hesse's *Demian* (1919), the play *The Skin of Our Teeth* (1942), by Thornton Wilder, and Jose Saramago's novel *Cain* (2012). In many of these works Cain is the bearer of ideas and intellectual speculations—characteristics of a new version of masculinity.

I will not mention allusive references to Cain and non-explicit rewritings here—I have already covered the topic more exhaustively in my monograph (Di Gennaro 2015); but I will say something on one novel in particular, where Cain is vastly and openly present: John Steinbeck's *East of Eden* (2000). Though written in 1952, the vicissitudes of this family saga take place around the Great War. A couple of generations of Cain and Abel pairs move in the time-frame of the novel, through the country from North to South and from East to West. In this novel, wandering is the movement of seasonal workers, of searchers for land, of those who enlist in the army and die for reasons they will never really understand. It is a forced wandering, made tangible to the reader through Steinbeck's almost epic style and his mythical touch. In this novel, Cain is the eponym of a country and of a precise historical moment, as in many other novels, poems, and films of 1950s America; a period in which Cain's myth takes over from the Adamic myth. This is the short-circuit of World War II, an epoch in which a fratricidal war seems to be necessary for the conservation of the species.[12] At this point the guilt of humanity is cherished as an axiom, as is Cain's story. According to Steinbeck, the Salinas Valley was undoubtedly the East of Eden; the myth of Cain was one of the narratives which most characterises man: without this story, or rather, without the "sense" of this story, psychiatrists would have nothing to do, he says, because, together with the story of the Fall, it may be at the basis of all neurosis.[13] However, if the story of the Fall established the dominion of female will on humankind, the story of the first murder, the first conceived human being who turns out to be also the first killer of another human being, in one way or another established some of the stereotypes related to manhood in Western society.

The first couple of Cains and Abels in the story are the stepbrothers Charles and Adam Trask—they have the same first name initials as Cain and Abel. Charles is cruel, aggressive, and beats his brother severely for nonsensical reasons. Adam remains passive; he gives presents to his stepmother, who believes that they come from her son Charles—a misunderstanding of some sort is necessary to amplify fraternal tragedy. And, later on, another problem with presents more or less appreciated by the father (a knife versus a puppet) gives rise to fraternal hate. Adam is blond, while Charles is dark-haired, and gets a dark brown scar on his face too, which makes him even more reticent and antisocial.

Let us now look at the second couple, represented by Adam's (or maybe Charles's?) twin sons, Cal and Aron (again a C and an A). Their mother, Cathy Ames (also C and A), is the most devilish character in the novel, devil at heart while angelic in appearance. Again, Cal is dark-haired and always ready for a fight, while Aron is blond, shy, fragile, childlike, lighthearted, and more sociable than the solitary brother. Inadvertently, at the end, again Abel will be killed by his brother, not by a stone out in the fields, but in the city by an overtly emotional shock—knowledge, the acknowledgment of his mother's true nature.

Therefore, in what is perhaps the most overt rewriting of the story of Cain and Abel in the middle of the twentieth century, the stereotype of an aggressive, solid man as the villain is maintained—although in the film adaptation directed by Elia Kazan the more delicate James Dean was chosen to play Cal—and this makes it palpable that queering is often more a process than a ratio; and also, of course, that sometimes marketing dynamics go beyond ideology and coherency. But again, as in any archetype, the retellings are suggestive rather than comprehensive.

This is perhaps particularly evident in the ways Cain has been portrayed, recently, in a totally different genre: comics. An interesting example is a very complex comic book, which is impossible to summarise here, called *The Unwritten* (written by Mike Carey with artwork by Peter

Gross 2009–2015), whose last issue was published in the Unites States in 2014. Here, Cain is the original nature of the villain of the story, Pullman: he is drawn as the rough one, while Abel is the one with the fairest hair, nice dreadlocks, a Greek profile, and moderate in disposition. Another example is a webcomic, again an American one (I will not mention the Japanese *manga* and *anime* here, as they deserve a different study).[14] It is called *Starfighter* (by HamletMachine 2008) and is a homoerotic science fiction webcomic. Here Cain and Abel reproduce perfectly the stereotypes of the *yaoi manga*, the Japanese homoerotic *manga*, with a *seme* (攻め "assailant") and a *uke* (受け "receiver"). Extremely dislocated in time and space, the biblical pair reflects the ancestral dichotomy, amplified by new temporal vision of roles and local structures and ideology.

5 Queering the Peer

Cain and Abel are the most successful pair of brothers to have represented brotherhood in its most typical and paradigmatic feature: the dual relationship made of difference within equality. In one way or another, contemporary fiction has "queered" the two characters, either with brutal features or effeminate characteristics. It is an utterly masculine bond, as the word brotherhood, but also fratricide, implies—just like the French *fraternité*, which was part of the motto on which modernity is based.

It is no surprise then that comradeship can only be shared by men—bromances, brothers-in-arms, and all the other phrases about comradeship invariably portray the same concept in modern and contemporary culture. In fact, as Ricardo Quinones says, "as the masculine dominated language of brotherhood would indicate, it is hard for brotherhood not to be exclusive, not only of sisters but of others as well. […] We do not want great heroes to have brothers; brothers are not for the sons of destiny. […] The hero may travel with an entourage, even disciples, but he should have no brother. Achilles, Orestes, and Hamlet may have friends or confidants, but no brothers".[15] Cain must be the hero, the strongest part to survive—both physically and psychologically—because he has to become the true progenitor of mankind—though, according to most texts, the *evil* part of mankind. Again quoting Quinones, "brotherhood and blood were habitually conjoined. One drank blood from a cup with a sworn brother, and this practice summarizes the more fundamental enterprise in which comrades are engaged—that of risking and shedding blood".[16]

Therefore, Abel is the representative of herd mentality, while Cain is the "other", the outsider, the Jew, the black man: Cain is queer by archetypal and mythological characterisation, Abel is queer by successive, perhaps more ideological representations—almost by osmosis: the two ancestral brothers had to give a mirror reflection of their peer. Cain is the epitome of the difference within similarity, which occurs in brothers and even in twins, as it will often be in postromantic literature.

Cain is the other when enclosed in stereotypes, from which only rarely he succeeds in coming out in contemporary literature—as happens for example in Alexander Trocchi's novel, *Cain's Book* (1960), where in a beat surreal atmosphere Cain is the typical "played-out post-World-War-II existential hero, homosexual, and druggie artist".[17] The masculine, aggressive archetype has been queered too.

Also, let us not forget that another male character, another basic type, as Erich Auerbach calls them, bears a scar which makes other people recognise him: Ulysses. Just like him, Cain is a monomyth, an archetypal hero, whose stereotype implies that he must be a man. An evil man, but a man, whose actions are extreme, a figure who is rough and masculine. He is the villain in the fight, sometimes even his antagonistic self; as Philo believed, perhaps, when Cain kills his half—and I would add, his feminine half—he might actually be killing himself. One of the reasons why, at least up until twentieth-century literature, Cains are ambiguous and not easily defined from a psychological point of view, is that these characters do not self-confess. They are characters of status; they do not fulfil the procedure of individualisation that Foucault described as the way to know the truth of oneself.[18] We must also add that, as supposed by Derrida, "since the other is always already an aspect of the self, then absolute distinctions are logically impossible: discrete entities do not, and cannot, exist".[19] Thus brotherhood has sometimes become twinhood over the centuries.

Obviously, these are more or less stereotypical representations of the pair of brothers, but it is a matter of fact that in the modern world the questioning, dissatisfied, intellectually critical Cain is somehow more "masculine" than the "non-aspirant",[20] accommodating Abel—quite the opposite of what they were in the classical Christian era. Nonetheless, Cain keeps a vague roughness, sternness, and a greater vision—as the antifeminist stereotypes want to bestow on men. To queer such a character is also an act of destabilisation of common belief and is often an ideological engagement.

6 Conclusion

Within the borders of humanness, in the impossibility of coming out of intrinsic social behaviours, one of the most significant issues at stake with Cain's archetype is, as we have seen, the fact that he is the one expelled from the community, the one whose representations imply a nostalgic depiction of the community itself—and this is a central idea in Zygmunt Bauman's *Community: Seeking Safety in an Insecure World* (2000). Community is seen as a "paradise lost" or a paradise yet to be found. In postmodern society, Sullivan argues, critics of Queer Theory often represent it as "an example of a more general postmodern malady, a sort of a homesickness",[21] at least partially sharing Freud's ideas expressed in *Civilization and its Discontents*: community "embrace" traded off for your freedom.

We may conclude by observing that in the Cain and Abel paradigm the "queer one" in the most traditional way is usually the one who is not expelled by someone else—Cain's destiny—but eradicated from the earth itself by murder. Abel, the delicate, the more feminine, is destined to extinction together with his progeny. The impure survives and literature has only recently attempted to queer the survivor too. Over the last few decades the contemporary artistic imagination has been experimenting and familiarising itself with new forms of decontextualisation, which is quite often related to gender and, more in general, with all forms of identity *bildung*. These new archetypal characters perform their role in a way which goes against what is seen as normal or acceptable for the period and society that they represent in a fictional work. In doing so, not only do they "queer" mainstream society's idea of what it means to be a man, but also what an archetypal literary type is in its pliantness and permeability.

Notes

1. See Lyotard, J.-F. (1984). *The Postmodern Condition: a Report on Knowledge*. Minneapolis: University of Minnesota Press.
2. Halperin, D. (1995). *Saint Foucault: Towards a Gay Hagiography*. Oxford: Oxford University Press, p. 62.
3. References to the Bible are from the New International Version.
4. See S. Cannon, A., Hand, W.D., Talley, J. (1984). *Religion, Magic, Ghostlore: Popular Beliefs and Superstitions from Utah*. Salt Lake City: University of Utah.
5. See Williams, D. (1982). *Cain and Beowulf: A Study in Secular Allegory*. Toronto: Toronto UP; Mellinkoff, R. (1981). *The Mark of Cain*. Berkeley: University of California; O'Donoghue, H. (2003). What Has Baldr to Do with Lamech? The Lethal Shot of a Blind Man in Old Norse Myth and Jewish Exegetical Traditions. *Medium Aevum*, 72(1), 82–107; Bandy, S.C. (1973). Cain, Grendel, and the Giants of Beowulf. *Papers on Language and Literature*, 9, 235–249.
6. Wagner, E. (2013). Keeping It in the Family: Beowulf and the Tradition of Familicide in the Kin of Cain. *Hortulus Journal* 9(1), p. 36.
7. Ibid., p. 27.
8. Hodges, H.J. (2007). Cain's Fratricide: Original Violence as "Original Sin" in *Beowulf*. *Chungse Yongmunhak Medieval English Studies* 15(1), p. 32.
9. *The Woman's Bible* (1974), written by the nineteenth-century feminist Elizabeth Cady Stanton and a "Revising Committee", is one of the first attempts by women to evaluate the Judeo-Christian legacy and its impact on women's lives. Stanton does not go as far as to affirm that "God is a woman", but there are several contributions which discuss the gender of God.
10. One example is the 1999 film *Dogma*, where God takes the shape, among other terrestrial figures, of the pop singer Alanis Morissette.

11. Sullivan, N. (2003). *A Critical Introduction to Queer Theory*. New York: New York University, p. 190.
12. "The Cain myth must have seemed to a non-theological age to be more closely related to history than the Adamic myth" (Stock, E. (1977). Chaos, the Self and the Cain Myth: John Hay and Henry Adams. MLA session *The Cain and Abel Theme in Literature*, cited in Quinones, R.J. (1991). *The Changes of Cain: Violence and the Lost Brother in Cain and Abel Literature*. Princeton: Princeton University Press, p. 267, note 1.
13. Quinones, R.J. (1991). *The Changes of Cain*, p. 136.
14. In the Japanese vampire anime *Shiki* (2010), for example, there are numerous references to Cain and Abel, as the story is described as a metaphor where Cain and Abel are two sides of the same person, and in which the murder of Abel reflected Cain's rejection of God. In the famous series of light novels, *Trinity Blood* (2001–2005), the multiple Christian themes of the post-apocalyptic plot also include references to Cain and Abel: Cain Knightlord (Krusnik 01, also significantly referred as Contra Mundi) is Abel's older twin brother, depicted, with some variations in the novels, *manga*, and *anime*, with blond hair and piercings in both ears. A cover sees him being portrayed with red roses and a red banner inscribed with "igne natura, renovatur integra" ("through fire, nature is reborn whole"), the Christian medieval identification of the five petals of the rose with the five wounds of Christ. In other *manga* versions he is portrayed as a white-eared White Rabbit, as opposed to his brother, the black-eared rabbit, or with a ram's head, a reference to Baphomet, an occultist figure usually associated with evil. As a child, before his fusion with the nanomachines, Cain is compassionate and sensible, and demonstrates a wisdom far beyond his years. However, after his fusion with the machines, he becomes unstable as he combines his good nature with the nanomachines' bloodlust, becoming apathetic and remorseless, incapable of processing the consequences of his actions, or even totally careless: "The resulting being went completely insane, desiring the eradication of all life on Earth while maintaining an outwardly upbeat, childish, and somewhat air-headed demeanor" (source: http://trinityblood.wikia.com/wiki/Lilith_Sahl). In the same series Abel Nightroad (Krusnik 02) is the main protagonist, a member of a division of the Vatican's Ministry of Foreign Affairs. Abel has long silvery hair, tied with a black ribbon, blue-gray eyes, and wears small round glasses. He also wears a black priest's robe with embroidered crosses and white gloves. Originally he

hates humans, but ultimately changes his mind after the death of another Krusnik called Lilith Sahl.

15. Quinones, R.J. (1991), *The Changes of Cain*, pp. 5 and 7.
16. Ibid., p. 4.
17. Ibid., p. 206.
18. Foucault, M. (1980). *The History of Sexuality*. Vol. 1: *An Introduction*. New York: Vintage, p. 59.
19. Sullivan, N. (2003). *A Critical Introduction to Queer Theory*, p. 144.
20. Quinones, R.J. (1991), *The Changes of Cain*, p. 13.
21. Ibid., p. 144.

References

Auerbach, E. (1991). *Mimesis: The Representation of Reality in Western Literature*. Princeton: Princeton University Press.

Bandy, S. C. (1973). Cain, Grendel, and the Giants of Beowulf. *Papers on Language and Literature, 9*, 235–249.

Bauman, Z. (2000). *Community: Seeking Safety in an Insecure World*. Oxford: Polity Press.

Carey, M., art by Gross, P. (2009–2015). *The Unwritten*. New York: Vertigo.

Di Gennaro, P. (2015). *Wandering Through Guilt. The Cain Archetype in the Twentieth-Century Novel*. Newcastle-upon-Tyne: Cambridge Scholars.

Foucault, M. (1980). *The History of Sexuality, Volume 1: An Introduction*. New York: Vintage.

Halperin, D. (1995). *Saint Foucault: Towards a Gay Hagiography*. Oxford: Oxford University Press.

HamletMachine. (2008). *Starfighter*. Retrieved September 24, 2016, from http://starfightercomic.com/comic.php

Hesse, H. (1919). *Demian*. London, Chester Springs: Peter Owen.

Hodges, H. J. (2007). Cain's Fratricide: Original Violence as 'Original Sin' in *Beowulf. Chungse Yongmunhak Medieval English Studies, 15*(1), 31–56.

Léonard-Roques, V. (2003). *Caïn, figure de la modernité*. Paris: Champion.

Léonard-Roques, V. (2007). *Caïn et Abel. Rivalité et responsabilité*. Paris: Éditions du Rocher.

Lyotard, J.-F. (1984). *The Postmodern Condition: A Report on Knowledge*. Minneapolis: University of Minnesota Press.

Mellinkoff, R. (1981). *The Mark of Cain*. Berkley, Los Angeles, London: University of California Press.

Quinones, R. J. (1991). *The Changes of Cain: Violence and the Lost Brother in Cain and Abel Literature*. Princeton: Princeton University Press.

Saramago, J. (2012). *Cain*. London: Vintage.

Unamuno (de), M. (1917). *Abel Sanchez and Other Stories*. Washington, DC: Regnery Publishing.

Wagner, E. (2013). Keeping It in the Family: Beowulf and the Tradition of Familicide in the Kin of Cain. *Hortulus Journal, 9*(1), 27–51.

Williams, D. (1982). *Cain and Beowulf: A Study in Secular Allegory*. Toronto: Toronto UP.

7

An Effortless Voice: Queer Vocality and Transgender Identity in Kim Fu's *For Today I Am a Boy*

Serena Guarracino

1 Introduction

This chapter offers some reflections on the social and cultural relevance of vocal identity in the embodiment of queer subjectivities through a reading of Kim Fu's 2014 novel *For Today I Am a Boy*. Here, readers follow the *bildung* of Peter Huang, a young Canadian of Chinese descent, as she[1] undertakes the slow and painful journey from boy to woman, from "Peter" to "Audrey". This eccentric journey is mapped out through a web of intertextual references that this contribution aims at unravelling: my starting point is the title of the novel itself, a direct reference to the song "For Today I Am a Boy" by Antony Hegarty (see Antony and the Johnsons 2005). Antony's voice frames the story of Asian-American Peter as he grows into Audrey, as the song (quoted in the novel's epigraph) goes: "One day I'll grow up, I'll be a beautiful woman/[…] But for today, I am

S. Guarracino (✉)
Dipartimento di Studi Letterari, Linguistici e Comparati,
Università degli Studi di Napoli "L'Orientale", Napoli, Italy

P. Baker, G. Balirano (eds.), *Queering Masculinities in Language and Culture*,
Palgrave Studies in Language, Gender and Sexuality,
https://doi.org/10.1057/978-1-349-95327-1_7

a child. For today, I am a boy" (Fu 2014). Choosing the title—the only one in a narrative rather devoid of musical references—as a privileged "point of hearing"[2] allows for the relevance of vocal positioning to emerge, in the novel as well as in wider elaborations of queer positionalities.

By tracing references to vocal practices as diverse as Italian and Chinese opera and contemporary pop music, I attempt to trace a (necessarily partial) cultural history of the high male voice and its undermining of biologically assigned gender identities. My point is that *For Today I Am a Boy* bears traces of this history with its open reference to Antony, but also via subtler hints to cultural practices from the different backgrounds that shape the main character's journey. The novel features voice as "a particularly intense site for the emergence of the queer" (Jarman 2011, 4); however, although its narrative is concerned with a male-to-female transition, the term "queer" as used in the following pages does not simply designate either a transgender or a lesbian, gay, bisexual, trans, and/or intersex (LGBTI) identity. On the contrary, "queer" is intended here as a radical undermining of *any* fixed construction of subjectivity, be it along the lines of the sex-gender axis, of racial embodiments, or of cultural histories and formations. As José Esteban Muñoz has famously argued in *Cruising Utopia*, queer is "the rejection of a here and now and an insistence on potentiality or concrete possibility for another world" (2009, 1).

Antony's voice, as the heir of a long tradition of queer "assigned male" vocalities, embodies this utopian drive for another world. It is also the most evident element in an imaginary landscape where intertextuality works not just as a more or less explicit reference to another text, but as what Julia Kristeva notoriously identified as a practice undermining the unity of both the subject and object positions (see Oliver 1993, 93). The novel hence makes use of what could be called "queer intertextuality" to unmake masculinity as a heteronormative discourse, but also femininity as a unified arrival point of the transition process. Queer intertextuality also tackles the cultural conflicts spun out in Fu's novel, where the character's Asian descent—he is the third out of four children and only son of a Cantonese family living in Fort Michel,[3] Canada—emerges as a major constituent of the heteronormative paradigm.

At the beginning of the novel, growing into a Chinese man appears to be the only option available to the boy Peter. Hence, when Peter becomes

Audrey he not only becomes the "beautiful woman" evoked in Antony's song, but also grows into an "Audrey Hepburn" persona, apparently morphing into a white, British woman. *Sabrina* (1954), Hepburn's iconic performance referenced multiple times in the novel, works as a counterpart of the "transvestite Oriental" stereotype, the mark of shame for Chinese effeminacy. The dialogue between these two tropes expose how the novel's gendered discourses are interrupted by racial and cultural difference; it also makes Peter/Audrey's journey utopian, quite literally aiming at a non-place, as none of these models represents a safe place of arrival.

Thus, in this chapter, I trace the trajectory of high-ranged male vocality in Western performativity (with a short detour on Chinese musical theatre) in order to shed light on the intertwined cultural histories that converge into the making of Peter/Audrey's utopia. To do this, I will first explore the history of the high male voice in Western music, where it has been constantly cherished while at the same time disparagingly associated with effeminacy and other forms of deviancy from the heterosexual norm. Then I will trace the association of male falsetto with ethnic difference, to highlight the intersectionality of race and gender as complementary but also competing paradigms in Peter/Audrey's journey. Finally, I will offer a queer reading of the novel's voices to show how Fu's main character does not perform a straight trajectory from a male to a female identity; on the contrary, Peter/Audrey's is a quest whose ending, paradoxically, both overlaps with its starting point and looks at more journeys to come.

2 What Makes a Male Voice?

Near the end of the novel, Peter dresses up as Audrey Hepburn for Halloween and, in a self-defining gesture, introduces herself to some guests with the name she will eventually choose as her own: "'Hello-*o*', I said. I added a melodic whistle to the name when I said it myself, the voice *effortless*. 'My name is Audrey'" (Fu 2014; my italics). Audrey's voice, as she finally enjoys the feeling of being comfortable in her own skin, is significantly "effortless"—a voice fitting perfectly with her newly donned female persona. This is rather uncommon in narratives about transsexual experiences, where the voice often emerges as an element resistant to transitioning because its range and tone are determined by elements—such as hormonal patterns and larynx conformation—that are supposed to be more rigidly related to biological sex.[4] The very word used to define the high male voice—"falsetto"—speaks of falseness and trickery, the very opposite of Peter's voice as it finally becomes Audrey's.

Voice pitch is indeed a pivotal index of gender identity in everyday communication, but also one that exposes how difficult it may be to attribute a given feature to either biological factors or social and cultural conditioning. In their fundamental contribution to sociophonetics, Paul Foulkes, James M. Scobbie, and Dominic Watt state that "some gender-appropriate speech behavior must be learned in childhood rather than being determined solely by anatomical differences between the sexes", leading to the conclusion that "[i]t can therefore be difficult, even impossible, to disentangle socially influenced variation from variation which is the product of biology and physics" (Foulkes et al. 2010, 706). In the same individual, voice pitch may vary according to many factors, such as ageing and hormone therapies; it can also be manipulated through more or less self-conscious vocal positioning, which can be altered not only through time but also according to social context. Moreover, pitch often becomes a meaningful category in relation to gender identity only when it differs from socially expected voice ranges: "Most of us are familiar with the sensation of hearing a person speak, and noticing voice characteristics that do not conform to our vocal stereotypes, e.g. a man with a high and shrill voice, or a woman with a deep and sonorous voice" (Biemans 1998, 41).

In this area, falsetto voices—and especially male falsettos—occupy a peculiar position as social and cultural signifier. Robert J. Podesva, in his study on the role of voice quality in creating a public persona for speakers, defines falsetto as follows:

> The glottal configuration for falsetto gives rise to rapid vocal fold vibration, correlating acoustically with a high fundamental frequency (f0) level which can range from 240 Hz to 634 Hz in the speech of men. This contrasts sharply with the average modal voice f0 level for adult men of approximately 100 Hz. (Podesva 2007, 480)

Rapid vibration of vocal folds is not by any means unique to men, and women can use falsetto to produce voices higher in frequency than their "average" pitch as well. Yet, as Podesva clearly notes, male falsetto is invested with major significance in relation to the production of a gendered identity, as it contrasts with the cultural capital that a deep voice confers in relation to socially constructed perceptions of masculinity. Podesva explicitly talks about "gay-sounding voices", stating that "using the high f0 levels characteristic of falsetto phonation is a socially marked behavior, at odds with more culturally normative pitch practices for men, and may be involved in the performance of stereotypical gay identity" (Podesva 2007, 480).

While sociolinguistics has only recently started to investigate the significance of pitch, music offers a long and complex history of vocal manipulation; differently from everyday practices, however, the individual elements of a musical performance—including voice range and its relationship with the gendering of the performing body—are subordinated to the pleasure that can be aroused in listeners. This does not mean that the musical voice works independently from the "everyday" speaking voice: on the contrary, the two realms often intersect with each other. The singing voice puts into operation a complex mechanism of identification in listeners which has been subject to a great deal of scrutiny; in particular, practices such as sing-along and lip-synching may function to mark a person's identity positioning in relation to different social realms, among which gender emerges as crucial (see Jarman 2011). As Michael Chanan writes, "if the experience of music is subjective then this subjectivity is not so spontaneous and naïve as usually supposed, but is constructed by the subject's own social, cultural and historical situation and self-interest" (Chanan 1994, 8). "Public" voices, such as singers', play a central role in how any subject places or perceives herself/himself vocally, as they offer a recognizable gendered (but also racialized) identity which the subject may intend to partake in.

In this context, male high voices emerge as a crucial cultural nexus rather early in the history of European classical music—a nexus that, as I have explored elsewhere, is intertwined both with gender politics and with British national identity discourses (see Guarracino 2004, 2011). This is especially the case of the Italian *castrati*, who embody with specific historical relevance the gender politics of eighteenth-century English theatre: singers such as Nicolini, Farinelli, or Senesino offered to amazed Londoners the spectacle of heroes (such as Julius Caesar from Handel's *Giulio Cesare*, 1724) endowed with a soaring voice that far exceeded the perceived "natural" male range (see e.g. Dame 1994). In the English press of the time, these freakish "capons"—generally poor or orphaned boys from Southern Italy who had been mutilated in early youth in order to preserve their extraordinary voices—were routinely accused of being effeminate, and Italian opera was cast as England's "feminine other" (McGeary 1994, 17).[5] *Castrati* were to disappear from European stages: while the last one to perform in a theatre was Giovanni Battista Velluti in 1825, and the last known castrato, Alessandro Moreschi, died in 1922, by the end of the eighteenth century the high male voice had already fallen into disrepute in theatres throughout Europe.[6]

Yet England retained its own, centuries-old tradition of male altos—not in theatres though, but in churches, and, having not been subjected to any mutilation, these singers perfected a falsetto technique that allowed them to sing in a higher than "natural" range. Differently from the Italian opera of the time, which disappeared with the *castrati* who interpreted it, this religious music has remained a lasting tradition throughout England; so much so that under the head "Falsetto" from the *The New Grove Dictionary of Music and Musicians* it is stated that "it is only in England that second-mode singing enjoyed an uninterrupted, widespread tradition, particularly in all-male cathedral and collegiate choirs, academia, and in the glee club tradition" (Negus et al. 2001, 538). Nonetheless, the *New Grove* prefers the diction "second-mode singing" to "falsetto", because "the phonatory mode known as 'falsetto' has been equated with 'unnatural' as opposed to 'natural', partly through misleading philological usage" (537).[7]

Falsetto's supposed unnaturalness exposes the complex cultural role played by male voices which do not conform to the standard range expected from men: hence in the *Oxford Dictionary of Music* it is stated that falsetto means a "singing method used by males, particularly tens. [tenors], to achieve a note or notes higher than comes within the normal range of their [voice]" (Kennedy et al. 2013, 278).[8] As the tenor is the highest of male voices in Western classification, it follows that falsetto resides in an aural realm associated with women. The cultural grounds for

Podesva's identification of falsetto as a gay male signifier start to gain historical consistency here: there is something definitely not "straight" in falsetto when used by a man. Indeed, cultural critic Wayne Koestenbaum writes that "falsetto is part of the history of effeminacy. [...] Long before anyone knew what a homosexual was, entire cultures knew to mock men who sang unconventionally high" (1994a, 165). The superimposition of homosexuality and effeminacy underplays the challenge male homosexuals represent for heteronormative masculinity by performing a conflation between the male homosexual and the feminine, a conflation that has only recently been challenged.

Readers have no way of locating the pitch of Peter/Audrey's "melodic whistle". Yet, the novel clarifies its symbolic distance from the taint of inauthenticity that accompanies the cultural history of a high voice coming from an assigned male body. In this, it mirrors recent trends in music performance which have both countered and exploited the socially perceived "unnaturalness" of the male high voice. This does not mean that the stigma associated with a man singing "high" has diminished over time: but this voice has also been appropriated in different ways to mark resistance to hegemonic masculinity. Pop music has offered a substantial contribution to the presence of falsetto voices in the public arena: Antony Hegarty, in this sense, may be considered the (temporary) point of arrival of a long history of high male singing as the voice rebelling against normative gender discourses. This history, from the eighteenth-century *castrati* all the way to the pop and rock experiences of the 1970s and 1980s, features falsetto as a shifting signifier, as it has been used with equal effectiveness by performers showing off an ostentatious (if sometimes boyish) masculinity such as Michael Jackson and Marvin Gaye, and by singers committed to the battle for gay and transgender rights, such as Jimmy Somerville and Sylvester.[9]

3 Beauty and the Butterfly

Simon Ravens offers an interesting map of the ways male altos may have made their way in contemporary music, underlining, for example the centrality of racial difference in some uses of falsetto in pop and rock, which trace back to African-American music. Yet, among the many and different lineages of the high male voice, Ravens concludes that "in truth, though, popular singers probably find and use falsetto simply because it is there" (2014, 203): falsetto is there, in any assigned male body, ready to come out. Antony, an England-born singer and founder of the Antony and the Johnson ensemble, uses falsetto intermittently and seamlessly with other registers, and the emotional impact of his songs does not stem from a virtuoso's ability to defy a gender assigned vocal range. On the contrary, as John Hodgman argues, Antony's voice shows "the pace and intimacy of breathing" (Hodgman 2005, n.p.). The performer's appearance mirrors this musical choice, functioning as an exploration of possibilities more than an assigned male assuming a female persona: "The makeup and silk slips he has worn onstage have never seemed to be an imitation of womanliness but more a pursuit of a kind of inclusive idea of beauty that he is still in the midst of defining" (Hodgman 2005, n.p.).

Beauty, this elusive category to which the male body has had intermittent access, in Antony's imaginary equates freedom, the freedom to grow up as a beautiful woman or as a bird—as the title of the album including "For Today I Am a Boy", *I Am a Bird Now* (Antony and the Johnsons 2005), suggests. The desire to explore the endless possibilities of one's own body emerges as a central preoccupation of Antony's writing, and in the speech "Future Feminism" the singer has explicitly linked transgender practices to a radical political involvement, based on the intimate relationship between the body and the material world: "I've been searching and searching for that little bit of my constitution that isn't of this place and I still haven't found it. Every atom of me, every element of me seems to resonate, seems to reflect the great world around me. […] I truly believe that unless we move into feminine systems of governance we don't have a chance on this planet" (Antony and the Johnsons 2012). Antony here casts herself/himself as spokesperson of a queer utopia where, as in Fu's novel, the "feminine" is not a biologically, anatomically, and/or socially gendered identity but a radically antagonist vision of the human's place in the universe. Indeed, in much the same way, the "beautiful girl" from "For Today I Am a Boy" is not a normative bodily standard but, on the contrary, the embodiment of the multiple possibilities to happiness inscribed within the body.[10]

This possibility finds a painful counterpoint in the novel, where a six-year-old Peter goes into a crying fit when bluntly told by his older sister Helen that he cannot grow up to be pretty like their eldest sister, Adele: "'You can't, Peter. You can be handsome, like Father or Bruce Lee. [...] You're a boy" (Fu 2012, position 211). Peter immediately rejects this socially imposed "handsomeness"; although imbued with advantages of its own (something his three sisters will always be a painful reminder of), the novel highlights the curtailing of possibilities and the entrenchment of desires that heteronormative masculinity embodies in a rigid system of familial and social expectations. Moreover, Bruce Lee, as a viable model of masculinity, works as an intertextual reference to the context of Chinese migration to North America. Masculinity for Chinese, and more generally East Asian, migrants has historically been a vexed question, as David Eng has argued in exploring the feminization of Asian-American men through an analysis—among other texts—of David Henry Hwang's well-known play *M. Butterfly*. Here, the traumas of sexual and racial difference are negotiated by the white male subject through the symbolic emasculation of the Chinese male body (see Eng 2001, 138–166). Yet the gendered identity of *M. Butterfly*'s Asian Other—aptly named Song—is elaborated through performance practices from Chinese opera, where female characters are traditionally played by men. In this context male falsetto, already tainted with effeminacy to the Western ear, also becomes the cultural mark of racial difference: "Falsetto constituted a significant part of the Chinese theater experience. [...] This situation constituted, conveniently for the nineteenth-century Western tourists, a rendition, a dramatization, and a sonification of effeminate Chinese" (Rao 2015, 55).

There is very little of the multiple possibilities of a queer masculinity or femininity in the shadow of the transvestite Oriental as emerges at the intersection between gender and racial hegemonic discourses. Yet, when it is featured in the novel, this stereotype marks two significant moments in Peter's road to her queer utopia. The transvestite Oriental appears for the first time in the tales of Chef, head of the kitchen where young Peter is working as a dishwasher while still at his parents' in Fort Michel. Chef, a big man with hands "large enough to eclipse mine completely" (Fu 2014, position 968), features as Peter's first love interest, and embodies a powerful but benign masculinity whose potential for violence is only subtly hinted at. He distorts Peter's family name—making everyone call him Wong instead of the correct Huang—and avowedly likes the new employee because "I feel like I could whip you into shape. Like you're not anything yet" (position 973). The possible negative impact of Chef's paternalistic stance is played down when he actually saves Peter from Simon Hughman, his co-worker and former schoolmate. Simon bullies Peter repeatedly and eventually traps him in the kitchen cooler. Being rescued and swept from his knees into Chef's arms offers the main character, half-dazed by the cold, the first awareness of the sexual nature of his attraction to his boss: "As I woke more fully, I leaned on him [Chef] harder, letting myself enjoy the firmness of his body, his smell of smoke and cooking meat and burned hair and spices and something more delicious besides" (Fu 2014, position 1269).

Chef introduces in Peter's and the novel's imaginary sexual desires and practices that do not conform to the biological assignation of the bodies involved. He is a champion of male heterosexuality and prowess, and his tale of when "I fucked a guy in Montreal" (position 1160) comes as quite a surprise for his interlocutors as well as for the readers. Still, this tale not only comes at the end of a long list of sexual adventures with women, but is meant to be a part of the same narration: "Not much to tell. I met a girl, I fucked her, and she turned out to be a he" (position 1164). The scene, told in graphic detail, echoes the misunderstanding at the core of Hwang's *M. Butterfly*, where the main character Gallimard has a relationship with a Chinese male singer believing for years that he is in love with a suitably bashful—but sexually available—Chinese woman. In much the same vein, the body of Chef's lover, though never racially marked as Asian, is described as "smooth as a baby's", with a behind "like perfect, firm pillows and round as peaches" and covered by a "short, sexy kimono thing" (Fu 2014, position 1172). The kimono, actually a Japanese traditional garment, reinforces the parallel with the *M. Butterfly* narrative, where Gallimard falls in love with Song as he listens to his performance of excerpts from Puccini's *Madama Butterfly*.[11]

A Chinese man dressed in a kimono is here elected as a suitable object of sexual desire for a Caucasian heterosexual male such as Chef—an authorization which does not get lost on Peter who projects this fantasy over his own body: "I turned my back to the mirror and looked over my shoulder. […] My robe became a silk kimono, black with a red rash, tied loosely. I pulled it slowly up, clutching what I needed to at the front, lifting it high. *Round as peaches*, Chef said, squeezing each one, testing for ripeness" (Fu 2014, position 1293; italics in the text). This body, as Teresa de Lauretis has argued for *M. Butterfly*, is nothing but "an orientalist fantasy based on hierarchies of gender, race, and colonial and political domination" (de Lauretis 1999, 308); yet this is also, at the beginning of the novel, the only fantasy that allows Peter's assigned masculinity to experience the disturbing pull of the queer. At this point in the narrative, Peter has no other resource than to "pull a Butterfly", a popular expression mentioned by Hwang in the afterword to his play meaning "playing the submissive Oriental number" (Hwang 1989, 95): in the aforementioned episode when Chef saves him from the cooler, the narrating "I" exposes how Peter's assumption of a vulnerable persona saves his life, as he exploits Chef to have Simon fired on the spot: "I buried my face in Chef's armpit, trying to go limp, to seem as pathetic as possible. My eyes watered from the strong light. I let the tears flow" (Fu 2014, position 1271).

The ability to "pull a Butterfly" allows Peter to survive to a world where his needs—his desire to wear high heels, or his sexual attraction to Chef—must remain hidden from public censure; yet it also represents a hindrance to his eventual metamorphosis into Audrey. His submissiveness to other people's vision of him only gives him access to the patriarchal vision of femininity *and* to the Western vision of Asianness,[12] both of which he impersonates in his relationship with Margie. An older woman with a soft spot for "exotic" younger men, she is introduced to the reader clasping a diamond bracelet to Peter's wrist and telling him: "I always wanted a little China boy […]. I've never had one before" (Fu 2014, position 1531). Their relationship is immediately articulated through an overturning of traditional gender power relations—it is the woman who takes on a younger lover seducing him through costly gifts—but one that reinstates racial ones: Margie hence works obsessively to make Peter her own "little China boy", plucking his sparse body hair, making him "wear a brocade hat with a braid built into it from a novelty store" and "fake an accent, a cruel mimicry of my father" (Fu 2014, position 1566).

Given the intersection of racial and gender codifications, Margie's sometimes violent coercion becomes a way for Peter to further explore how to queer his assigned male status. Now the split between the narrating "I" and "Peter Huang", the boy-to-become-man persona, becomes explicit: "Peter should have protested, punched her on behalf of Asian men everywhere. But I was—I was—drunk. The name that had never fit slipped completely out of my grasp" (Fu 2014, position 1551). It is with her that Peter dresses as a woman in front of another person for the first time, and although the complex ritual staged by Margie—first making him wear her own underwear, then painting his face with elaborate make-up—is devised to humiliate him for not being able to engage with her sexually (climaxing in her choking him with a feathered boa), Peter still introduces the episode as "the best thing" (Fu 2014, position 1571) that happens during their short and stormy affair. As their relationship progresses, Peter becomes more and more aware that he cannot bring himself to feel any sexual desire for Margie; his tentative explorations of her body make him aware of the fact that he wants Margie's body not to "possess" sexually but as his own: "From this angle, it was perfect, it was just where it was supposed to be. It was between my legs" (Fu 2014, position 1561).

In both episodes, with Chef and with Margie, Peter is significantly mute, as it is the other characters that tell the story—Chef about his man in a kimono, and Marge of the "little China boy" she is going to mould him into. Peter's eventual voice—Audrey's effortless 'Hello-*o*'—emerges only after the main character has gone through a complex network of identifications and disavowals with the voices of other characters—a dynamics where, Jarman argues, "a site for the emergence of queer [is contained]" (2011, 2). Jarman finds this interplay in the relation with the singing voice; thanks to the musical frame symbolically offered by the novel, here it can be related to "everyday", speaking voices as well. The first is Simon's, his antagonist and colleague at the restaurant in Fort Michel, who is remembered because "he has a notoriously squeaky voice, as immortalized on the boys'-room wall: *Simon Hymen/forever a virgin/voice so high/the girls won't screw him*" (Fu 2014, position 1047). The novel does not give out any hint about Simon's sexual orientation, but his "high, wounded voice" (Fu 2014, position 1064) or "painful contralto" (Fu 2014, position 1148) is strongly remindful of Podesva's "gay-sounding voice". Yet Simon resists this social identification—and the stigma that comes with is—through behaviour Chef will derogatorily define as "macho fuckup" (Fu 2014, position 1060). His final violent gesture shows the wound of his endangered masculinity, and the insulting rhyme marks Peter's victory as Simon is fired: "Simon Hymen, forever a virgin, voice so high the girls won't screw him" (Fu 2014, position 1276). Simon's high-pitched voice features here as any man's nightmare, a "natural" voice exposing the male body's vulnerability to ridicule in a social context that values deep voices in men and associates high voices derogatorily with effeminacy.

Peter's straightforward disidentification with Simon is due to the violence associated with the character, but also to the disgrace of having a voice that does not collocate with the apparent gender of the body that produces it. Such a voice queers the pitch of heteronormative paradigms, in the sense of "to interfere with, to spoil the business" mentioned by Wayne Koestenbaum in the introduction to the miscellany *Queering the Pitch* (1994b, 1). Yet as the narration proceeds, queer pitches start to have a very different effect on Peter. As he is engaged in a relation with Claire, an activist from a fundamentalist Christian church called The Pathway, one such voice calls out to him. Claire, a lesbian who is trying to redeem herself from what she believes is the result of a sinful nature, is taking Peter on a round of distributing flyers for Pathway at the Village in Montreal, and here they are approached by "a woman [...]. Her voice was throaty, awkward. False. [...] Thick-limbed, thick-shouldered. Square jaw smothered in orange-toned foundation, fake eyelashes in the daytime. Still somehow convincing" (Fu 2014, position 2091). The slow recognition of the assigned male body that transpires in the woman confronting them in angry tones pulls Peter off balance, reminding him of his own desire to grow up and become a beautiful woman: "I felt a sinking sensation, like the sidewalk had gone soft under my feet" (Fu 2014, position 2091).

The same feeling will overcome Peter when confronted with the "deep and rich" (Fu 2014, position 2460) voice of John, his new employer in Montreal after he breaks up with Claire: "I thought of the bar employee who had sent me and Claire across the street while we were preaching, her artificial falsetto, the way the pavement had melted" (Fu 2014, position 2460). The woman's "artificial" falsetto and John's deep voice mark both bodies as a result of a painful process of self-definition, and yet

John's "natural voice" (Fu 2014, position 2570) matches his muscular figure and light beard more than his original assigned female status, making Peter doubt that he could have ever been born a girl. Peter's change of perception—from "artificial" to "natural"—appears to be caused by a shift in listening practice: at the moment of the first encounter he perceives the high-pitched voice coming from a male body as "false"; while the second case represents a pivotal moment in Peter's road towards a queer utopia, as it is through John that he becomes acquainted with the practices and politics of the queer movement. The fact that Peter finds no discrepancy between John's almost hyper-masculine "veiny forearms [with] visible seams of muscle" (Fu 2014, position 2060) and his voice marks Peter's recognition of the many engendering possibilities of any body, including his own.

And yet, in some way, John and his partner Eileen's attitude towards Peter mirrors Chef's and Margie's, wanting to shape Peter into a person fitting their own desires:

> [John and Eileen] beamed at me like proud parents. They'd made me into a project. [...] As soon as I said it, as soon as I said what they wanted me to say, everything would change. And I still didn't believe them—you couldn't just rename yourself, you couldn't tear down the skyline and rebuild and think there wouldn't be consequences. (Fu 2014, position 2754)

Peter/Audrey's queer utopia cannot be found here, not even in the overtly white-centred universe of queer activism the character is confronted with. The novel shows how it is impossible for Peter to fit seamlessly into the new family John, Eileen, and their friends have created. What separates them, in a way that the novel does not try to resolve, is Peter's experience as a Canadian of Chinese descent who lacks the cultural privilege of whiteness. Eng convincingly argues, in reference to Judith Butler's work, that "heterosexuality gains its discursive power through its tacit coupling with a hegemonic, unmarked whiteness" (Eng 2001, 13). This discursive power is supported by the emasculation of the racial other, and this emasculation is not a queer practice, as it repeats hegemonic narratives of racial difference and still casts femininity as a diminutive subject position, and not as an empowering realm of bodily possibilities.

The gender binary that constructs femininity as a diminished masculinity is interrupted by racial difference when Peter dresses up as Audrey Hepburn: "There she stood, at last: the iconic Audrey, only with Adele's almond eyes, her sloping cheekbones" (Fu 2014, position 2764). Adele, Peter's elder sister and prominent icon of beauty during his early years, surfaces under the Audrey Hepburn's costume as the actual model of Peter's transition. Adele's identification with Hepburn is explored earlier in the novel, when the four children go to the local cinema to watch Hepburn's *Sabrina*: in the darkness of the cinema theatre, Adele "looked just like Audrey Hepburn—the gamine smile, the swan-necked beauty" (Fu 2014, position 2764). In the process of growing up as a beautiful woman, Peter/Audrey does not join a new family but returns to her own, as she migrates to Berlin to join with her sisters, ironically following her father's footsteps.

The final passage breaks the flow of the novel, juxtaposing a scene from the past and one from the future in a narrative voice which does not feature the first person readers have by now become accustomed to. The first scene offers a brief flashback of Audrey's father, leaving for Canada: "Guangzhou and Beijing. Father in an airport, after his father bribed a doctor and a bureaucrat and a friend in Hong Kong who pretended to be a relative. […] Go, his father says. Go and be reborn" (Fu 2014, position 2897). The second, set in a dreamlike Germany, sees the four sisters finally reunited in a family picture: "'We're sisters', Bonnie says. '*Wir sind Schwestern.* This is Adele, Helen, and Audrey'" (position 2901). Migration seems here to be the ultimate queer utopia, so that Peter can "go and be reborn" as Audrey just as his father had been reborn as a respectable Western businessman in the move from China to Canada. Migration foregrounds Muñoz's "concrete possibility of another world" to be always on the verge of happening, Antony's "feminist future" to be always in the making. This also means queering masculinity to disempower its hegemonic narrative; Peter/Audrey's father, his toxic masculinity resulting from the painful fracture of migration, becomes the locus where a queer utopia can start to be imagined.

4 Conclusion

For Today I Am a Boy coalesces different public fantasies—Bruce Lee, the Oriental woman, Audrey Hepburn—as possible points of identification for Peter's self-fashioning. Among them, Antony is never mentioned if not in the title and epigraph of the novel, hinting in a subtle way to the journey through voices (Chef's, Margie's, John's) and silences (Peter's, but also his sisters') spun by the novel. Through Antony's voice, Peter's *bildung* can be read as emphatically *not* a story of transitioning from one hegemonic model—masculinity, whiteness—to another—femininity, the 'Oriental'—which would eventually end up reinforcing the first. On the contrary, the novel supports a notion of the fluidity of gender roles and personas and the truth of a voice that belongs to its own body, independently from its expected pitch or received gender assignation, such as Antony's. Welded together by different cultural refractions, these two voices—one musical and embodied, the other literary and disincarnated—show the overlapping of gendered and racial discourses on the high-ranged male voice, marking its prominence as cultural signifier today. Antony's voice shows the effortlessness of high pitch as one possible voice of an assigned male body, thus overturning the long story of ostracism and freakishness associated with it; starting from Antony's echo, *For Today I Am a Boy* overturns and disrupts normative expectations on gender and racial identity by shaping a character whose effortless voice does not need vocal coaching or hormone therapies, but only the possibility of being breathed out.

Notes

1. Pronouns are a sensitive issue in transgender identity politics: Kim Fu's novel does not address them directly, as the use of a first person narrator reduces references to the main character as he/she to a minimum. In discussing the novel, I will use the male pronoun for the main character when I discuss passages from the novel before the character starts her

transition; for passages coeval and following this moment I will use the female pronoun.

2. I am borrowing this expression from Adriana Cavarero's well-known insight on sound, and particularly the human voice, as a relational positionality opposed to the all-encompassing economy of the visual (Cavarero 2005, 121).
3. Fort Michel is the name with which the place is referenced in the novel, although the town in Ontario is actually spelled Fort Mitchell. This makes Peter's hometown an imaginary as well as a material place: the new name more explicitly expresses the negotiation between English (Mitchell) and French (Michel) in Canada, and thus references to the main character's own cultural predicament as a Canadian person of Chinese descent.
4. For example, see the opening sequence of the film *Transamerica*, which shows a voice training tutorial video for M to F transition: rather significantly, the only complete phrase—among many vocalizations—used to try out different inflexions in order to find the perfect voice for the newly gendered body is "This is the voice I want to use" (see *Transamerica*, dir. Duncan Tucker, USA 2005).
5. Yet, both McGeary (2000) and Helen Berry in her biography of the castrato Giusto Ferdinando Tenducci, who in 1765 eloped with an Irish girl from a wealthy family, convincingly argue that *castrati* were not just emasculated men who transgressed into femininity. More dangerously, they elaborated an alternative masculinity where their physical deficiency could be compensated by other qualities such as honour, reputation, and artistic taste—an emerging paradigm in the Georgian period, "a kind of polite masculinity to which castrati not only subscribed but acted as admired cultural leaders" (Berry 2011, 70).
6. For a thorough history of *castrati* in European theatres see Heriot (1956).
7. More recently, male altos have starred in the early music revival, a performance movement mostly stemming from Elizabethan and Restoration musical practices. Today, the rediscovery of early music has become a global phenomenon in Western classical performance, with more than one generation of singers—now called "countertenors" rather than the more culturally tainted "falsettists"—bringing the male high voice on the forefront of celebrity classical singing. For a thorough history of the movement see Haskell (1996).

8. Here I am purposefully not taking into account musical discourses that distinguish between falsetto and head voice as two different ways of producing a higher vocal pitch in men. This distinction is in itself controversial (see e.g. Ravens 2014, 11), and rests on the centuries-old disparaging of falsetto as inauthentic and effeminate. Moreover, even if applicable, this is a distinction that would not be necessarily perceptible to the untrained ear, and as the chapter moves into the realm of pop music this will become a major issue in my argument.
9. This connection between *castrati* and contemporary pop icons is drawn in the documentary *Heavenly Voices*, to which I worked as consultant alongside singer and performer Ernesto Tomasini. Although this contribution veers towards different textualities, I want to thank Ernesto for the inspiring exchanges we have had through the years, and for sharing with me his priceless insights on the issues of voice pitch and identity (gendered and otherwise) that he has been exploring in his performances; see *Heavenly Voices*, dir. Gino Pennacchi and Alessandro Scillitani, Germany 2013.
10. This approach resonates in the use of gendered pronouns for this artist, which has recently witnessed a notable shift. Antony has apparently never dictated any policy in this respect, and Hodgman does indeed use the male pronoun in his 2005 interview; yet in the recent controversy over her refusal to attend the 2016 Academy Awards ceremony the artist, under the gender-unspecific name of Anohni, is consistently referred to in the feminine in the press covering the issue (see e.g. Finger 2016; Walker 2016). In the communication explaining her refusal to attend the ceremony due to the fact that she was not asked to perform, Anohni straightforwardly defines herself as "an androgynous transwoman", and ascribes her exclusion from the prestigious evening's line-up to the "system of social oppression and diminished opportunities for transpeople that has been employed by capitalism in the U.S. to crush our dreams and our collective spirit" (quoted in Pitchfork 2006).
11. Gallimard's blindness to cultural specificities as regards "the Orient" is actually made fun of in the play; as he praises her "convincing" performance of Butterfly, the Chinese singer retorts: "Convincing? As a Japanese woman? The Japanese used hundreds of our people for medical

experiments during the war, you know. But I gather such an irony is lost on you" (Hwang 1989, 17).

12. Peter's father, on the other hand, emancipates himself from the emasculated Asian male stereotype by endorsing an uncompromising masculinity he means to pass on to his son: this cultural self-fashioning includes both not allowing his children to learn Cantonese and taking a white mistress, in a landscape where the sexual politics of the Western nuclear family model tightly intertwine with the cultural clash experienced by Chinese migrants in North America.

References

Antony and the Johnsons. (2005). *I Am a Bird Now.* Secretly Canadian.

Antony and the Johnsons. (2012). Future Feminism. In *Cut the Word.* Rough Trade Records.

Berry, H. (2011). *The Castrato and His Wife.* New York: Oxford University Press.

Biemans, M. (1998). The Effect of Biological Gender (Sex) and Social Gender (Gender Identity) on Three Pitch Measures. *Linguistics in the Netherlands, 1,* 41–52.

Cavarero, A. (2005). *For More Than One Voice: Toward a Philosophy of Vocal Expression* (P. A. Kottman, Trans.). Stanford: Stanford University Press.

Chanan, M. (1994). *Musica Practica. The Social Practice of Western Music from Gregorian Chant to Postmodernism.* London and New York: Verso.

Dame, J. (1994). Unveiled Voices. Sexual Difference and the Castrato. In P. Brett, E. Wood, & G. C. Thomas (Eds.), *Queering the Pitch. The New Gay and Lesbian Musicology* (pp. 139–151). New York and London: Routledge.

Eng, D. L. (2001). *Racial Castration: Managing Masculinity in Asian America.* New York: Duke University Press.

Finger, B. (2016, February 25). Transgender Oscar Nominee Anohni Explained Why She Will Not Be Attending in a Powerful Essay. *Jezebel.* Retrieved March 11, 2016, from http://jezebel.com/transgender-oscar-nominee-anohni-explained-why-she-will-1761360670

Foulkes, P., Scobbie, J. M., & Watt, D. (2010). Sociophonetics. In W. J. Hardcastle, J. Laver, & F. E. Gibbon (Eds.), *The Handbook of Phonetic Science* (2nd ed., pp. 703–754). Oxford: Wiley-Blackwell.

Fu, K. (2014). *For Today I Am a Boy*. Kindle ed. Boston and New York: Mariner Books/Houghton Mifflin Harcourt.

Guarracino, S. (2004). Voicing the Archive. Sexual/National Politics in Early Music. *Anglistica AION, 1–2*, 185–201.

Guarracino, S. (2011). Voices from the South: Music, Castration, and the Displacement of the Eye. In L. Cazzato (Ed.), *Anglo-Southern Relations: From Deculturation to Transculturation* (pp. 40–51). Nardò: Salento Books.

Haskell, H. (1996). *The Early Music Revival. A History*. Mineola, NY: Dover.

Heriot, A. (1956). *The Castrati in Opera*. London: Calder and Boyars.

Hodgman, J. (2005, September 4). Antony Finds His Voice. *The New York Times*. Retrieved November 10, 2015, from http://www.nytimes.com/2005/09/04/magazine/antony-finds-his-voice.html?_r=1

Hwang, D. H. (1989). *M. Butterfly*. London and New York: Penguin.

Jarman, F. (2011). *Queer Voices: Technologies, Vocalities, and the Musical Flaw*. London: Palgrave.

Kennedy, M., Rutherford-Johnson, T., & Kennedy, J. (2013). *The Oxford Dictionary of Music*. Oxford: Oxford University Press.

Koestenbaum, W. (1994a). *The Queen's Throat. Opera, Homosexuality, and the Mystery of Desire*. London: Penguin.

Koestenbaum, W. (1994b). Queering the Pitch: A Posy of Definition and Impersonation. In P. Brett, E. Wood, & G. C. Thomas (Eds.), *Queering the Pitch. The New Gay and Lesbian Musicology* (pp. 1–5). New York and London: Routledge.

McGeary, T. (1994). Gendering Opera: Italian Opera as the Feminine Other in Britain, 1700–42. *Journal of Musicological Research, 14*, 17–34.

McGeary, T. (2000). Repressing Female Desire on the London Opera Stage, 1724–1727. *Women and Music, 4*, 40–58.

Muñoz, J. E. (2009). *Cruising Utopia. The There and Then of Queer Futurity*. New York and London: New York University Press.

Oliver, K. (1993). *Reading Kristeva: Unraveling the Double-Bind*. Bloomington and Indianapolis: Indiana University Press.

Pitchfork. (2006, February 25). Anohni: Why I Am Not Attending the Academy Awards. *Pitchfork*. Retrieved March 11, 2016, from http://pitchfork.com/news/63773-anohni-why-i-am-not-attending-the-academy-awards/

Rao, N. Y. (2015). From Chinatown Opera to *The First Emperor*. Racial Imagination, the Trope of "Chinese Opera", and New Hybridity. In M. Ingraham, J. So, & R. Moodley (Eds.), *Opera in a Multicultural World: Coloniality, Culture, Performance* (pp. 50–67). London: Routledge.

Ravens, S. (2014). *The Supernatural Voice: A History of High Male Singing*. Woodbridge, Suffolk and Rochester, NY: Boydell Press.

Walker, T. (2016, February 27). Oscars 2016: British Singer Anohni Says She Will Boycott Event Because She Was Not Invited to Perform. *The Independent*. Retrieved March 11, 2016, from http://www.independent.co.uk/arts-entertainment/music/news/oscars-2016-british-singer-anohni-says-she-will-boycott-event-because-she-was-not-invited-to-perform-a6900496.html

8

Painting Social Change on a Body Canvas: Trans Bodies and Their Social Impact

Emilia Di Martino

1 Introduction

This chapter explores the life and artistic production of a trans feminine-presenting individual as a specific, contextualised ("locally specific") case of non-hegemonic positively aimed "deviant" masculinity. It aims to show how the performer of such a complex identity consciously attempts to reverse the "othering" practices (Staszak 2009) that dominant discourses on masculinity (and femininity) often carry out at the expense of other competing discourses.[1] While it may appear controversial to include a trans female-identifying individual under the umbrella of masculinity (or at least in a volume on masculinity), this is a provocative way of bringing attention to the fact that women and transwomen produce performances and models that contribute to changing ideas around traditional maleness and masculinity. This is in line with Milani's assertion that "women and transgender and intersex individuals *also* perform a variety of different masculinities that serve a plethora of competing agendas"

E. Di Martino (✉)
Facoltà di Lettere, Università Suor Orsola Benincasa, Napoli, Italy

P. Baker, G. Balirano (eds.), *Queering Masculinities in Language and Culture*, Palgrave Studies in Language, Gender and Sexuality,
https://doi.org/10.1057/978-1-349-95327-1_8

(Milani 2015b: 2). On the one hand, this chapter addresses Connell's (2005 [1995]: 848) invitation "to give much closer attention to the practices of women and to the historical interplay of femininities and masculinities" than research on masculinity has traditionally done. Indeed, the life and artistic production of the transgender person under consideration here (media celebrity Laverne Cox) is analysed as evidence of the crucial impact that discourses on masculinity have on the definition/redefinition of patriarchy: "focusing only on the activities of men occludes the practices of women in the construction of gender among men. As is well shown by life-history research, women are central in many of the processes constructing masculinities—as mothers; as schoolmates; as girlfriends, sexual partners, and wives; as workers in the gender division of labour; and so forth" (*ibid.*). On the other hand, Milani's invitation to "move the field of language and masculinities beyond an exclusive focus on male-born, male-bodied individuals" (Milani 2015b: 4) and dislocate masculinities from maleness is another aspect addressed here. Indeed, Cox's identity is explored in its complex picking and mixing of multiple aspects that may be separately (or traditionally) ascribed to masculinity or femininity. I focus on the counter-discourse of social improvement produced by the media celebrity chosen for this study (see also Di Nuzzo in this volume for another recent example of transgender counter-discourse). This counter-discourse helps to deconstruct and review (while clearly also apparently re-confirming, from a traditionally binary perspective) the Bourdesian view of masculinity as interlocking with aggressiveness and violence, insofar as it is constructed within the serious games of competition that men play with each other (Bourdieu 1990, 1997, 2001). Both feminine and masculine indices in transwomen can indeed offer an insight into masculinity, and though the "essence" of the latter obviously remains elusive even when looked for and analysed in its absence, it may become more marked in the process of the conscious or unconscious silencing and counter-enactment of certain elements (or indices) that is performed on it by individuals who were "assigned to a male gender role at birth" (see Zimman 2015).

A key point that this chapter will seek to make is that—while incorporating certain aspects of masculinity (and femininity) perceived as positive—the discursive practice focused on fails to produce other signs, performances, and languaging[2] commonly deemed "appropriate" across the diversity of personal differences and transmitted as common sense through the power of persuasion, particularly via the media. In doing so, it "queers" (Halperin 1995, 2012; Sullivan 2003) social conditions which "promote and produce heterosexualities as natural, self-evident, desirable, privileged and necessary" (Cameron and Kulick 2003: 55). Indeed, the term "positively aimed" aims to convey the idea that the discourse in question implies an openly declared purpose of producing a counter-discourse intended not so much to balance out power distribution within the existing range of possible manifestations of masculinity (and femininity) as, rather, to bring about wider social improvement. Such a discourse actually represents one of the "well-crafted responses to racial/ethnic marginalisation, physical disability, class inequality, or stigmatized sexuality" discussed by Connell and Messerschmidt (2005: 848), and/or similarly crucial counter-action to other forms of social injustice. Whereas dominant discourses tend to "other" practices that do not conform to the implicit "norms" dictating the "prototypical" forms of masculinity and femininity, the discourse analysed here consciously attempts to overturn such "othering" practices through the production of messages directly aimed at combating violence and more generally ameliorating human behaviour in society.

As for the decision to focus on a specific, contextualised instance of masculinity (and femininity), this stems from the view that identity is dynamic, changing in relation to different contexts and actors. As already hinted, gender is not looked upon as a stable system but rather as a reality which constantly creates and re-creates itself in relation to the degrees of masculinity/femininity of others and in different contexts: "'masculinity' does not represent a certain type of person but, rather, a way that men[3] position themselves through discursive practices" (Connell and Messerschmidt 2005: 841).

While regarding masculinity (and femininity) as a multidimensional phenomenon in this sense, the chapter sets out to study the body representations and language production of the specific model identified as a "sexed text" (Baker 2008) or "sexed sign" (Milani 2014), based on the conviction that "*all* media producers have the *potential* to rescale social, cultural and symbolic capital, and thereby 're-shuffle' authority and expertise on particular issues" (Milani and Johnson 2009: 6). Indeed, Cox is analysed in terms of how she is both an object of external gaze and the subject of a "political" discourse, focusing on linguistic and visual issues within both female and male representation at the intersection of gender, sexuality, and cultural belonging. Language and body are viewed as loci of identity formation, expression, and contestation, and Cox's performative (linguistic and visual) manifestations and her media portrayal do not simply seem to "choose those discursive positions that help [...] ward off anxiety and avoid feelings of powerlessness" (*ibid.*: 842), nor to "promote self-respect in the face of discredit" (*ibid.*). On the contrary, they seem to articulate a more complex, forward-looking agenda.

The structure of this chapter revolves around the analysis of Cox's linguistic and body manifestations and her media portrayal, which follows this introduction and represents the core of the study, drawing from a mixture of frameworks. For visual analysis, Berger's theory of the male gaze (1972) is incorporated within the structure of multimodal analysis (Kress 2010; Kress and van Leeuwen 2006 [1996]) and focus on magazine, TV, and social media images of Cox. For textual analysis, reference will be made to Tannen's views on conversational style (1990) within the general frame of Discourse Analysis (Gee 1996 [1990] but also, among others, Wodak and Meyer 2009) and focus will essentially be on interviews and extracts from the television series *Orange Is the New Black*. The concluding section pulls together the points emerging from the analysis in order to look to the future, connecting emerging insights both with recent reports on transgender identity, and with research focused on bias towards transgender people and prejudice at large.

2 Laverne Cox's Fluid Transgender Identity as a Powerful Discourse of Social Change

Laverne Cox is the "transperson"[4] or "sexual and gender variant identity/expression"[5] singled out in this chapter as a specific, contextualised case of non-hegemonic positively aimed "deviant" masculinity (and femininity). Language is a crucial aspect of the analysis as linguistic choices need to be made in order to refer to the case identified (e.g. should a gendered or gender-neutral pronoun be used?). It is opportune that this section—which must also further delimit the field of analysis through a viable definition of its object of study—should refer to the proliferation of categories and the explosion of gender binarism witnessed in Gevisser 2015, and to Fleming's concurrent observation that the prevalent attitude to transgender identity, that is, "that the person really is the new gender, not merely that s/he/other designation is perceived as such" (Fleming 2015: 116). Fleming's radical view is that "[g]ender is mutable until it mutates" but this sounds unsatisfactory due to its being clearly paradoxical: all this seems to mean is that "those who change genders are now in the position of those who didn't have to or want to change—meaning what? That their gender was in fact solid all along? That it was in fact their sex? The theoretical overreach of transgender theory is in a situation common to all outsiders who want to claim that the status quo is illegitimate—until they become the status quo" (*ibid.*). Despite possibly sounding over-sweeping, this perspective on the current attitude to transgender identity does seem to find real-life evidence in some countries' responses to (and re-appropriations of) the issue (see the quotations from Gevisser 2015 presented in the conclusion). However, the position adopted in this chapter will differ considerably, based not only on the idea that a person may still feel, act, and campaign (and be perceived and reacted to, particularly by the media) as transgender once the transition process is complete, but also on the conviction that every single individual displays and performs a variety of both male and female aspects and roles. Moreover, "sexual and gender variant identities/expressions" will be referred to as "transgender individuals" and "transgender persons" in this chapter, using pronouns and address terms favoured by Cox when focused on herself, and which coincide with her "new" gender. Finally, it is also worth considering that, as Eliason argues, "[w]e sometimes pride ourselves for being on the outside of the 'establishment' and consider ourselves to be activist-scholars, and there are certainly advantages to having the outsider perspective. On the other hand, there are huge benefits to being a part of the system, so that we can change it from the inside out. Being part of the system requires some level of compromise and following the 'rules'" (2014: 173).

The remarkable progress of transgender individuals in the USA, in terms of social visibility, collective awareness, and legal recognition of rights over the last few decades, is both typified and helped by Laverne Cox's Emmy nomination, her appearance on the cover of *Time* magazine, and the recent decision to install her wax figure at Madame Tussaud's, all three of which are historic firsts for a transgender person (see, e.g. Vanderhorst 2015). *Orange Is the New Black* (2013, and at the time of writing in its fourth season), the television series about Piper Chapman sentenced to 15 months in a federal prison on a drug trafficking conviction and whose life crosses the stories of other women struggling with incarceration, probably features the most successful of Cox's roles as transgender inmate Sophia Burset (for which she was nominated for Outstanding Guest Actress in a Comedy Series at the Emmys in 2014). Despite implicitly re-enforcing criminality as one of the common tropes of reporting on transpeople[6] (see, e.g. Baker 2014), the series is an excellent example of director Kohan's female-centred programming as well as her intervention in post-feminist representational paradigms. Progressively showing how "the civility and niceness" that Piper "experiences 'inside' as her innate character, herself, utterly depends upon the civil, racial, and economic privileges and protections that exist 'outside' of that self" (McHugh 2015: 22), the series disallows "the neoliberal, postfeminist framework of personal choice, freedom, and independence" (23–24), placing Laverne Cox and the transgender individual at the intersection of many paradigms and facing several crucial issues. However, the character of Sophia Burset, a former fire-fighter serving time for credit-card fraud, and the prison's hairdresser, represents an advancement in itself considering, as Cox argues, that "when folks want to write a trans character, the first thing that they think of is sex work" (NPR 2013).

The episode in which the public learn how she was sent to prison ("Lesbian Request Denied," directed by Jodie Foster) was one of the most poignant of the first series. The episode also reveals that Sophia (whose role before surgery was played by Cox's twin brother, musician M. Lamar) has a son, and that her wife supported her through her gender-reassignment process. The four seasons of episodes available at the time of writing focus on a variety of interesting and often topical issues. However, due to space constraints, this chapter will only briefly look at one episode in the show, episode 12 in Season 3, which, due to its raising questions of maleness and masculinity, appears as particularly relevant and possibly conducive to fruitful discussion in the present context.

Cox has her own equally powerful story to tell in real life, as an advocate for trans rights both in words (she delivered, amongst other things, a stirring speech at the Creating Change 2014 conference for LGBT Equality) and deeds (she gently but firmly stopped journalist Katie Couric's intrusive questions on trans surgery and, above all, publicly supported CeCe McDonald, an African-American transwoman sentenced to 41 months in prison for a killing that, she claims, occurred in self-defence) (see Cox 2014). So visible is her presence in the US mainstream media that her omission from 2014 *Time*'s people of the year list caused outrage; the magazine editors later decided to make her the cover story for one issue, suggesting that a "tipping point" may have been reached in the transgender "movement" (see the photo of Cox published on the cover of *Time* magazine, 29 May 2014).[7]

Cox's performance (or at least perceived performance) of gender is a fluid one, encompassing both masculinity and femininity.[8] On the cover of *Time*, her image stands out as both hyper-feminine and womanly, statuesque in her tall and robust figure, and masculine in her clearly—however partly mitigated—assertive body positioning. A maximally assertive pose would have probably implied feet firmly planted and far apart and hands on hips, however the photographer's choice for a pose which can certainly not be described as relaxed with chest thrusting forward and lack of smile reflects a self-protective, self-reliant stance. More recently, Cox has been portrayed on the cover of *Variety* (Fig. 8.1[9]) and *Entertainment Weekly*'s LGBT Issue (as Lady Liberty), where again her stance comes across as confident, bold, and therefore subtly masculine, if one agrees with the fact that many people would still associate hegemonic masculinity with "strength, independence, dominance, and confidence" (Baker 2015: 34). On the *Variety* cover she wears a trouser suit, with no display of emotion on her face, and one elbow leaning on the arm of the chair, which creates an assertive undertone while also allowing the figure to take up more space on the page in the picture; on a cover for *Entertainment Weekly* she strikes a defiant pose with well-toned arms crossed in the foreground, chin resting on a Statue-of-Liberty-torch/training-weight and looking directly into

Fig. 8.1 Cox as photographed by Emily Hope for the cover of *Variety* (6 May 2015)

the camera, with a sly grin on her face[10]: all subtly masculine indices, particularly considering that it is quite unusual for women to be depicted in a training pose, against "a current conceptualisation of hegemonic masculinity […] now more firmly entrenched in the notion of a muscular physique" (*ibid.*: 51); muscularity seems indeed to be "the preserve of men" (*ibid.*).[11] On displaying a combination of masculine and feminine indices, all these pictures implicitly play with and subvert assumptions based on gender.

This display of gender liminality may not appear to be consistently anti-normative if one focuses on the verbal and visual stress on the feminine side in reports on the celebrity's private life. Indeed, despite the fact that self-identification as transfeminine suggests an affiliation whose nature can vary considerably (see Zimman 2015), Cox seems to be adamant on the nature of that affiliation in *her* case, describing herself as "a black transgender chick from Mobile, Alabama" in a 2015 *Guardian* interview by Nicholson. Moreover, she is normally quoted and pictured as dating heterosexual men,[12] and this stress on her relationships with ostensibly heterosexual males could be regarded as a sort of political "domestication," even if unconsciously carried out, which may become exclusive of less mainstream forms of transgender identity, a sort of "hegemonic transgender identity." Very much in tune with Fleming's representation of current attitudes to transgender identity (2015), this may even appear as "a 'new equilibrium' in Gramscian terms, a point at which dominant discourses have opened up slightly to include those gender challenges (i.e. gender-conforming "wrong body" identities) that are the least threatening to dominant gender norms, while still maintaining a much more exclusionary/marginalising approach to identities that might provoke a rethinking of gender norms" (Barker-Plummer 2015). However, a close look at Cox's nude portrait in *Allure*,[13] which has been described by herself as another milestone for transgender representation ("I felt this could be really powerful for the communities that I represent," People 2015: 84), again seems to offer a much more complex and sophisticated picture.

While the unconventional depiction of a transgender person tastefully framed in black-and-white as a desirable body may, from a certain perspective, help shape society's opinion of transgender individuals in different terms, it may also, in stressing such a body as recognisably feminine, function as a gender spectacle for cis-audience consumption. Cox's lack of gaze is notable in the picture, and would seem to re-enforce the classic theory of the male gaze in post-Renaissance sexual imagery: "Men 'act' and women 'appear'. Men look at women. Women watch themselves, being looked at" (Berger 1972: 47). As a result, the story behind the picture may function rather as an "ultimate makeover" than as a real gender challenge: "These narratives minimise gender ambiguities, queerness, racial, or other complexities, and present audiences with a heteronormative, gender-conforming identity which is then allowed to stand in for all kinds of trans experience. Such a limited representation does little to change dominant gender discourses or practices more generally" (Barker-Plummer 2015).

However commodifiable and commodified Cox's image may be as an object of external gaze, the discursive performance of femininity played in the picture does not strike as fully straightforward. Rather, it seems to project a model of masculinity-absorbing (or non-hegemonic) femininity; it seems to suggest a gender performance that cannot easily be pigeonholed into a "neat" category and as such may easily become the subject and carrier of a strong and powerfully narrated "political" discourse. The first element that appears to break the visual script of femininity is the large, manly (despite wearing nail varnish) hand resting on Cox's forehead, which is made salient in the picture by being placed in the top-right corner, which foregrounds it. The same dissonant function seems to be achieved by the oil-smooth muscular limbs that appear to divide the image into different subsections, pointing to the hemp, monochrome (most probably grey) stone-washed sheets, which could, with a certain degree of verisimilitude, be more recognisable as "masculine" bedding than their silk, brightly coloured, or floral equivalents. As a model of masculinity-absorbing (or non-hegemonic) femininity, one may apply/adjust to Laverne Cox's case Green's judgement of female-to-male transpeople when commenting on Fertig's statement that the latter are "some of the sexiest men on the planet" (1995):

> [...] they are men who have the capacity to fully integrate feminine experience, qualities, and behaviors (however limited or unexpressed in their masculine psyches) without feeling threatened. They have a very real sense of the compatibility of the two extremes of gender because they have brought them together in dynamic combination, and they have found a home in their bodies for the conscious balance they have found in their psyches. For transmen, it is the bodily confirmation of the male identity that matters. Once that has been achieved to a transman's satisfaction, he can start to integrate his personality in the same ways that non-transpeople

do. Trans or nontrans, when individuals realize that they can give up the struggle of trying to prove who they are, or how butch they are, or how male, or how masculine, they can realize that whatever qualities of character they have, they are all part of the package. (Green 2005: 298–299)

Cox's nude portrait seems to beautifully integrate masculine and feminine as "part of the package," considerably contributing to the image of the media artist's unique sexiness while also making room for a view of gender as essentially fluid not only before but also after transition.

Equally powerful is Cox's more personal message, which only starts off as the typical account of a minority discursive position aiming to promote "self respect in the face of discredit" (842):

Running around Alabama in a zebra robe and a turban, I got bullied a lot. It was rough. When kids would bully me, I would say, "One day I will be rich and famous and I'll show you. And that's what got me through my childhood." (WWD 2014)

Indeed, the media artist's first-person performative (linguistic and visual) manifestations primarily seem to articulate a complex, forward-looking social agenda[14]:

I've gotten in trouble by saying this publicly, that most of the street harassment I've experienced has been from other black folks. [...] I think the reason for that is there is a collective trauma that a lot of black folks are dealing with in this country that dates back to slavery and to the Jim Crow South. [...]

I believe that a lot of black folks feel that there is this historic emasculation that has been happening in white supremacy of black male bodies. I think a lot of black folks dealing with a lot of post-traumatic stress see trans, my trans woman's body, and feel that I'm the embodiment of this historic emasculation come to life. [...]

I understand that as trauma. I have love. I have so much love for my black brothers and sisters who might call me out on the street, 'cause I get it. I understand. They're in pain.

I feel so often our oppressors are in a lot of, lot of pain. I think whenever someone needs to call out someone else for who they are, and make fun of them, it's because they don't feel comfortable with who they are. (Cox 2013)

Cox's criticism over the US census' inability to represent transgender people in its current form[15] and her *The T Word* documentary for MTV[16] are only the latest items on the list. This social agenda, presented as a mixture of *rapport*/private (connection-establishing, traditionally feminine) and *report*/public (negotiating and maintaining status, traditionally masculine) talk (Tannen 1990; also Seidler 1989), in Cox's interviews and talks, calls upon the philosopher and activist Cornel West as an inspirer and can be roughly summed up in the mantra "love is the answer": "What are we going to do about that? I think love is the answer. Cornel West reminds us that justice is what love looks like in public. I love that, because I feel that love, if we can love trans gender people, that will be a revolutionary act" (Cox 2013).

While mobilising such masculine indexical resources as articulate and informed languaging, and an assertive tone, Cox seems to distance herself from, and clearly place herself in contrast with, language indexing the model of rigid masculinity that urban men traditionally define themselves against. In lieu of toughness, it emphasises how crucial, powerful, and far-reaching an ideal of universal love can be, an objective that is, in Cox's intentions, targeted at social improvement at large: "'If I'm going to have a public platform, I want to use it not just to elevate myself but to elevate issues that are important to me' she says now" (Breen 2014). This appears as a conscious attempt at reversing the "othering" practices that dominant discourses often perform at the expense of all other competing discourses and producing a counter-discourse of wider social improvement based on the construction of "points of reference that are humanizing" and that help demystify difference, as well as placing the protection of children and self-help conversations across the differences at the heart of this process, as Cox's *Time* magazine interview and her Creating Change 2014 speech show. In the *Time* interview she was asked about an event where she had spoken in San Francisco. In that event a woman had brought with her a child named Soleil who had asked Cox about what to do about being bullied at school. Cox's reply in the interview was:

> What was really emotional for me is Soleil is six years old. I forget how young six years old is. Soleil is a baby and is being told that they can't be themselves. I think about when I was that age and my gender was being

policed and how deeply painful it was and how it made me feel like I was wrong, at my very core, that every instinct I had, to reach for this and be who I was, was wrong. And seeing Soleil, I just thought about how young six years old really is and how innocent six years old really is. And how we need to protect this child. And we need to protect our children from that and allow them to be themselves. (*Time* 2014)

The following excerpt is taken from Cox's Creating Change 2014 speech:

Some days I wake up and I'm that sixth grader who swallowed a bottle of pills because I did not want to be myself anymore because I did not know how to be anybody else. And who I was, I was told was a sin, a problem, and I didn't want to exist. Some days I wake up and I am that black, trans woman walking the streets of New York City hearing people yell, That's a man, to me.

And I understand, I've come to understand that when a trans woman is called a man, that is an act of violence.

[...]

We are more than our bodies. The criminalization of trans people is, is so pervasive in this culture. CeCe McDonald's case is one example, and I am sure many of you are aware of a sixteen-year-old girl in California by the name of Jewlyes Gutierrez. Sixteen years old and, and was bullied like so many transgender youth; 78% of trans youth in grades K-12 experience harassment and bullying in school. Seventy-eight percent—that is unacceptable. (Cox 2014)

In a recent paper, Lawson reminds us that "over the past 50 years, a large body of research has argued that masculinity and violence are closely related, especially in Western society" (2015: 53).[17] As Messner contends, the present model of masculinity no longer corresponds to the Terminator/Rambo model that arose as a "remasculinization of America" response to the Vietnam War (Jeffords 1989), and yet in the new model softness is still looked upon as definitely undesirable:

[...] the ascendant hegemonic masculinity combines the kick-ass muscular heroic male body with situationally expressive moments of empathy, grounded in care for kids and a capacity to make us all feel safe. Feminism,

> anti-war movements, health advocates, and even modern business human relations management have delegitimized pure hypermasculinity. But many people still view effeminacy as illegitimate in men, especially those who are leaders. So, neither hard nor soft is fully legitimate, unless the two are mixed, albeit with a much larger dose of the former than of the latter. (2007: 469)

While clearly colluding with dominant masculinist discourses that value toughness and violence, Cox does not trade in one gender "norm" for another. Her fluid transgender identity, which, as hinted at above, seems to openly appropriate traditionally positive "masculine" indexing, seems to adjust this "not too hard not too soft" standard to her own personal context and personality, weaving it into a unique form of conscientious assertiveness which conjugates a strong, confident verbal and body language with a message of understanding and compassion, and a strongly and openly conveyed desire to change things for those who experience unfair hostility or overt oppression. Indeed, on the one hand, the media artist seems to authenticate her status as a woman through willingly accepting and valuing not only the loss of privilege that comes with being recognised as male but also the stigma that arises from the combination of the two minority conditions of femininity and blackness with the further, consciously acquired minority condition of having transitioned from male to female, which makes her a potential target for both male and female,[18] both white and black people's[19] verbal and physical aggressiveness. The unique form of hostility at the intersection of cis-sexism, transphobia, and misogyny that transwomen often experience is indeed further complicated for transwomen of colour like Cox by the intersection of "transmisogyny" (Serrano 2007)[20] with racism, a condition referred to as "misogynoir," since racism normally equals anti-blackness.

With the fictitious character played by Cox in *Orange Is the New Black* being similarly targeted, episode 12 in Season 3 is an excellent example of the type of complex transphobic attention a transgender male-to-female (let alone black) individual may receive, with three of Sophia Burset's fellow inmates asking to ascertain the truth of her sex, confronting her about her allegedly, unfairly privileged condition of "man" in a women's prison and Sophia being sent to solitary confinement at the Security Housing Unit, "for her own protection" as a result[21]:

> [...]
> [Reema] We just wanted to ask you a question. Spanish been saying how you still got your dick. That true?
> [Sophia sighs] What you got between your legs is your business—and what I got is mine.
> [Reema] Maybe. But my man is out at Lexington. He's having a real hard time. Hard. Meanwhile, you hiding out in here, "pretending" to be a female.
> [Gabby] Seems like you got it all figured out.
> [Sophia]You have any idea how ignorant you sound?
> [Gabby] We just want a little peek. Educate ourselves.
> [Sophia] Get the fuck out of my house.
> [Reema] Not till we see it. Fuck you, she-male! Damn, I told you he still had his man strength!
> [Sophia] Don't think I won't kill you, you fucking cunt!
> [Gabby] That's it, bitch! [Sophia grunting]
> [Sophia] Fuck you, bitches! Help me!
> [Sikowitz] I'll get Caputo.

Assertive transwomen, like Sophia—who has attained status at Litchfield as a professional—seem to be particularly targeted on the basis of their supposedly "male socialised behaviour." But Cox, like her fictitious persona, does not seem to choose to do without her natural (socially acquired as it may be) self-confidence to appear "more of a woman." Like the transmen Green describes, "who have the capacity to fully integrate feminine experience, qualities, and behaviors (however limited or unexpressed in their masculine psyches) without feeling threatened" (Green 2005: 298), she seems to have chosen to integrate this "masculine" index into her personal identity, her verbal and body language displaying a balance of compassion and determination, the latter being crucial for the former not to remain just a vague message of universal love for the world. She seems to have painted her need and invitation to social change on her body canvas, literally re-creating in her body that opening, that welcoming space, the cradle that a womb is so often described to be, while retaining a self-reliant posture which makes it only too clear that she will not easily give in and surrender her dream of change; nor is she unaware of how the world goes. She is not a martyr, despite her incredible capacity of forgiveness (see her 2013 interview above, where she understands and justifies the hatred and violence she gets from her "black brothers" and from people in general as the result of trauma). She has gone a long way and faced the stigma of diversity as well as many forms of open hostility to defend her beliefs; she now seems to be willing to take the next step and ready to support others in their daily battles against discrimination and social injustice, making her cause a universal one, but she also appears to have it clear in her mind that strong and beautiful is better and achieves more than weak and plain. Her complex and fluid identity which can combine empathy with the ability to keep her feet firmly on the ground makes her an exceptional model of mediation, of gender shuttle diplomacy geared to social improvement. Cox may have contented herself to construct an alternative performance of manhood and womanhood and chosen to leave her gender performance at the stage of "mere" challenge to heteronormative masculinity and femininity, if not, from a different perspective, simply shaped for herself a form of hegemonic transgenderism, as hinted at above. In taking the path that makes her an advocate of diversity, making do with "just" empowering herself, she seems to have offered the world a potentially powerful resource for social improvement. One such model would indeed provide a sustainable paradigm as much for masculinity as for femininity, for the generations to come. Cox has broken down many barriers as a black transwoman artist, and because her professional status is recognised worldwide, her achievements are not just personal. They are political. They have a larger significance, as their reach is global and may affect other people's lives, making her message of universal love more alluring and, ipso facto, captivating.

3 Conclusion

In his recent article in *Nation* mentioned above (2015), Gevisser argues in the subtitle that "[t]he transgender movement is coming out—and bringing with it a deeper understanding of what it means to be human."

It is precisely this understanding of humanity (in the twofold meaning of "human" and "humane") that the personality focused on in this chapter seems to emphasise, encouraging the performance of social change through a verbal and body language that combines sensitivity and vigour, understanding and force.

In stressing current gender fluidity, Gevisser foregrounds the dangers lying around the corner for gradually more mainstream forms of transgendering:

> To be sure, an embrace of transgenderism and its possibilities might perversely serve to reinforce the binary: if you have a son whose identity falls outside the box of conventional masculinity, you can solve your "problems" by turning him into a girl; your sissy-boy can become a princess. The extreme example of this is Iran, where homosexuality is illegal but gender transition is legal and subsidized by the government. And evidence suggests that the government pressures some gay people to undergo gender-reassignment surgery. (325)

Siebler also seems to embrace this position, stating:

> [...] trans people are, in fact, not queering binaries of sex/gender but reinforcing them. [...] Today, especially in digital spaces, the binaries and sex/gender ideologies are the dominant narrative, a sharp and dichotomous contrast to the trans rhetoric of the 1970s–1980s. In the digital age, there are few representations of trans people who have *not* had surgeries and hormones to 'align' their gender with a constructed sex. (Siebler 2016: 131–132)

However, Gevisser also seems to foresee the possibility of a wider social impact of transgender identity and ultimately of its influence on patriarchy as well:

> Many of the genderqueer kids in today's liberal America are what Charlotte Wolf calls "transtrenders," using gender as a form of social provocation or sub-cultural bonding. The majority may later marry and assume the conventional gender roles, much as Japanese boys become company men after being allowed their very structured anime rebellion. But an increasing

> number will stay in the borderlands and, in so doing, redraw our gender frontiers—and with them, the patriarchy itself. (*ibid.*)

Hardly anything has been written, to date, on how transgender identity may affect masculinity or femininity. This chapter has tried to start filling this gap, inviting reflection on how a specific instance of transgender identity which has recently brought international attention to the transgender community may help re-shape, or at least deconstruct the nexus between masculinity and violence, and simultaneously yield positive social consequences.

It remains to be seen if such a focus on social change is actually true of most forms of transgender identity (also see Di Nuzzo in this volume on this issue), and whether or not this aspect can (or will) ultimately be perceived as desirable and therefore appropriated (as is to be hoped) by mainstream forms of gender performance, in consideration of the "dialectical pragmatism" described by Demetriou:

> [...] hegemonic masculinity appropriates from other masculinities whatever appears to be pragmatically useful for continued domination. The result of this dialectic is not a unitary pattern of hegemonic masculinity but a "historic bloc" involving a weaving together of multiple patterns, whose hybridity is the best possible strategy for external hegemony. A constant process of negotiation, translation, and reconfiguration occurs. (2001)

For the time being, after a number of outcries and scandals (Bohannon 2016), a recent study (Broockman and Kalla 2016) on prejudice, specifically focused on negative attitudes towards the transgender community, which appear to be more persistent than other forms of discrimination and as such urgently in need of investigation, has shown that "the canvassing strategy" can effectively influence biases, and the positive change recorded has been proved to last for a period of at least three months at the moment of writing. This strategy, a persuasion technique pioneered by the Los Angeles LGBT Center, implies the interviewed individual taking an analogic perspective aimed at awareness-raising: "By inviting someone to discuss an experience in which that person was perceived as different and treated unfairly, a canvasser tries to generate sympathy for the suffering of another group—such as gay or transgender people" (Bohannon 2016).

This brings new hope for the possibility of improving the personal lives of transgender individuals, and for the feasibility of widening the reach of the universal message of peace and understanding delivered by such an outstanding model of gender mediation as the one analysed in this chapter. This should in turn result in better understanding and respect for the multitude of ways that we are human.[22]

Notes

1. The term "Discourse" in this chapter refers to the use of language to convey ideas, based on the view that "discourse" does not conflate with "language use," but encompasses both language and life, thus revealing more, that is the world and our way of being in it. It corresponds to what Gee designates as Discourse (with a capital D): "[…] a socially accepted association among ways of using language, other symbolic expressions, and artifacts, of thinking, feeling, believing, valuing and acting that can be used to identify oneself as a member of a socially meaningful group or 'social network'" (Gee 1996 [1990]: 131).
2. "Languaging" is here meant as "the simultaneous process of continuing becoming of ourselves and of our language practices, as we interact and make meaning of the world," in a view of language as "an activity rather than a structure, as something we do rather than a system we draw on, as a material part of social and cultural life rather than an abstract entity" (Pennycook 2010: 2, 8).
3. Following Milani (2015a), I would actually say "people (both male- and female-identifying)."
4. To use a more traditional label, meant as "a broad umbrella term in common usage in many community settings, recognizing the many debates over appropriate terms and terminology as all raising important points about the need to depathologize and recognize difference among people who may or may not see themselves falling under its purview" (Matte and Johnson 2009: 44).
5. To opt for a more recent definition, meant as "people who by their self-identities, behaviors, relationships, desires, public presentation, or attractions, do not fit mainstream normative sexuality or gender" (Eliason 2014: 163).

6. Sophia is actually incarcerated because she stole credit cards in order to pay for sex-reassignment surgery.
7. It was not possible to obtain permission to reproduce this image, but it can be found online at http://www.huffingtonpost.com/nicholas-snow/laverne-cox-time-magazine_b_7238884.html
8. "Transituated strategic discourse" queering the binaries in Cromwell's terms (Cromwell 2006 [2001]).
9. Photographer Emily Hope generously allowed free reproduction of the picture she took for *Variety*.
10. It was not possible to obtain permission to reproduce this image, but it can be found online (at the time of publishing) at http://ew.com/article/2015/06/10/laverne-cox-entertainment-weekly-cover
11. On this topic, also see Nelson (1994), Birrell and Cole (1994), Kolnes (1995), Halbert (1997), Choi (2000), Russell (2007), and the definition of the female athlete as deviant in Veri (1999).
12. See, for example, The Huffington Post (2016 [2015]) and US Magazine (2016).
13. It was not possible to obtain permission to reproduce this image, but it can be found online at http://www.papermag.com/see-laverne-coxs-stunning-nude-portrait-for-allure-1427540754.html
14. The Promotional Trailer for FREE CeCe! is available at https://www.youtube.com/watch?v=-pW8oHJ7zqg&t=10s. The video from the public dialogue with bell hooks at The New School is available at https://www.youtube.com/watch?v=9oMmZIJijgY
15. The video from Wochit News is available at https://www.youtube.com/watch?v=uzxuD3qtE48
16. The documentary is available at https://www.youtube.com/watch?v=mDy0DhfuxfI&t=496s
17. Also see the "toughness" masculine ideology expressed in freestyle rap performances (Williams 2015).
18. See Michael (2015), (Steinmetz 2015), and the experience narrated by Thom: "The idea is that transwomen, with our 'masculine' bodies and having been 'raised as male,' receive all kinds of privilege that ciswomen don't, such as relative safety from sexual harassment, social preference in school and the job market, and so on. As a result of this perspective, transwomen are often excluded from women-only spaces on the basis that we might be violent, or make ciswomen uncomfortable, or that we are already served by male institutions" (Thom 2015).

19. See Cox (2013) above.
20. Transmisogyny is a controversial concept: central in transfeminism and intersectional feminist theory but rejected by those feminists who do not see transwomen as female.
21. A short video from episode 12, Season 3 of "*Orange Is the New Black*" is available at https://www.youtube.com/watch?v=1sC6VA--cNs
22. Ultimately, for the ineffability of the other, "who is not disclosed through speech but leaves a portentous shard of itself in its saying, a self that is beyond discourse itself" (Butler 2015 [2001]: 192).

References

Baker, P. (2008). *Sexed Texts: Language, Gender and Sexuality*. London: Equinox.

Baker, P. (2014). Bad Wigs and Screaming Mimis: Using Corpus-Assisted Techniques to Carry Out Critical Discourse Analysis of the Representation of Trans People in the British Press. In C. Hart & P. Cap (Eds.), *Contemporary Critical Discourse Studies* (pp. 211–236). London: Bloomsbury.

Baker, P. (2015). Two Hundred Years of the American Man. In T. M. Milani (Ed.), *Language and Masculinities* (pp. 34–52). New York and London: Routledge.

Barker-Plummer, B. (2015). *The Ultimate Makeover: US Media, Celebrity, and the Commodification of Transwomen*. Talk presented at the 2015 annual conference of the International Association for Media and Communication Research (IAMCR), Montreal, Canada, 12–16 July 2015.

Berger, J. (1972). *Ways of Seeing*. London: BBC and Penguin Books.

Birrell, S., & Cole, C. L. (Eds.). (1994). *Women, Sport, and Culture*. Champaign, IL: Human Kinetics Publishers.

Bohannon, J. (2016, April 7). For Real This Time: Talking to People about Gay and Transgender Issues Can Change Their Prejudices. *Science Magazine, American Association for the Advancement of Science (AAAS)*. Retrieved from http://www.sciencemag.org/news/2016/04/talking-people-about-gay-and-transgender-issues-can-change-their-prejudices

Bourdieu, P. (1990). La Domination masculine. *Actes de la Recherche en Sciences Sociales, 84*, 2–31.

Bourdieu, P. (1997). Eine sanfte Gewalt: Pierre Bourdieu im Gespräch mit Irene Dölling und Margareta Steinrücke. In I. Dölling & B. Krais (Eds.), *Ein alltägliches Spiel. Geschlechterkonstruktion in der sozialen Praxis* (pp. 318–230). Frankfurt am Main: Suhrkamp.

Bourdieu, P. (2001). *Masculine Domination* (R. Nice, Trans.). Stanford, CA: Stanford University Press [French edition: Bourdieu, P. 1998. *La Domination Masculine*. Paris: Seuil].

Breen, M. (2014, August/September). Laverne Cox: The Making of an Icon. *Advocate*, Issue 1074.

Broockman, D., & Kalla, J. (2016). Durably Reducing Transphobia: A Field Experiment on Door-to-Door Canvassing. *Science, 352*(6282), 220–224.

Butler, J. (2015 [2001]). Doing Justice to Someone. Sex Reassignment and Allegories of Transsexuality. In S. Stryker & S. Whittle (Eds.), *The Transgender Studies Reader* (pp. 183–193). New York and London: Routledge.

Cameron, D., & Kulick, D. (2003). *Language and Sexuality*. Cambridge: Cambridge University Press.

Choi, P. Y. L. (2000). *Femininity and the Physically Active Woman*. London: Routledge.

Connell R. W. (2005 [1995]). *Masculinities*. Berkeley, CA: University of California Press.

Connell, R. W., & Messerschmidt, J. W. (2005). Hegemonic Masculinity Rethinking the Concept. *Gender & Society, 19*(6), 829–859.

Cox, L. (2014). *Talk. Creating Change 2014* [Transcript]. Retrieved November 28, 2015, from https://www.youtube.com/watch?v=6cytc0p4Jwg

Cromwell, J. (2006 [2001]). Queering the Binaries. Transituated Identities, Bodies, and Sexualities. In S. Stryker & S. Whittle (Eds.), *The Transgender Studies Reader* (pp. 509–520). New York and London: Routledge.

Demetriou, D. Z. (2001). Connell's Concept of Hegemonic Masculinity: A Critique. *Theory and Society, 30*(3), 337–361.

Eliason, M. J. (2014). An Exploration of Terminology Related to Sexuality and Gender: Arguments for Standardizing the Language. *Social Work in Public Health, 29*, 162–175.

Fertig, J. (1995, August 24). The World's First FTM Conference Held in SF. *San Francisco Bay Times*.

Fleming, B. (2015). The Vocabulary of Transgender Theory. *Society, 52*, 114–120.

Gee, P. J. (1996 [1990]). *Social Linguistics and Literacies: Ideology in Discourses*. Bristol, PA: Falmer Press.

Gevisser, M. (2015, June 4). Engendered: Beyond the Binary. *Nation, 300*(14), 233–235.

Green, J. (2005). Part of the Package: Ideas of Masculinity among Male-Identified Transpeople. *Men and Masculinities, 7*, 291–299.

Halbert, C. (1997). Tough Enough and Woman Enough. Stereotypes, Discrimination, and Impression Management among Women Professional Boxers. *Journal of Sport and Social Issues, 21*(1), 7–36.

Halperin, D. M. (1995). *Saint Foucault: Towards a Gay Hagiography*. New York: Oxford University Press.

Halperin, D. M. (2012). *How to Be Gay*. Cambridge, MA: Belknap Press.

Jeffords, S. (1989). *The Remasculinization of America: Gender and the Vietnam War*. Bloomington: Indiana University Press.

Keppler Speakers. (2013). *Cox, Laverne. "On Bullying and Being a Trans Woman of Color"*. Retrieved November 28, 2015, from https://www.youtube.com/watch?v=7zwy5PEEa6U

Kolnes, L.-J. (1995). Heterosexuality as an Ongoing Principle in Women's Sport. *International Review for the Sociology of Sport, 30*(1), 61–75.

Kress, G. (2010). *Multimodality: A Social Semiotic Approach to Contemporary Communication*. London and New York: Routledge.

Kress, G., & van Leeuwen, T. (2006 [1996]). *Reading Images: The Grammar of Visual Design*. London and New York: Routledge.

Lawson, R. (2015). Fight Narratives, Covert Prestige, and Performances of "Tough" Masculinity: Some Insights from an Urban Center. In T. M. Milani (Ed.), *Language and Masculinities* (pp. 53–76). New York and London: Routledge.

McHugh, K. (2015). Giving Credit to Paratexts and Parafeminism in *Top of the Lake and Orange Is the New Black*. *Film Quarterly, 68*(3), 17–25.

Messner, M. A. (2007). The Masculinity of the Governator: Muscle and Compassion in American Politics. *Gender & Society, 21*(4), 461–480.

Michaels, S. (2015, June 26). It's Incredibly Scary to Be a Transgender Woman of Color Right Now. *Mother Jones*.

Milani, T. M. (2014). Sexed Signs. Queering the Scenery. *International Journal of the Sociology of Language, 228*, 201–225.

Milani, T. M. (Ed.). (2015a). *Language and Masculinities*. New York and London: Routledge.

Milani, T. M. (2015b). Introduction: Language and Masculinities … 20 Years Later. In T. M. Milani (Ed.), *Language and Masculinities* (pp. 1–7). New York and London: Routledge.

Milani, T. M., & Johnson, S. (2009). Introduction. In S. Johnson & T. M. Milani (Eds.), *Language Ideologies and Media Discourse: Texts, Practices, Politics* (pp. 3–14). London: Continuum.

Nelson, M. B. (1994). *The Stronger Women Get, The More Men Love Football: Sexism in the American Culture of Sports*. New York: Harcourt Brace.

Nicholson, R. (2015, June 14). Laverne Cox: "Now I Have the Money to Feminise My Face I Don't Want To. I'm Happy That This Is the Face God Gave Me". *The Guardian.*

NPR (National Press Release). (2013, August 8). *Laverne Cox: Transgender Actress on the Challenges of Her "New Black" Role.* Retrieved November 28, 2015, from http://www.npr.org/2013/08/07/209843353/orange-is-the-new-black-actress-calls-role-complicated

Pennycook, A. (2010). *Language as a Local Practice.* London and New York: Routledge.

People. (2015, June 1). *Body Moments of the Year.*

Russell, K. (2007). "Queers, Even in Netball?" Interpretations of the Lesbian Label among Sportswomen. In C. C. Aitchison (Ed.), *Sport and Gender Identities. Masculinities, Femininities and Sexualities* (pp. 106–121). London and New York: Routledge.

Serano, J. (2007). *Whipping Girl: A Transsexual Woman on Sexism and the Scapegoating of Femininity.* Emeryville, CA: Seal Press.

Siebler, K. (2016). *Learning Queer Identity in the Digital Age.* Basingstoke: Palgrave.

Staszak, J.-F. (2009). Other/Otherness. In K. Rob & N. Thrift (Eds.), *International Encyclopaedia of Human Geography* (Vol. 8, pp. 43–47). Oxford: Elsevier.

Steinmetz, K. (2015, August 17). Why Transgender People Are Being Murdered at a Historic Rate. *Time.*

Sullivan, N. (2003). *A Critical Introduction to Queer Theory.* New York: New York University Press.

Tannen, D. (1990). *You Just Don't Understand. Women and Men in Conversation.* New York: Ballantine Books.

The Huffington Post. (2016 [2015]). *Queer Voices. Laverne Cox: Men Dating Trans Women Are Probably "Stigmatized More Than Trans Women".* June 18, 2015. Updated Feb. 2, 2016.

Thom, K. C. (2015, October 4). Still Think Trans Women Have Male Privilege? These 7 Points Prove They Don't. *Everyday Feminism.*

Time. (2014, May 29). *Laverne Cox Talks to TIME about the Transgender Movement.*

US Magazine. (2016, February 1). *Laverne Cox Has a Hot Boyfriend Named JonoFreedrix—All the Details.*

Vanderhorst, B. (2015). Whither Lies the Self: Intersex and Transgender Individuals and a Proposal for Brain-Based Legal Sex. *Harvard Law & Policy Review, 9*(1), 241–274.

Veri, M. J. (1999). Homophobic Discourse Surrounding the Female Athlete. *Quest, 51*(4), 355–368.

Williams, Q. E. (2015). Emceeing Toughness, Toughing Up the Emcee: Language and Masculine Ideology in Freestyle Rap Performances. In T. M. Milani (Ed.), *Language and Masculinities* (pp. 77–99). New York and London: Routledge.

Wodak, R., & Meyer, M. (Eds.) (2009 [2001]). *Methods of Critical Discourse Analysis*. Los Angeles/London/New Delhi/Singapore/Washington, DC: Sage.

WWD (Women's Wear Daily). (2014, August 21). *Laverne Cox: With Fame, Comes Responsibility*, 208(38).

Zimman, L. (2015). Transmasculinity and the Voice: Gender Assignment, Identity, and Presentation. In T. M. Milani (Ed.), *Language and Masculinities* (pp. 197–219). New York and London: Routledge.

9

Neapolitan Social-Transgenderism: The Discourse of Valentina OK

Annalisa Di Nuzzo

1 Introduction

Anthropologie du proche (Augé 1996) offers a problematic definition of the "anthropological view", debating the meaning and the duties of an "anthropology of everyday life". According to this view, the anthropologist's job is to make over-interpretations on the cultural behaviours of a certain society which risks either "over"signifying elements or banalising them, thus producing a loss of epistemological identity. Certain aspects of contemporary social life such as kinship, marriage, gift-giving, and exchange are well suited to anthropological research (Héritier 2002). However, the use of material from anthropological observation creates the problem of developing a language and an *écriture* of diversity, as well as the choice of the materials themselves. Del Lago (1995: 41) conceptualises the description of a culture as being "a creative activity that we must take to an extreme as "writing about diversity". I mean rewriting from the point of view of

A. Di Nuzzo (✉)
Dipartimento di Scienze dell'Educazione,
Università degli Studi di Salerno, Fisciano, Italy

P. Baker, G. Balirano (eds.), *Queering Masculinities in Language and Culture*,
Palgrave Studies in Language, Gender and Sexuality,
https://doi.org/10.1057/978-1-349-95327-1_9

others as a way of documenting their voice, as the presence of the "other" in anthropological practice, and as a covering for the other literary genres" [author's English translation].

Thus, the search for "contiguous" knowledge calls upon different academic fields and textual sources including anthropology, sociology, the novel, and drama, providing each of them with a continuous self-construction of their identities. So the anthropologist will keep on doing anthropology, the novelist will keep on writing novels, and the sociologist will keep on doing sociology, even though each one of them will draw on the others' work. Undoubtedly the excess of meaning that Augé (1996) speaks about contributes to enriching the complexity of the notion of time and space in traditional research and offers new defining horizons. Because of changes in space-time and its rapid transformation, the contemporary world has an ever-increasing need of an anthropological perspective able to provide a renewed and systematic consideration of otherness.

Against such a theoretical backdrop, this paper sets out to analyse the verbal and body language of the late Neapolitan transwoman Valentina OK,[1] a transperson who adopted and re-shaped the traditional figure of the *femminiello*. This figure represents a particular form of crossing over of gender that can be understood as social because it is accepted by the rest of the community and is found in most traditional cultures. The paper hinges on an analysis of media portrayals of Valentina OK and aims to stress their culture-specific ("locally specific") aspects. Following this introduction, Sect. 2 discusses how different cultures accommodate the presence of a gender that has both male and female elements, focusing on the Neapolitan context, while Sect. 3 introduces the television personality Valentina OK. I discuss how she played an important role in guiding young people and fostering acceptance of gender crossing. In the world of *femminielli*, of which Valentina OK represents an evolution, the dimension of constant change may be said to be a constitutive element. Their ability to adjust to time and contexts allows *femminielli* and Valentina OK to take on new roles. Following this discussion, in the conclusion, I argue that the consideration of and reflection upon Valentina's identity can contribute to a fuller understanding of gender.

2 Subtle Cross-Cultural Ambiguity: Crossings and Rituals in Cultures and Neapolitan Specificity

The combination of aspects of male and female gender identity is common to many cultures. In this process of gender definition there may be room for the existence of diversity, or better still for what is usually referred to as not normal or natural. According to Ruth Benedict, normal is culturally expected and socially approved behaviour, while abnormal is behaviour that is perceived as alien to the cultural model of a society (Benedict 1934). So each culture establishes what is normal and what is not, and some cultures develop ways to expel what is different while other cultures tend to integrate such elements. On the one hand, the notion of abnormal supports practices of social exclusion that Lévi-Strauss calls anthropoemic, that expel deviants, while on the other hand, anthropophagic societies digest abnormalities, integrating them into the group through specific functions and rituals (Lévi-Strauss 1966). Generally speaking, many traditional societies had a strongly ambivalent conception of abnormality that was able to combine positive and negative, lewdness and decency, norm and transgression. To make this liminality "acceptable", abnormality is sometimes endowed with magic powers linked to the extra-human, bestowing upon it divine and metaphysical power. These powers depend on its belonging to a dimension that escapes normal categorisations, providing the deviants with knowledge and ways of organising life. This unknown and mysterious dimension is perceived as a well of both beneficial and harmful power. "There is an energy, a surplus of meaning that circulates in the interstices of the categories into which the world is arranged. For this reason, the attitude towards the abnormal is mingled with fear" (Scafoglio 2006a: 158, author's English translation). A peculiar form of abnormality is deviance defined through choices of ambiguous sexual construction.

While each culture creates its own specificity, we can recognise some shared aspects, similar but not identical to, those that we find in the Neapolitan *femminiello* in the Native American *berdache* and in some Iatmul practices of transvestism studied by Bateson (1988) as well as in the Hijra, a particular caste in Pakistan, India, and Bangladesh (Reddy 2005). The common trait of the protagonists of these practices is that they are not male, not female; in different contexts they can be seen as homosexual, transgender, or queer. All these figures have a special relationship with the sacred and are welcome at public ceremonies as bringers of good luck and abundance. They look after children and elderly people and know effective cures and treatments for illness. Until her death, and still today in the Neapolitan collective memory, the figure of Valentina OK represented a continuity and a significant reshaping of this aspect of the sexuality of traditional cultures in post-modernity.[2]

Neapolitan culture is a great container of popular cultural traditions. However, we can ask questions about how definitions of cultural traditions are made and who makes them. For most of the nineteenth century, popular wisdom indicated what belonged to the community as a whole, to the exclusion of the "high" culture enjoyed by intellectual minorities. In this way, popular wisdom is a synonym of the non-intellectual, the traditional, and the archaic. Yet this nineteenth-century definition does not do justice to the articulate and significant internal diversities that make up a society.

With regard to our specific case study, reality is full of hybrid forms of popular rituals and mass culture, that require decoding. In Naples the difference between high and low culture has some very specific features. From the seventeenth century onwards, the nobility lived in close contact with the lower classes: there was a continuous transmission of the popular culture to the aristocracy. It was a sort of mutuality that would lead to the sharing of symbols, values, and meanings, which would bring about a cultural "circularity" among the different social classes (Scafoglio 1996).

Naples is a unique, extremely tolerant and open-minded city: some have called it "the big Mediterranean sponge", the porous city (Velardi 1992) absorbing and then releasing heat; a city which can condense, contain, and conciliate. It is in this context that the transgender person we are investigating here belongs. In all its manifestations, Naples-ness (or *napoletanità*) is full of ambivalence and seeming polarisations that bring about integrations which would be unconceivable in other societies. Valentina's role is certainly divergent compared with the socially codified definitions, namely the correspondence between anatomical sex and social role, but at the same time it is accepted across the community and all social classes, just like the fluid crossing over between male and female that the *femmeniello* or *femmenella* has been able to interpret for such a long time. Neapolitan tolerance and the popular culture embody and render this a famous figure of diversity and liminality (Goddard 1987). In Neapolitan popular culture, the "*femminiello*" (a Neapolitan dialect word connoting an "effeminate man", a "sissy") is an icon of diversity and tolerance. For centuries, *femminiellos* have spent most of their lives in the alleys (in Mediterranean seaside cities, and towns, streets, and alleys are the places where social bonds are created and maintained), making up their faces, and constructing their body images and their place in society.[3] They have taken care of and protected others through a sometimes extreme theatricalisation that, according to Thomas Belmonte (1997), is part of every gesture and movement in Neapolitan culture. Some even argue that the construction of Neapolitan femininity as the strongly emotive and distinctively bodily-marked phenomenon it is, as represented by such icons as Sophia Loren, is the result of the *femminiello* being in charge of children's education. Theatricalisation not only involves transvestitism or the *femminiellos*' interpretation of their role, but also the way of interpreting male and female roles socially and emotionally. In this sense, in Neapolitan popular culture, being a *femminiello* is not an excess, but a way of living out liminality.

In Naples, *femminielli* marry in the traditional way. They walk through the streets with their grooms and go to restaurants that organise banquets for the whole community; they stand on the church parvis (the Catholic Church considers such unions blasphemous so they would not be allowed inside), they kiss each other, and make their wedding vows dressed in traditional wedding garb: the white dress and all the accessories including veil and flowers. After nine months, a child is born—always a boy—and the birth becomes a ritual representation which takes place within a house and is carried out more discreetly than the other rites. In same-sex couples where one partner is a *femminiello*, the latter pretends to be pregnant and carries out the famous rite known as the *figliata*, where all the phases of pregnancy are enacted: a swollen belly, relaxing on the bed and giving birth to a boy, generally a wooden puppet the size of a new-born baby with a huge phallus to highlight his male sex and strength (for a detailed literary description of this event, see Malaparte 1981 [1949]). Sometimes, during the christening, the couple show him off, and a woman from the community brings the newborn baby around to make it look like a real baptism.[4] Thus, awareness of having a common social dimension is manifested in a concrete sense. The miracle is that the couple manage to carve out a definition of a role that in reality they do not have. This happens in a continuum of social sharing that does not take place anywhere else in such a ritualised way: "in Naples transvestism is not to be considered as a consequence of disguised virility, but the condition of a present integrated and fully recognised reality" (Simonelli and Carrano 1985: 27, author's English translation).

This is the context from which Valentina OK came. Within Neapolitan circles, as we shall see, she was more than accepted—she was loved. In the following section I show how she created an identity which yielded such a positive response from her audience.

3 Valentina OK

Valentina OK was a transperson who adopted and re-shaped the traditional *femminiello* figure. She used transvestitism and aesthetic surgery as the first steps towards image re-shaping (she died before undergoing transition surgery), internalising the values of *femminiello* culture, establishing continuity between old and new practices and using local television to spread what had all the appearance of a true social message.[5] (See also Di Martino in this volume on this issue.) Rosalia Porcaro, a comic actress who worked for the TV programme *Telegaribaldi* from 1998 to 2000, often did impersonations of Valentina OK: a transvestite imitated by a woman who disguised herself as Valentina. Perhaps it is true to say that only in Naples was it possible to play on the specular reciprocity of genre construction in a comic key.

A critically acclaimed singer, Valentina OK hit the headlines in local and regional news coverage and was written about in the national newspapers in the late 1990s; John Turturro devoted a few seconds to her singing act in his film *Passion* (2010). For several years, she hosted a television show where she would sing songs requested by audience members phoning in, dedicating them to friends or relatives, following a format and structure that were particularly popular with the local networks. She had blond hair, a supermodel physique and an extremely melodic voice, and she reached the peak of her career when she was in her early twenties. Her transidentity, which bridged the established dichotomy between gender identity and anatomical sex, was the result of her choice to undergo a de-construction/re-construction process of her body: new breasts, hips and thighs, hair loss, beard removal and hormone and silicone injections produced a new, complex sexuality (as illustrated in Fig. 9.1). But the most unexpected fact—which immediately made

Fig. 9.1 Valentina during one of her shows

Valentina OK an atypical transperson, especially taking into account that the context was Southern Italy in the 1990s—was the extreme youth of most of her audience: children and pre-teens were her most devoted followers. The phenomenon may seem unusual at first, but is perhaps not totally unexpected in a city like Naples.

Her show was broadcast on Sundays in an early afternoon time slot, which implied a mainly family audience and, twenty years on, the family still represents the main target of these small local networks. Valentina OK interpreted her role as both a host and a singer by means of a personal communication strategy and an active use of the television medium, constantly referring to her sexual ambiguity. The camera angles were often fixed; in addition, the numerous close-ups were not only the result of her directors' inexperience but the consequence of a precise strategy that Valentina adopted in order to strengthen her personal empathetic relationship with viewers. Her glance, directed towards the camera, was engaging and fundamental in establishing contact with the audience. Her language was simple and apparently trifling, based on the stereotypical repetitiveness of the "phone call-musical request" format. A naive and familiar colloquial tone and "simplicity" were the strengths of her communication code—the OK in her name perfectly fitting with the mundane, repetitive nature of her small talk. And yet, Valentina addressed her viewers with conscious ability. She was determined to further a detailed social agenda on such issues as maternity, family, parenting roles, and the possibility of integrating transgressive gender definitions with serenity, respect, and tolerance, especially in those neglected and marginalised contexts where violence is commonly encountered. During phone calls, she often asked male viewers whether they were in a relationship and what their girlfriend's name was, focusing her conversations on life as a couple. Through their repetitiveness, these claims produced a celebration of stereotypes as well as feelings of a shared respectability which might have appeared incompatible with her character.

Table 9.1 shows a brief exchange taken from one of Valentina's many television programmes:

Her communication strategy was to appeal to different kinds of audience, as she clarified in an interview that I carried out in 1999 (Table 9.2).

Table 9.1 Extracts from the Telegaribaldi programme "Valentina"

Valentina: Ciao, Pronto chi sei amore	Valentina: Hello, who are you, love?
Spettatrice: Sono Katiuscia e ti voglio bene e voglio sentire la tua voce e la tua canzone	Viewer: I'm Katie and I love you and I want to hear your voice and your song
Valentina: Quale vuoi che ti dedico?	Valentina: What do you want me to dedicate to you?
Spett: Una qualunque basta che la scegli tu e la canti in diretta al telefono così io la posso cantare con te ... (Iniziano a cantare insieme...)	Viewer: Anything as long as you choose it and you sing it live on the phone so I can sing along with you ... (They start to sing together...)
Valentina: Un bacio fortissimo ti voglio bene e ti auguro ogni bene	Valentina: A big kiss I love you and I wish you every happiness
In un'altra telefonata Valentina porta avanti una sorta di monologo ecumenico in cui saluta tutti e tutta la città di Napoli nominando tutti i quartieri uno per uno:	*In another call Valentina makes a sort of speech to the city and the world where she greets everyone and the whole city of Naples, naming all the districts one by one*:
Valentina: Un bacio fortissimo per Elena, ai quartieri spagnoli, un bacio e un saluto per Enzo, per la mamma, per tutti quelli che soffrono, e che hanno problemi, vi voglio bene a tutti e un saluto per tutti i quartieri: Sanità. Forcella, e un bacio dappertutto e per chi non è libero "presto a libertà".	Valentina: A big kiss to Elena, to the Spanish Quarter, a kiss and a hello to Enzo, to mum, to everyone who's suffering and has problems, I love you all and I want to say a big hello to all the different districts: Sanità. Forcella, and a kiss everywhere. And for anyone who is not free, "get out soon".[a]
Spettatore: Grazie Valentina ti vogliamo bene, sei tutti noi, sei una brava ragazza, sei OK, canta per me	Viewer: Thanks Valentina we love you, you're all of us, you're a good girl, you're OK, sing for me

[a]The last comment is a coded message that many Neapolitans use to wish that anyone in prison be set free very soon

Valentina always achieved the desired result. In a similar way to the much-loved UK radio comedy characters Julian and Sandy, two gay men who also broadcast for a family audience on Sunday afternoons (see Baker 2002), part of her charm was that she was accepted and successful because she was seen as unthreatening: she was kind, interested in others, and she engaged in small talk. Her female audience expressed solidarity with her; Italian women, who usually do not establish positive

Table 9.2 Extracts from an interview carried out by Annalisa Di Nuzzo at the headquarters of Telecolore Salerno, Naples 28 June 1999

I: Perché il tuo successo e chi è il tuo pubblico?	I: What makes you such a success and who are your audience?
V: Io non voglio piacere solo agli uomini ... io voglio piacere a tutti e non mi interessa essere comm' Pamela Prati na' bambola tutta sesso ... io voglio essere amica di tutti quelli che mi telefonano ... voglio far ascoltare la mia musica ... e voglio dire una parola per i loro problemi, per quelli che soffrono, che stanno in carcere e poi voglio sentire i bambini ... Il mio programma è la voce di tutti senza differenze e le mie canzoni parlano della vita e dell'amore. Proprio come quando parlo in diretta con il mio pubblico io dico quello che penso ... io non faccio nessuna recita ... sono spontanea	V: I don't just want men to like me ... I want everyone to like me and I don't want to be like Pamela Prati, just a sex doll ... I want to be a friend to everyone who phones me ... I want people to listen to my music ... and I want to say a word or two about their problems, something for everyone who suffers, something for those in prison, and I want to hear from the kiddies ... My programme is the voice of everybody, without distinction, and my songs talk about life and love. Just like when I talk live with my audience I say what I think ... it's not a performance ... I'm just myself

relations with transpeople due to their strong Catholic upbringing—especially at that time—acknowledged the criteria of a fully shared beauty in her, due to her simplicity and lack of excessive ostentation, just like a good family girl.

Feminine but "no sex doll", Valentina claimed the right to express her opinion on her audience's problems and showed energy and strength in her decisions, clearly displaying a leading role as social guide, one which is traditionally masculine ("and I want to say a word or two about their problems, something for everyone who suffers: those in prison, and I want to hear from the kiddies ... My programme is the voice of all, without distinction"). In this way she offered a distinct verbal model of positively aimed masculinity. Assertive but not violent or vulgar, feminine but not submissive or meek, Valentina displayed both the feminine abilities of the skilled conversationalist that Fishman 1980 describes as necessary to negotiate uncooperative male behaviour and the self-confidence and advice-giving role typical of male conversation (Tannen 1990). She did not live long enough to undergo full gender reassignment surgery,

Table 9.3 Extracts from an interview carried out by Annalisa Di Nuzzo at the headquarters of Telecolore Salerno, Naples 28 June 1999

I: Come hai vissuto il tuo corpo? V: Man mano che crescevo mi sono sentita prigioniera volevo esprimere i miei desideri e le mie emozioni attraverso un'altra me stessa che non voleva i peli sul viso, le mani nodose ma fianchi morbidi e seni femminili e desiderava allo stesso tempo essere forte decisa non volgare, trasgressiva e scandalizzare ... io ci credo alla famiglia ai sentimenti di fedeltà e di rispetto, di amore verso i bambini che sono la mia gioia ... volevo i miei valori senza ricorrere alle "arti femminili" per raggirare gli uomini. Ho sofferto molto per raggiungere il corpo che ho ... Medicinali, cambiamento dei miei muscoli ... un metabolismo stravolto ... ma ho raggiunto il mio benessere e non sarà solo l'operazione chirurgica finale a cambiarmi, io sono unica e sonoinsieme più cose...	I: Tell me about your relationship with your body V: As I grew up I felt like a prisoner: I wanted to express my desires and my emotions through another myself who didn't want hair on her face or muscly hands, but soft hips and feminine breasts and at the same time I wanted to be strong and determined, not vulgar, transgressive, scandalous ... I believe in the family, and feelings of loyalty and respect, and love for children, who are a real joy to me ... I wanted my values without resorting to "feminine wiles" to get round men. I suffered a lot to get the body that I have ... Medicine, changes to my muscles ... my metabolism turned upside down ... but I've found my peace of mind and it won't just be the final operation that will change me ... I am unique and at the same time lots of things...

but as she clearly understood, the final operation would not have changed the unique being that she was (Table 9.3).

The repetitive obsessiveness of ritual phrases such as "Ti amo/I love you", "Mando un bacio a tutti/I blow a kiss to everyone", "OK", "Saluto.../I say hello to...", emphasises the phatic communication function of her speech, giving her viewers a sense of reassurance and belonging to a community, which is a typical aspect of private Neapolitan TV networks. It was (and is) an extremely varied world, which cannot simply be connoted as media for the underclasses, but one which shares a transversal element: social marginality. The peculiar composition of Neapolitan society implies a clarification of the role of the marginal classes. Marginality does not fall under the categories determined by one's social function or the related role one plays in the more or less consolidated traditional hierarchy of the social classes; it depends on a series of distinguishing components and economic powers. Therefore, the peddler who owns a large truck and goes to every regional market is marginal; the person with a criminal record who rips others off using new information technology is marginal; the civil servant who "uses" bureaucracy to personal advantage is marginal. A chain of values is therefore established which is no longer ascribable to a typical census. The Valentina OK character understood this perfectly, and she interpreted her communicative text and based her role of social representation on the element of reassurance. The consequent message produced new schemes of gender definition together with values of diversity integration.

There was a strong, noticeable, and immediately engaging desire for clarity and acceptance in Valentina OK, even in personal contacts. Her hands (Fig. 9.1) highlighted the irreducibility of her masculine origin, pointing to a complicated diversity: an *abnormality* to be accepted. The audience shared this identity-alterity dialectic, the homogenisation of diversity found in the very marginality of those watching the show.

Needing a workable and new definition of "transgender", Valentina especially used her unique gender performance to talk to children and establish a special, engaging relationship with them, revealing a deep-rooted maternal dimension. During her show, the phone calls she received from this specific audience were characterised by a particular empathy, full of serenity and sweetness, together with Valentina's ability to access and share the world of the child with easy spontaneity. Sometimes the fatuous dynamics of the conversations opened up to reveal unsuspected relational skills, paving the way for real dialogue. So Valentina talked about the toys, childhood friendships, and habits of her callers as well as the importance of parents, especially the mother. Valentina's young followers almost saw her as a nouvelle Alice leading them to an (albeit provincial) TV Wonderland. Valentina continuously highlighted an atavistic but also present-day feeling in males, the biologically impossible but culturally desired feeling of maternity, which was more intensely lived out in her desire to lay claim to her acquired femininity.

Thus, like the most highly acclaimed stars in traditional Anglo-Saxon culture, she went to the children's hospitals in the city, bringing gifts to the neediest patients, gifts which she herself had received from more fortunate children. She was at ease moving through the hospital wards, asking about the health of the patients, hugging and cuddling them, and the "event" was filmed each time to add a new scene to her tried and tested script. Ward nurses contributed spontaneously to the scene, greeting her warmly, kissing her and calling blessings down upon her in a surprising "order-disorder" contamination. A double ancestral need seems to emerge during these events, as identified by Simonelli and Carrano (1985): on the one hand the masculine expression of control and responsibility on the future generations (which is inevitably jeopardised in such crucial physiological moments as childbirth or breastfeeding, when the woman is the real protagonist), on the other hand the implicit declaration of freedom from feminine power on those same generations that Valentina OK has "adopted". Valentina OK's behaviour is a manifestation of these ancestral needs which still exist and characterise contemporary Neapolitan society, but also other contexts, where maternity has always represented a true matriarchy. A mainly matriarchal family structure still exists in Naples, with a significant influence on the children and their behaviours (Scafoglio 2006b) in an economically disadvantaged city with a lack of stability in masculine models. According to a line of research dating back to the 1960s,[6] in the context of the Neapolitan family and the social reality described above, a son may simultaneously repudiate and interiorise the maternal model, ultimately making a transgender choice. It was as an intrusive and power-wielding mother that Valentina OK talked to children, well aware of the seductive game she was sometimes playing with her young audience, in an almost subliminal way. Today, the narrow backstreets of Naples that provided a specific context and distribution of roles are disappearing and have been replaced by a sort of virtual backstreet within the local television networks, where the younger generations have an outlet for self-expression and entertainment offered by a new-found media visibility.

Valentina would ask questions, especially about the pre-teens' everyday lives. During a programme broadcast by the national TV network RAI 2, she repeatedly declared her particular interest in pre-teens, calling herself their confidante. She referred in particular to those children aged thirteen to fourteen going through a difficult puberty, especially if they were becoming aware of a gender identity different from their anatomical sex. This reference to age groups does not reflect those rigidly schematised by developmental psychologists (obviously Valentina was not abreast of academic developments), but it shows how she instinctively understood the importance of this transitional phase from childhood to adulthood. Her interest in youngsters starts from childhood, with the young spectators who follow her and then she feels responsible, guiding and supporting them in the difficult phase when they become aware of their sexual orientation. The help of a person like Valentina could be crucial in finding what she herself defined as "the courage necessary to be what you really are, to establish your own identity in spite of everything, always with the help of the Lord, avoiding foolish, impulsive actions or selling out" (RAI 2 1998).

Valentina explained the reason for this unexpected success with a very young audience in an interview (Table 9.4).

Table 9.4 Extracts from an interview carried out by Annalisa Di Nuzzo at the headquarters of Telecolore Salerno, Napoli, 28 June 1999

I: Perché tanti ragazzi ti seguono? V: Forse perché sono diventata la loro confidente ... specialmente per quei ragazzi di 13–14 anni che stanno passando un momento difficile perché si sentono diversi da quello che li vogliono far essere. Io posso essere per loro un esempio ... non li voglio far soffrire ma piuttosto rendere possibile quello che è successo a me anche con l'aiuto della famiglia ... si può trovare il modo. Per me la televisione è anche questo Valentina lo può fare per dire che si può trovare quel coraggio necessario per essere ciò che si è, per affermarsi a dispetto di tutto, ma con l'aiuto del Signore, senza colpi di testa, senza svendersi. I ragazzi di oggi che amano e seguono Valentina quando saranno adulti non si comporteranno come molti adulti di oggi, sono convinta che saranno diversi e non costringeranno i loro figli, se ci saranno problemi, a nascondersi, a fuggire, credo che da questo punto di vista sarà un mondo certamente migliore	I: Why do young people like you so much? V: Perhaps because I've become their confidante ... especially for those aged 13–14 who are going through a bad patch because they feel different from what the others want them to be. I can be an example to them ... I don't want to make them suffer, but to make possible what happened to me, also with the help of the family ... you can find a way. Television is about this too. Valentina can go on TV to say that you can find the courage needed to be what you are, to affirm yourself despite everything, but with the Lord's help, without doing anything impulsive, without selling out. The kids who love and follow Valentina won't behave like a lot of adults today, I'm quite sure they'll be different and won't force their children to hide or run away if there are problems. I think it'll definitely be a better world from that point of view

During television interviews she would stroke a soft toy while sitting on a bed in a room that could have belonged to one of her followers, one of those children joining her numerous fan clubs in Naples and the surrounding area (she herself still lived with her parents). So it almost seemed natural that the Italian national television network would ask her to host a national show for children, an idea which was eventually shelved mainly because the rest of Italy was not ready to accept her progressive social message as Naples had done.

This is due to the history of the city, which has made possible the circulation of values beyond differences in wealth, role, or class. Over the years, Naples has been less influenced by the religious puritanism and bourgeois ideas of decency that Catholic culture (that censors any form of sexuality which is not targeted to Catholic marriage and family) has imposed on the rest of Italy. Pasolini[7] used to say that Neapolitans would not allow themselves to be changed because their culture is close-knit and cuts through class differences. For some, this has been a sign of provincialism and a rejection of modernity, but in this case it is a question of greater openness and autonomy.[8] Valentina knew what she was managing to achieve and how effective her communication was, as she herself put it: "Above all I would really appreciate it if people understood that I am a slightly different kind of transsexual person: I am not the kind of person who seeks to cause a scandal on TV or to exploit my looks and my body. I have my own sensitivity as an artist, which is why mothers choose to let their children watch my shows" (Elia 1997, author's English translation). Valentina was therefore trying to reach out to the whole family sphere, positively affirming her own diversity in order to bridge and mediate teenage conflicts and crises, avoiding social fracture and presenting herself as an example of someone who emerged from her own crisis in a positive way. Parents acknowledged her role, trusting her, following her on television, and expecting her to fulfil the function of teaching "openness towards the world" and towards the universe of feelings for "the other". She still performs this role even after her death, claiming positive values such as family, religion, and maternity to be passed on to future generations.

4 Conclusion

This chapter has tried to illustrate the fascinating process of integration of the different layers that coexist in Neapolitan culture. Naples has explored and reshaped the theme of sexual diversity through the figure of the *femminiello*. Identity is not built up through a simple play of opposites, but through gender transgression, side by side with social constructs. Indeed *femminielli* enjoy weddings, baptisms, and a series of other rites, in which all the others from the alleys (*vicoli*[9]) participate. They are also essential guests at traditional gatherings and rituals marking births, deaths, and marriages. Like all self-respecting communities, *femminielli* have ritualised these fundamental moments of their "being in the world". So there is a queer dimension that is implicit in some aspects of Neapolitan culture. This dimension, consciously ambiguous in relation to the different genders that coexist, is a deliberate choice to remain suspended between the two dimensions of masculine and feminine. Its starting point is the lacerated forms of the relationship between corporality and sexual identity, as Valentina shows, resulting then in new harmonies, "working" on the body to re-establish different relationships between identity and gender.

Judith Butler speaks of *Bodies that Matter* (1993), and of freeing oneself as Valentina did, from what she (Butler) calls *gender performativity*. Western culture has always tried to divide sex and gender, associating sex with matter (the body) and gender with culture. What makes Valentina remarkable is her alignment with a way of being that is essentially post-modern where the result consists of an integration of masculine and feminine identities that become and continuously cross over into each other, sustaining and problematising each other. To identify as transgender is often to endure a long and arduous process that combines pleasure and pain, a request for legitimate happiness and transgressive serenity. In interviews with, and statements by, Valentina the need emerges to overcome the logic of duality and to be seen as including both masculine and feminine elements, in other words as queer (Alfano Miglietti 2002). Each identity category—lesbian, gay, bisexual, transgender, and heterosexual—can coalesce into a general queerness that does not result in an ambiguous chaotic vortex, but a mutual recognition. The challenge of queerness consists in the perpetual questioning of the established unity of sexual identity, which can constantly be redefined.

As Valentina suggested in our last meeting: "If you want to say who Valentina is, or what Valentina does, you can't. No one can". The construction of the personage is complete, like that of the mystery. The impossibility of definition is a characteristic of our time. It is the essence of "queer", as Halperin (1995: 61–62) describes it: "Queer is by definition whatever is at odds with the normal, the legitimate, the dominant. There is nothing in particular to which it necessarily refers. It is an identity without essence".

Being female, male, or transgender, becomes an element of social visibility, a new category of socio-cultural transformation of which Valentina is a unique herald, detached from corporeality, from nature, a dream in the anthropological imaginary. The culture of the city of Naples, which tends to go beyond mere tolerance, to understand diversity and to be a cultural laboratory of post-modernity in which tradition is innovation, is ahead of its time and simultaneously an original reinterpretation. A city in which purity and danger, order and disorder, lawful and the unlawful, obscenity and purity, and the perverse and the ordinary continue to live without the need to reiterate modalities, rituals, and sanctions, Naples is a fascinating and multifaceted polymorph. It is rich in sensuality that restores zones of interdiction and offers original reinterpretations. Valentina was one of the thousand faces of this Neapolitan kaleidoscope.

Notes

1. Valentina died in September 2014.
2. On these comparisons see: Zito E. and Valerio P., *Corpi sull'uscio, identità possibili. Il fenomeno dei femminielli a Napoli*, Naples, Filema, 2010; Ferrari F., *Non gender specifico nel XXI secolo nell'Asia Meridionale.* "Trickster", n.3. università di Padova 2007; Butler J., *La disfatta del genere* Meltemi, Rome 2004; Zito E. and Valerio P. (eds), *Genere: femminielli. Espolarioni antropologiche e psicologiche*, Libreria Dante & Descartes, Naples, 2013; D'Agostino

G., *I Femminielli napoletani: alcune riflessioni antropologiche, in Genere: femminielli. Espolazioni antropologiche e psicologiche*, Libreria Dante & Descartes, Naples, 2013; pp. 75–106; Callender Ch., Kochems L. M., The North American Berdache, "Current Anthropology", 24, 4 (Aug.–Oct.). 1983; Héritier F., Dissolvere la gerarchia. Maschile/femminile II, Raffaello Cortina, Milan, 2004; Herdt G., *Guardians of the Flautes. Idioms of Masculinity*, McGraw-Hill, New York, 1981.

3. As I will clarify in the following paragraphs, *femminiellos* meet up on the occasion of traditional celebrations like weddings and christenings. The *vicolo* (the narrow street where she has her home, a *basso*, a one-room flat at street level where eyes peep in and out) is the place where social relationships are maintained.
4. In seventeenth-century England, men known as Mollies conducted weddings among themselves, as well as enactments of childbirth (Norton 1992). They were not widely accepted like the *femminiellos*: in fact, they were criminalised.
5. For more details about Valentina OK and the changes in postmodernist Neapolitan culture, cf. Di Nuzzo (2007, 2009, 2013).
6. Victoria Goddard's research confirms the essential role of women in conserving group identity in the marginal classes in Naples. Maternal power is consolidated through the control and exclusion of males from areas of domestic skills. Victoria Goddard, "Women's Sexuality and Group Identity in Naples", in *The Cultural Construction of Sexuality*, ed. Pat Caplan (London: Tavistock, 1987). See also Sydel Silverman, "The Life Crisis as a Clue to Social Function" in *Anthropological Quarterly*, 40 (1967): 127–138.
7. Pasolini P. P., *La napoletanità*, in Saggi sulla politica e sulla società, Walter Siti and Silvia De Laude (eds), vol. I, Milano, Mondadori, 1999, pp. 230–231.
8. Giddens A., Identità e società moderna, Napoli, Ipermedium, 1999.
9. See footnote 3.

References

Alfano Miglietti, F. (2002). *Identità mutanti. Dalla piega alla piaga: Esseri delle contaminazioni contemporanee*. Milan: Costa & Nolan.

Augé, M. (1996). *Non Luoghi*. Milan: Eleuthera.

Baker, K. A. (2002, June 8). *Organizational Culture* [Online]. Retrieved from www.au.af.mil/au/awc/awcgate/doe/benchmark/ch11.pdf

Bateson, G. (1988). *Naven. Un rituale di travestitismo in Nuova Guinea.* Turin: Einaudi.

Belmonte, T. (1997). *La fontana rotta. Vite napoletane: 1974–1983.* Rome: Meltemi.

Benedict, R. (1934). *Patterns of Culture.* New York: Houghton Mifflin.

Butler, J. (1993). *Bodies That Matter.* New York: Routledge.

Del Lago, A. (1995). *I nostri riti quotidiani.* Genoa: Costa e Nolan.

Di Nuzzo, A. (2007). Valentina e le altre. In D. Scafoglio (Ed.), *L'odore della bellezza. Antropologia del fitness e del wellness* (pp. 52–63). Milan: Delfino edizione.

Di Nuzzo, A. (2009). La città nuova: Dalle antiche pratiche del travestitismo alla riplasmazione del femminiello nelle nuove identità mutanti. In F. Scalzone (Ed.), *Perversione, Perversioni e Perversi* (pp. 143–153). Rome: Borla edizione.

Di Nuzzo, A. (2013). Napoletanità e identità post-moderne. Riplasmazioni del femminiello a Napoli. In E. Zito & P. Valerio (Eds.), *Genere: Femminielli* (pp. 131–159). Naples: Libreria Dante & Descartes edizioni.

Elia, P. (1997, July). Valentina la neomelodica. *Corriere del Mezzogiorno.*

Fishman, P. (1980). Conversational Insecurity. In H. Giles, W. P. Robinson, & P. M. Smith (Eds.), *Language: Social Psychological Perspectives* (pp. 127–113). Oxford: Pergamon Press.

Goddard, V. (1987). Women's Sexuality and Group Identity in Naples. In P. Caplan (Ed.), *The Cultural Construction of Sexuality* (pp. 166–192). London: Tavistock.

Halperin, D. M. (1995). *Saint Foucault: Towards a Gay Hagiography.* New York and Oxford: Oxford University Press.

Héritier, F. (2002). *Maschile e femminile. Il pensiero della differenza.* Bari: Edizioni Laterza.

Lévi-Strauss, C. (1966). *Antropologia strutturale.* Milan: Il Saggiatore.

Malaparte, C. (1981 [1949]). *La pelle.* Milan: Oscar Mondadori.

Norton, R. (1992). *Mother Clap's Molly House.* London: GMP Books.

RAI 2. (1998). *Intervista a Valentina OK.* Author's personal script.

Reddy, G. (2005). *With Respect to Sex: Negotiating Hijra Identity in South India.* Chicago: University of Chicago Press.

Scafoglio, D. (1996). *Contesti culturali e scambi verbali nella Napoli contemporanea.* Salerno: Gentile Editore.

Scafoglio, D. (2006a). *Introduzione alla ricerca etno-antropologica.* Naples: CUES.

Scafoglio, D. (2006b). Le forme lacerate. Fenomenologia e semantica dell'osceno. Special Issue of *L'immagine riflessa. Esibire il nascosto. Testi e immagini dell'osceno*. Alessandria: Edizione dell'Orso, pp. 70–120.

Simonelli, P., & Carrano, G. (1985). Mito e seduzione dell'immagine femminile a Napoli. In S. M. Raso (Ed.), *Sessualità e sessuologia nel Sud* (pp. 17–23). Naples: SEN.

Tannen, D. (1990). *You Just Don't Understand: Women and Men in Conversation*. New York: Ballantine Books.

Turturro, J. (dir.) (2010). *Passion*.

Velardi, C. (1992). *La città porosa*. Naples: Cronopio.

10

Undoing Black Masculinity: Isaac Julien's Alternative Grammar of Visual Representation

Emilio Amideo

1 Introduction: Looking for a Black Queer Genealogy, or Queering Black Masculinity

Looking for Langston is a black and white film produced in 1989 by the Anglo-Caribbean visual artist and filmmaker Isaac Julien. The short film, of about 40 minutes, is the fifth one that Julien produced with the *Sankofa Film and Video Collective* which he co-founded in 1983.[1] Winner of numerous awards, including a *Teddy* for best short film at the Berlin International Film Festival in 1989, *Looking for Langston* is a "poetic meditation" (Mercer 1994: 223), partly drawing on the documentary genre, which explores the ambiguous black queer subtext of the 1920s Harlem Renaissance and of the 1980s London and Washington DC. By combining the realistic aspect of archival footage with imaginative newly

E. Amideo (✉)
Dipartimento di Studi Letterari, Linguistici e Comparati,
Università degli Studi di Napoli "L'Orientale", Napoli, Italy

P. Baker, G. Balirano (eds.), *Queering Masculinities in Language and Culture*,
Palgrave Studies in Language, Gender and Sexuality,
https://doi.org/10.1057/978-1-349-95327-1_10

scripted scenes, and through the presence of important intellectual figures from the 1920s to the 1990s (including Richard Bruce Nugent, Langston Hughes, James Baldwin, and Essex Hemphill), Julien focuses on a diasporic representation that enables him to express a truly liberating black queer experience and to reconstruct, in a way, its genealogy.

Together with the coeval *Tongues Untied* by the African American filmmaker Marlon Riggs, *Looking for Langston* represents one of the first filmic explorations of black queer experience and has therefore been at the centre of numerous critical debates. While focusing on Julien's articulation of an alternative black masculinity outside of the dominant stereotypical discourse that surrounds it, this chapter proposes a new reading of the film through a semiotic approach, partly drawing on the work on multimodality by Kress and van Leeuwen (2006) and strongly influenced by the theoretical tradition of the Caribbean diaspora (especially Édouard Glissant and Edward Kamau Brathwaite) and, particularly, by the queer Caribbean diasporic experience (Rinaldo Walcott). If "reality is in the eye of the beholder" or better "what is regarded as real depends on how reality is defined by a particular social group" (Kress and van Leeuwen 2006: 158), Julien knows only too well how the long history of debasement of both black masculinity and homosexuality is dependent on hegemonic representations by the Western "racialized heteropatriarchy" (Allen 2012: 220). My reading of *Looking for Langston*, therefore, will emphasise the way in which Julien's images move in the context of Western culturally produced regularities (or "grammar" in Kress and van Leeuwen's terms) while at the same time disrupting them in order to propose alternative ways of seeing. This way of "queering" the gaze will demonstrate also how Julien partly displaces the prominence of the visual characteristic of Western tradition to highlight a more holistic perception which involves (and evokes) other senses, such as hearing and touch.

2 Queering the Gaze, Displacing the Visual

"[H]ow much pressure does it take to waken one?" asks the voiceover while in one of the central scenes of *Looking for Langston*—two male characters exchange a tender kiss (Fig. 10.1).

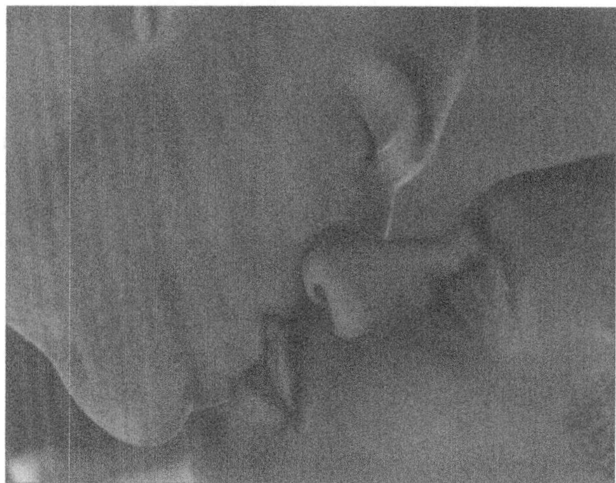

Fig. 10.1 Still from Isaac Julien's *Looking for Langston*, 1989

> [...] then he awoke. [...] Beauty was smiling in his sleep ... half his face stained flush color by the sun ... the other half in shadow [...] his lips were so beautiful ... quizzical [...] I would kiss your lips ... he would like to kiss Beauty's lips ... he flushed warm ... with shame ... or was it shame? [...] his pulse was hammering ... from wrist to fingertip. ...Beauty's lips touched his ... his temples throbbed. [...] Beauty's lips pressed cool ... cool and hard ... *how much pressure does it take to waken one?* [...] Beauty's lips pressed hard against his teeth, he trembled ... he could feel Beauty's body close against his ... hot ... tense ... and soft ... soft. (Julien 1989, adapted from Nugent 1926 [emphasis mine])

The voiceover cites, and adapts, an excerpt from Richard Bruce Nugent's *Smoke, Lilies and Jade* (1926), the first short story written by an African American writer to openly address homosexuality which appeared in *Fire!!*, an experimental literary magazine of the Harlem Renaissance. In his cinematic rendition, Julien quotes the interracial love affair at the centre of Nugent's story which involves Alex—a young African American artist—and Adrian, the Hispanic man with whom he spends the night, and who is renamed Beauty in honour of his allure. Their love affair is visually and aurally transposed as intraracial, through the elision of all the words that in the original text allude to Beauty's white skin. This choice is consistent with Julien's attempt to create a space for the recognition of black male beauty in order not only to contrast the stereotypical representations of black masculinity forged through colonial history, for example the black man as lazy, childlike, or its opposite, aggressive, hypersexual, instinctual (Staples 1982, 2006; Mercer 1994: 131–170; Hall 1997: 244–269; Milton 2012), but also to give visibility to black queer desire, ostracised both in the context of Black Nationalism and Western society as a whole.

The question "how much pressure does it take to waken one?"—only apparently referring to the quantity of pressure one should put into a kiss to waken a lover who is asleep—lingers on in the film. The director's insistence on tactility, as evoked by the term "pressure" is emblematic, especially if we consider the pivotal role that the visual has played in Western history. Starting from the Renaissance's monocular perspective, Western tradition has, in fact, always used the gaze as an instrument to define individual subjectivity and convey epistemological mastery over the representation of "reality" (Silverman 1996; Parisi 2004):

> Perspective, as a point of origin, a regulated and homogenous geometry of space, locates the eye of the viewer at the centre of the frame, controlling and defining what is to be seen, catalogued, described, explained. (Chambers 2001: 30)

This "western master narrative of visuality" (Ponzanesi 2015: 8) in which the subject knows and controls through his gaze—an equation represented by the pair of English homophones "I" (the subject) and "eye" (the organ of sight)—is inherent in cinematic representations where the observer is brought to identify with the camera. It is also particularly evident in certain types of documentary genres, such as ethnographic filmmaking which has often been used to fix the otherness of cultures and identities into an objectifying gaze (Shohat and Stam 1994; Ponzanesi 2015). With his focus on tactility, but also on sound suggestions, Julien displaces the centrality of the visual, which still remains very important in his representation, by hybridising and contaminating it. The result is a "perceptive synaesthesia" (Parisi 2004: 328 [translation mine]), in which sound, image, and evocation of the sense of touch combine to corroborate a perception which is continuous transition and resonance.

Julien's experimental artistic production crosses the boundaries between different arts and genres in order to construct powerful visual narrations that challenge naturalised knowledge and assumptions about "race", class belonging, and sexuality.[2] By rendering visible the choice, selection, and articulation of visual and sound material, Julien proposes a performative documentary (Nichols 2010) through which he suspends the presumed "objectivity" of Western historiography, and transports the audience into his world in order to allow them to share his perspective on black queer desire, whose voice is finally unearthed.

As Kobena Mercer recognises: the film's "fragmentary collage of archival and original material interrupts the transparency necessary for an 'objective' account to achieve a quality of critical reverie" (Mercer 1994: 59). This reading is especially fruitful as it highlights Julien's diasporic poetics in line with the concept of "usable past", firstly theorised by the American historian and literary critic Van Wyck Brooks, and widely used in the black diasporic tradition to signify the production, through narrative, of an otherwise irretrievable past. The same concept has been used by Édouard Glissant to define the last phase of Caribbean literary production: the "passion for memory" (the other two being "acts of delusion" and "acts of survival") that is "compensatory and recuperative" of the loss of history and is characterised by the artistic imagination that counters the common notion of history and re-symbolises it (Glissant 1997).[3] In Derek Walcott's words:

> In the Caribbean history is irrelevant, not because it is not being created, or because it was sordid; but because it has never mattered. What has mattered is the loss of history, the amnesia of the races, what has become necessary is imagination, imagination as necessity, as invention. (D. Walcott 1974: 6)

To respond to this necessity for imagination, Julien offers a poetic "meditation" (Hemphill 1991: 177–178) which not only restores "the love that does not dare speak its name", particularly "sinful" in the African American tradition where homosexuality is often considered a crime against the "race",[4] but he re-symbolises as well the common features associated with black masculinity while contesting them from within:

> [...] instead of avoiding the black body, because it has been so caught up in the complexities of power and subordination within representation, this [Julien's] strategy positively takes the body as the principal site of its representational strategies, attempting to make the stereotypes work against themselves. (Hall 1997: 274)

Julien brings the black male body at the centre of his film in order to show it under a new light. Focusing on a diasporic depiction which refuses essentialism, he strips "black masculinity" of its stereotypical attributes and affirms a truly liberating black (homosexual) identity.[5] In this context, then, his question "how much pressure does it take to waken one?" might be read as referring to the amount of pressure (or uneasiness) necessary to waken the spectator (black and white community alike) to the awareness of a very vulnerable desire which has otherwise been hidden. This is what Julien aims at in his film production: he wants to leave a mark using a direct representation which makes the spectator feel exposed, uncomfortable even, but never indifferent.

Considering the reaction of shame in some members of the audience during the first screening of the film, Julien affirms:

> [...] that kind of unease is important if we're going to progress, to learn how to look in a different way; I think that looking in a different way is what's threatening. And this response, this shame, is something that I think holds back important discourse around black male representation in the cinema—and in lived reality. (hooks and Julien 1991: 177)

The menace inherent in looking in a different way—of queering the gaze—but also the ambiguity of the look itself is what moved Julien to produce the film. It is not by chance that the verb "looking", with its multiple meanings, appears in the title. Julien starts his journey with the aim of "tracking" Langston (an overt reference to the twentieth-century African American poet Langston Hughes), but on his way he focuses on "watching", he "observes", "scrutinises" even, the past in order to find empowering means for the expression of a black queer desire in a racist and homophobic society. That is why he turns to the Harlem Renaissance, a movement whose main exponents were black and queer themselves, to include Nugent and the closeted Hughes, and who therefore represent a sort of genealogy for the expression of this particular kind of desire. A move that necessarily has to pass through a dismantling of the litany of stereotypical representations surrounding black males.

3 Undoing "Black Masculinity"

In *We Real Cool* (2004) the African American theorist bell hooks describes the condition of contemporary black men in what she defines "imperialist white-supremacist capitalist patriarchy" essentially as a vicious circle in which, for the price of visibility and recognition, they are forced to identify with the stereotype that society has moulded for them, either by embodying it or by living a life to prove to be other than that:

> In patriarchal culture all males learn a role that restricts and confines. When race and class enter the picture, along with patriarchy, then black males endure the worst impositions of gendered masculine patriarchal identity. Seen as animals, brutes, natural born rapists, and murderers, black men have had no real dramatic say when it comes to the way they are represented. They have made few interventions on the stereotype. As a consequence they are victimized by stereotypes that were first articulated in the nineteenth century but hold sway over the minds and imaginations of citizens of this nation in the present day. (hooks 2004: x)

If, effectively, in patriarchal societies all men have to conform to specific roles which are socially constructed and historically contingent, black men have (had) to deal with the additional burden of a type of masculinity defined through centuries of cultural debasement. Stripped of their masculine prerogatives during slavery (Staples 2006: 69), black men went from embodying the paternalistic stereotype of the "good negro" characterised by intellectual inferiority, laziness, and gluttony as shown in Minstrel Shows and Vaudeville Acts of the nineteenth century, to that of the "bad negro" during the Reconstruction Era when, after the abolition of slavery, legal segregation was reinforced in the United States. This latter image portrayed the black man as beastly, hypersexual, and aggressive, and subsequently merged in the myth of the "black rapist" (Milton 2012: 18).

In the 1950s a "purified" image of the black man started to make its appearance in the cinema as exemplified by the black film actor Sidney Poitier, often portrayed as an elegant, sophisticated, and intelligent man. This representation differed from previous stereotypes by offering—from a white liberal perspective—the image of a non-threatening (and also non-sexual) black man (Hall 1997: 252–253). In order to contrast this "racialized regime of representation" (Hall 1997: 249) which deprived black men of their agency, in the 1960s and 1970s Black Nationalism completely wiped out the image of the submissive and obedient "good negro" to substitute it with a provocative, revolutionary, even violent, image of the black American man (Hunter and Davis 1994: 23). If on the one hand this conceptual redefinition of black masculinity, that linguistically marked the passage from the term "negro" to the term "black", served as a propellant for social protest, on the other it almost eclipsed the issue of desire from the protest or nationalist cultural production of the twentieth century.

In spite of the inevitable sexual component of this idea of black masculinity (mainly associated with sexual prowess and manhood), the issue of desire, of eroticism intended as creative charge and means of empowerment—to use a suggestion from Audre Lorde in her renowned 1978 paper "Uses of the Erotic"—was largely ignored. To this image, recalled in the film by Robert Mapplethorpe's photographs from the *Black Book* (1986) in which naked black men are represented in rigid, almost marmoreal poses, Julien opposes a black male body which is softer, almost vulnerable, in order to create a malleability capable of capturing the complexities and ambiguities inherent in every human being, therefore opposing the reduction to a few essential features that are fixed in nature, characteristic of stereotyping (Hall 1997: 249). In Julien's words:

> I think that my own project has been one of discussing masculinity, black masculinity in particular, and in a way trying to point out the construction of black masculinity, and by creating gaps, or lacks, in the representations

> of black men in the films that I make, I try to show a more ambivalent black masculinity, which is something that is masked over. In black popular culture, of course, a black masculinist, hard representation is what's important in articulating polemics against [...] institutionalized racism. But if we're actually trying to create a discussion among ourselves or trying to show another kind of representation, it's important to portray the kind of construction of black masculinity that is something very fragile and vulnerable. (hooks and Julien 1991: 177)

In the film, then, Julien envisions a more ambiguous black masculinity, deprived of the mask it is forced to put on in the context of black nationalist rhetoric and of the attributes attached to it by racist discourse. In accordance with Hall's strategy defined above, Julien counteracts stereotypes by lingering on the details of black bodies, whose nakedness has been exploited by Western racist and sexist tradition as an instrument of humiliation and (physical and moral) subjugation, to rearticulate them. In a move that seems to embellish the past, Julien presents the spectator with highly aestheticised black bodies, of the kind one would see in advertisements, in opposition to the pervasive historical images of (more or less symbolically) scarred and anonymous black bodies, flogged or lynched, characteristic of the so-called pornography of pain. Highly voyeuristic in its nature, this phenomenon was typical of the late eighteenth- and early nineteenth-century Western cult of sensibility that redefined pain as unacceptable and, by making it a source of "illicit excitement, prurience, and obscenity" (Halttunen 1995: 325), eroticised it. The pornography of pain saw humanitarian reformers caught up in the contradiction of displaying certain practices (like the flogging of slaves or prisoners, the rape of women, etc.) with the aim of arousing popular opposition and eradicating them, and is still manifest nowadays in the pervasive spectacularisation of pain.

Julien does not succumb to this pitfall: he hints at violence and makes the viewer aware of its possibility, but he never actually shows it. For the first time, the spectator is brought to observe black masculinity and to gain a visual pleasure from it, instead of feeling threatened or menaced (hooks 2015: 199). Inspired by a photographic repertoire which includes the sensual male nudes of George Platt Lynes and the baroque funereal portraits of James Van Der Zee's *The Harlem Book of the Dead* (1978), Julien is driven by "the desire to eroticise and make sensuous Black bodies" (Julien interviewed by Shinhat 1990). In reproducing a fetishised gaze on the black body Julien undertakes a risky task, which could even seem counterproductive at first, but he is well aware that this expedient represents the most effective way of demonstrating to the spectator the mythic aspect of certain stereotypes. Julien deconstructs these stereotypes by making strange (by queering in a way), or de-familiarising, the act of looking itself (Hall 1997: 274), and thus proposes a desiring but not colonising gaze:

> Because of the historical inscription of male bodies in photography and in art generally, I was always worried about trying not to show the black male body in a particular construction that could be consumed for the white gaze. I was always worried about that gaze, and that meant that to an extent I annihilated my own ambivalent desire around the black male body. I think that was a problem, and I think that I resolved those things more successfully in *Looking for Langston* (1989), where I really wanted the black male body to be the site of pleasure. (Julien in hooks and Julien 1991: 172)

Destabilising the typical signifiers of racial, gender, and sexual difference, Julien shows the fabricated, artificial, and performative character of black masculinity, demonstrating how it can be constructed in different ways. At the same time, he expresses a homoerotic desire for the black male body freed from categories and hierarchies. This new way of looking at the male black body and at black masculinity stands out especially in the film's sequence that precedes and then flows into the quotation of Nugent's short story recalled at the beginning of this chapter.

In this scene the spectator is struck by the look that Alex (Ben Ellison) exchanges with Beauty (Matthew Baidoo), especially for the consequence that this intense and complacent look produces. Beauty is sitting at a table with a character modelled on Carl Van Vechten (one of the white patrons of the Harlem Renaissance) who reacts to the exchange of looks by banging a bottle of champagne on the table in order to call Beauty back to (his) attention. Here Julien addresses the patronage which linked black artists and white patrons at the time. A relationship that sometimes digressed in a sort of white fetishism for the black body and for black art, that the white patronage wanted to control and in which they expected to see "intuitions of the primitive"[6]:

> White patrons of the Harlem Renaissance wanted black artists and writers to know and feel the intuitions of the primitive. They didn't want Modernism. They wanted black art, to keep art and artists in their place. (Hall in Julien 1989)

This relationship is revoked later in the film when the same white character—Carl (John Wilson)—strolls among hanging portraits of black male nudes from Mapplethorpe's *Black Book* that he caresses. Simultaneously the spectator hears Essex Hemphill reading some of his poems on racism in the white homosexual subculture, before the scene ends with Carl paying a black character, in a gesture implying the commodification and objectification of his body. In this context, Julien's reference to the stereotypes surrounding black males, especially their being seen as phallic symbols is clear. As Frantz Fanon said in *Peau noire, masques blancs* (1952): "[o]ne is no longer aware of the Negro, but only of a penis; the Negro is eclipsed. He is turned into a penis. He *is* a penis" (Fanon 2008: 130). In Mapplethorpe's collection most men are in fact naked and, through the cropping and the light effects, the eye of the spectator is led to automatically associate the subject represented with his penis.

> The connotation is that the "essence" of black male identity lies in the domain of sexuality. Whereas the photographs of gay male S/M rituals invoke a subcultural sexuality that consists of *doing* something, black men are confined and defined in their very *being* as sexual and nothing but sexual, hence hypersexual. (Mercer 1994: 174)

The black male body is not only rendered hypersexual but also objectified through the male fantasy of domination and control which happens in the visual field: the eye as the almighty subject (eye/I) who can see without being seen. The dissecting of the body in fragments and details—chest, arms, buttocks, penis—invites, as a matter of fact, that scopophilic look in the exercise of control and domination that Laura Mulvey (1975) locates in the male spectator's gaze in Hollywood cinema.[7] In the scene, this fetishism interrupts the desiring gaze between the two black characters and Alex, who has lost Beauty's attention, turns towards the bar counter, looks straight at the camera, and begins to fantasise, dragging the spectator in his reverie.

According to Kress's and van Leeuwen's interactive metafunction this is achieved through a demand image mood which uses the close up on Alex's face (Fig. 10.2) to imply an identification with the viewer, his/her involvement through the frontal angle of the framing, and the revelation of the represented participant's (RP, Alex in this case) feelings (Kress and van Leeuwen 2006: 124–138).[8] Resulting from the representational metafunction the image represents a non-transactional action process since it only involves one reacter (Alex), while, if we consider the salience of the image (compositional metafunction), Alex's importance is emphasised by his position at the centre of the framing and by his sharpness of focus as opposed to the slightly out-of-focus background (Machin 2007: 51; van Leeuwen 2005: 273). The light coming from the left, finally, highlights whatever is portrayed on the right, so that the past (the given information is visually positioned on the left) metaphorically sheds light on the future (new information on the right) where two male figures

Fig. 10.2 Still from Isaac Julien's *Looking for Langston*, 1989

dance with each other. These two figures occupy the top framing, which for Kress and van Leeuwen represents the "ideal level", and therefore delineate queer desire as something which belongs to the imaginary. Alex's fantasising, on the other hand, is portrayed as real in its being located within the bottom framing.

The scene that follows represents the cinematic rendition of Nugent's *Smoke, Lilies and Jade*. Introduced by the sound of the sea waves—an aquatic image which visually and aurally returns on different occasions throughout the film—this scene appears suspended in time: both music and voiceover are absent while in an undefined room Julien quotes and re-inscribes a photograph by George Platt Lynes[9] which comes to life thanks to the slow movements of the camera that reproduce the back and forth flowing of the sea waves.[10]

The first movement is from left to right (Figs. 10.3, 10.4, and 10.5) and focuses on Alex lying on the bed. Here Julien appropriates the homoerotic perspective of Platt Lynes's photograph to represent the male black body in a pose which neither reproduces aggressiveness nor phallic associations, but imparts calmness, even a sense of vulnerability.

This is achieved not only through Alex's pose (he gives his back to the spectator, the palm of his hand is in an upward position) but also through

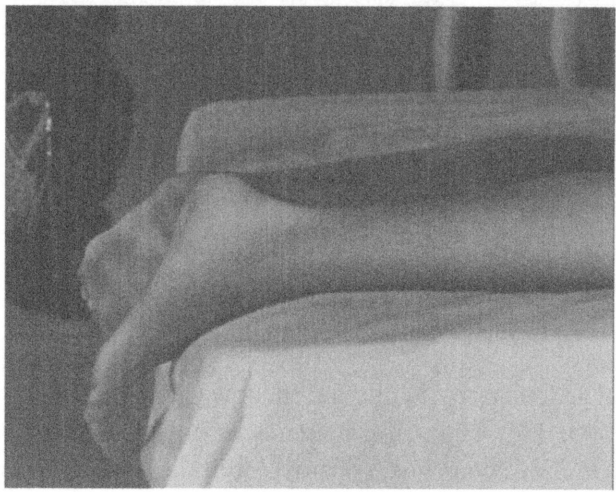

Fig. 10.3 Stills from Isaac Julien's *Looking for Langston*, 1989

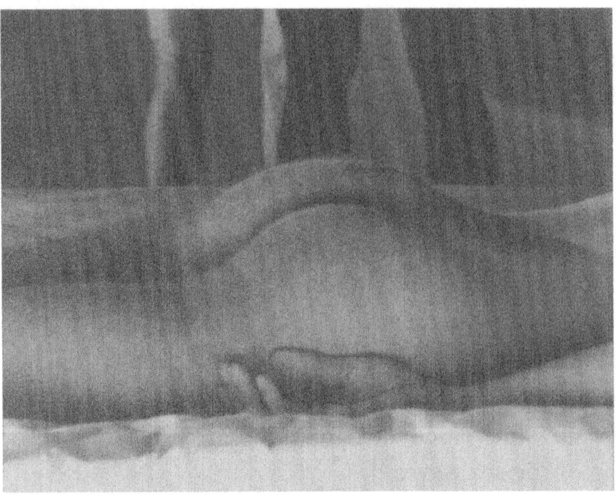

Fig. 10.4 Stills from Isaac Julien's *Looking for Langston*, 1989

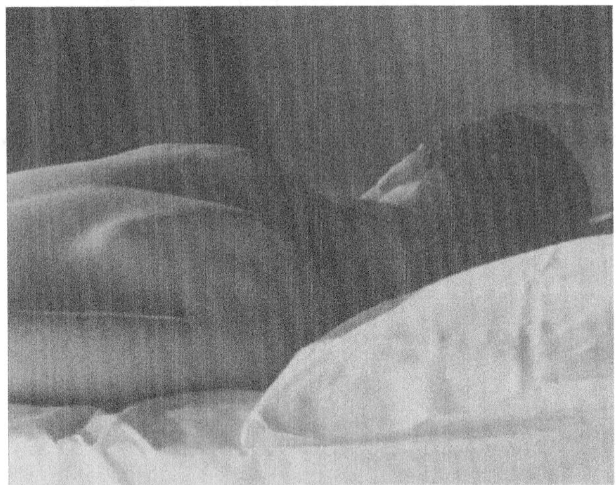

Fig. 10.5 Stills from Isaac Julien's *Looking for Langston*, 1989

the degree of articulation of light and shadow (Machin 2007: 45–57; van Leeuwen 2005: 160–176). The presence of only few shadows and the bright light on Alex's body give a positive/optimistic effect (Machin 2007: 54), while the low saturation of the black and white shooting suggests subtlety, tenderness, and a general moderation of feelings (Kress and van Leeuwen 2006: 233).

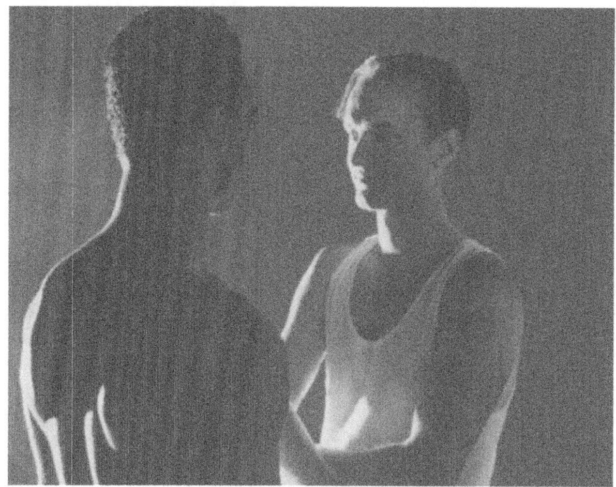

Fig. 10.6 Stills from Isaac Julien's *Looking for Langston*, 1989

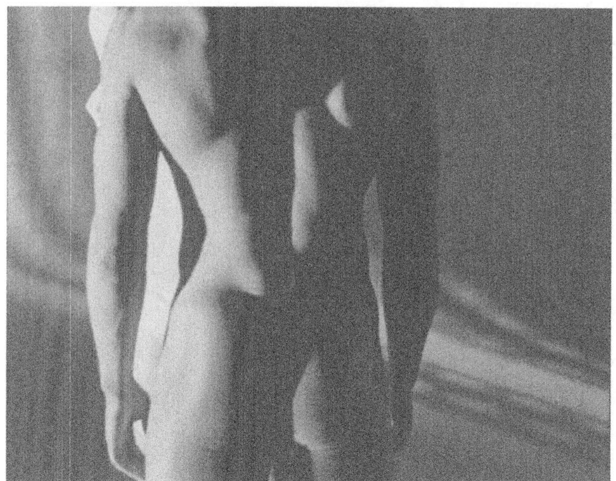

Fig. 10.7 Stills from Isaac Julien's *Looking for Langston*, 1989

The following movements of the camera are from right to left (Figs. 10.6, 10.7, and 10.8) and, back again, from left to right (Figs. 10.9 and 10.10), emphasising the longitudinal and transverse motions of the sea waves.

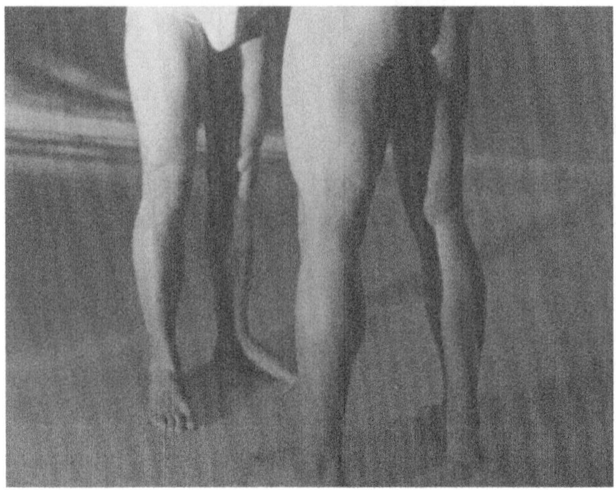

Fig. 10.8 Stills from Isaac Julien's *Looking for Langston*, 1989

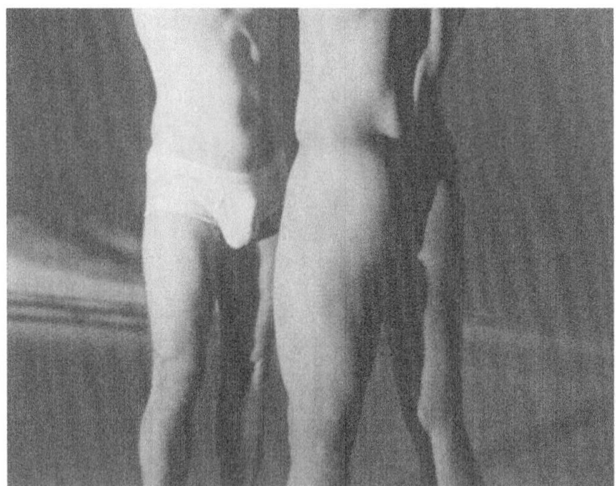

Fig. 10.9 Stills from Isaac Julien's *Looking for Langston*, 1989

Another strategy used by Julien in these sequences is the breaking up of the moving image which does not have the same objectifying effect of the fragmentation of the still image. While the latter invites a scopophilic approach resulting from a desire to control and possess the represented object, the breaking up of the moving image, on the contrary, allows for

Fig. 10.10 Stills from Isaac Julien's *Looking for Langston*, 1989

a refusal of fixation and, as a consequence, of a mortifying and objectifying power.

If the "still camera simultaneously 'kills' and affirms" (Silverman 1996: 199)—that is to say it freezes the subject in a representation which is outside of the lived experience while at the same time it "physically and socially actualizes it" (Silverman 1996: 199)—the moving image enables a less "stable and durable image of the self" (Silverman 1996: 198). The moving image, therefore, represents identity in flux, leaving a certain space for its re-articulation outside of fixed categories and hierarchies. This idea of identity in flux is enhanced by the constant reference to water throughout the film. Communicated in this scene visually through the back and forth movement of the camera and aurally through the sound of the sea waves, it fosters the feeling of ubiquity and suspension of time that Julien pursues in his film.[11]

The reference to water recalls Edward Kamau Brathwaite's notion of "tidalectics" which draws on the movement of the tides to explain the continuous washing upon each other of past and present that characterises our histories and life changes. In *ConVERSations* (1999) Brathwaite describes this movement through the image of an old woman who, early every morning, sweeps off the sand from her yard and who seems to be moving on water.

> Like our grandmother's—our nanna's—action [...] like the movement of the ocean she's walking on, coming from one continent/continuum, touching another, and then receding ("reading") from the island(s) into the perhaps creative chaos of the(ir) future. (Brathwaite 1999: 34)

Through the performance of a going out and a return movement which does not have an imposed resolution (Naylor 1999: 45), Brathwaite's cyclical, oceanic poetics of flows and currents is hence characterised by interruptions, repetitions, and returns. His evocation of the back and forth movement of the ocean, of history—the sea that is History, as Saint Lucian poet Derek Walcott would say (Walcott 2007)—conjures up the creation of a historical continuum that resists the synthesising thelos of Hegelian dialectics and that, exactly through its refusal of closure and with that erasure, remains open to an array of chaotic potentiality. The creative potential embodied by this gesture represents the capability to adapt, transpose, and hybridise characteristic of diasporic cultures that Julien seeks for his expression of a queer desire.[12] From a diasporic standpoint, Julien's position is necessarily one of movement in which identities and sexualities are perceived as fluid, shifting, thus emphasising the importance of "doing" over "being". As Rinaldo Walcott sustains:

> [...] it is queers of the global south who continue to keep sexuality in flux, often offering some of the most provocative ways of re-imagining what sexual minority practices might look like. (Walcott 2009: 14)

This interest in keeping identity and sexuality in flux, characteristic of queer theory as well, enables Julien to articulate a black masculinity outside the dominant homophobic discourse that affects not only the Caribbean and black communities in the diaspora (in which homosexuality is often perceived as antithetical to black skin) but also Western society as a whole.

In the scene that follows, Alex (still in his reverie) walks across a field wearing a tuxedo—the silence broken only by the bird's singing—where he meets the stark naked Beauty (Figs. 10.11, 10.12, and 10.13): culture meets nature.

Here Julien signifies on Nugent's story, where Alex is searching on his hands and knees in a field of black poppies and red calla lilies (Fig. 10.11),

Fig. 10.11 Stills from Isaac Julien's *Looking for Langston*, 1989

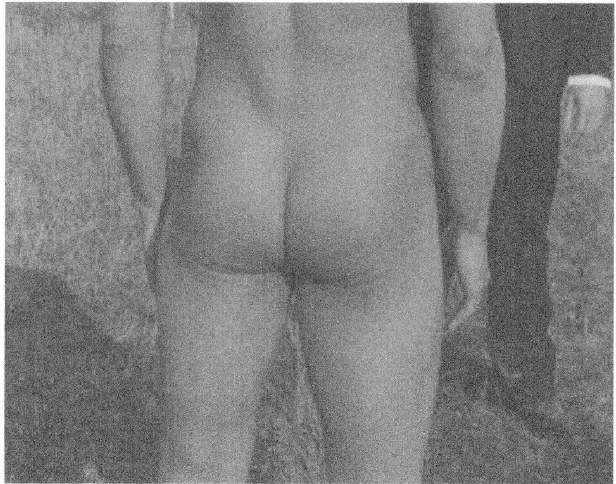

Fig. 10.12 Stills from Isaac Julien's *Looking for Langston*, 1989

in order to recall the production of texts (Glissant's "acts of delusion") by the colonial enterprise that were meant to justify both land and body possession in the Caribbean.

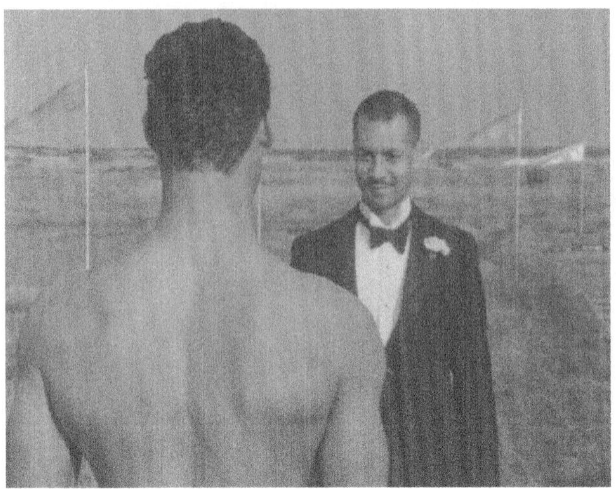

Fig. 10.13 Stills from Isaac Julien's *Looking for Langston*, 1989

The imperialist gaze of the European settlers seized the New World to create "landscapes" and "bodyscapes" (Pratt 2008) with which to present fantasised images of the land as empty, unknown, and free from ownership, and of the natives and slaves as desirous of being possessed (de Ferrari 2007: 22). This script, in which Alex appropriates the defining traits of colonialism and hegemonic masculinity (Connell 1995: 7) both involving domination (which is also sexualised), is interrupted by the first and only diegetic sound of the movie: Beauty saying "I'll wait" (Julien 1989).

The extreme close up (Bateman and Schmidt 2011: 10) on Beauty's mouth (Fig. 10.14) plays again with the colonial "bodyscaping" by defamiliarising and subverting it. The thick lips, usually fixed in the stereotype of the racialised and sexualised exotic body of the native, are portrayed in the act of speaking: the "native" regains his agency and interrupts this fixation by expressing his will to wait. Wait, in this case, until the desire will be available in a different script, one that would not reproduce the domination typical of the racialised heteropatriarchy. Alex is confused, he looks around searching for Beauty who meanwhile has disappeared; his desire interrupted and postponed.

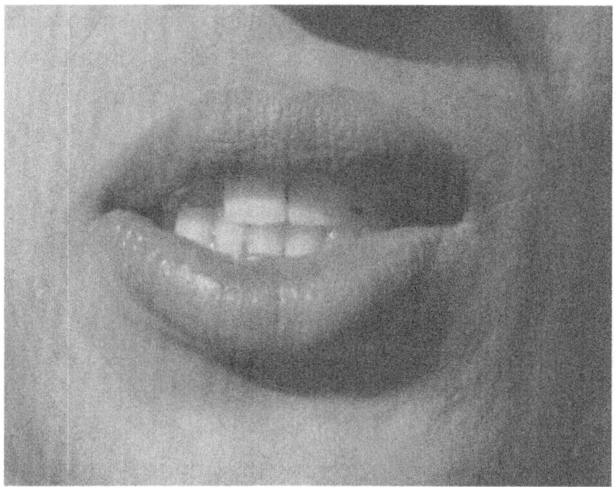

Fig. 10.14 Still from Isaac Julien's *Looking for Langston*, 1989

Fig. 10.15 Still from Isaac Julien's *Looking for Langston*, 1989

While the voiceover continues to read Nugent's story, the spectator sees Beauty listening to the sound produced by a conch shell (Fig. 10.15).

Used as a means of communication among the communities of runaway slaves in the Americas known as the Maroons in order to organise rebellions against the European settlers, in the Afro-diasporic tradition the conch shell (also known as "abeng") has come to symbolically epitomise not only hope, power, resistance, and self-determination, but also memory. This image, then, through an aural association with the reading of the homoerotic encounter in Nugent's short story, strengthens Julien's liberating message and his wish to articulate a black queer desire which consequently assumes revolutionary undertones.

The following scene, which draws on and emphasises another iconic photograph by George Platt Lynes (*Male Couple*, 1952), opens with a medium shot on Alex's and Beauty's faces and torsos (Fig. 10.16) to then represent Alex's fantasy (dream in the dream) which culminates in the tender kiss mentioned at the beginning of this chapter.

This sequence (Figs. 10.17, 10.18, and 10.19) shows the spectator two beautiful black males whose muscular bodies—positioned at the centre of the scene, their relevance emphasised by the plain background—retain a soft peculiarity, as accentuated by the way the light falls on them.

Here Julien uses the same representational strategies highlighted in the analysis of the previous sequence (Figs. 10.3, 10.4, and 10.5) so that the image of the black masculinity as aggressive and hypersexual is disrupted, this time especially through the tenderness of the exchanged kiss. The

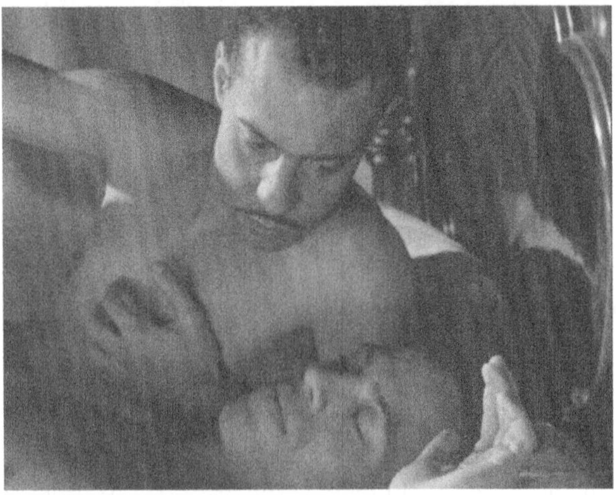

Fig. 10.16 Still from Isaac Julien's *Looking for Langston*, 1989

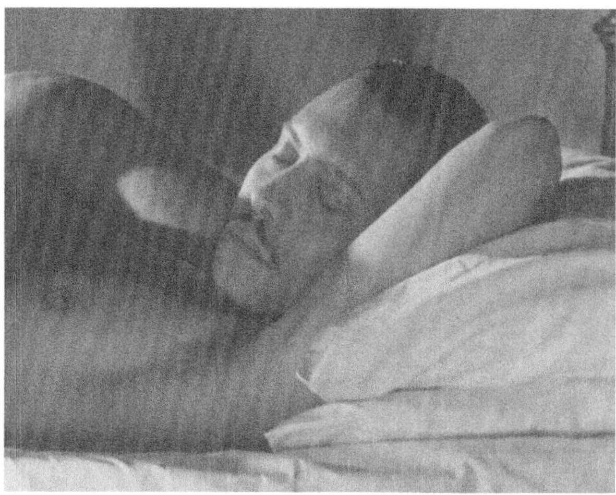

Fig. 10.17 Stills from Isaac Julien's *Looking for Langston*, 1989

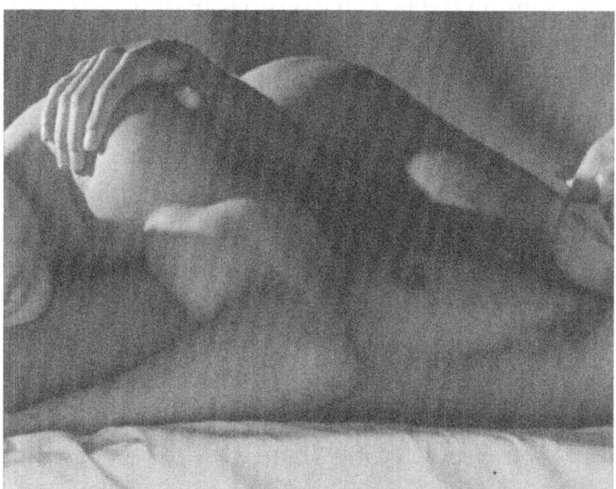

Fig. 10.18 Stills from Isaac Julien's *Looking for Langston*, 1989

panning of the camera from right to left (the movement is reversed this time), furthermore, shows no frontal nudes denying the association of the black man with his penis (Fanon 2008: 130), while the absence of superordinate and subordinate RPs conveys a feeling of mutuality.

Fig. 10.19 Stills from Isaac Julien's *Looking for Langston*, 1989

The medium shot on the faces has a subjectivising effect as opposed to the objectifying fragmentation in body parts, and the transactional reaction (between the two reacters Alex and Beauty) is portrayed through an offer image: the two RPs are "offered" to the viewer as "items of information, objects of contemplation, impersonally" (Kress and van Leeuwen 2006: 119). This impersonality is enhanced by the oblique angle signifying detachment, but is also balanced by the medium shot which retains a predisposition to intimacy and by the "camera-initiated" movement that positions the viewers towards what is being represented (Kress and van Leeuwen 2006: 261–262) as a more or less willing onlooker, witness, even voyeur.

Through his display of a number of aestheticized black male bodies, Julien focuses on a sensory coding orientation that is based on emotion and on the effect of pleasure and displeasure (van Leeuwen 2005: 22; Machin 2007: 59)—something that challenges the idea of objective reality (and its supposedly "real" stereotypical representations) since sensory coding is not independent from one's own perceptions.

His expression of queer desire, nevertheless, remains potential, as hope (Mercer 1994: 225), as emphasised by Beauty's uttering of the words "I'll wait" and by the fact that Alex's reverie is dictated by the impossibility of reaching his beloved who, in Julien's narration, stays with Carl. As a matter of fact, Julien shows the impossibility of fully articulating this kind of desire in a racist and sexist society which continues to impose dichotomous hierarchies and categories based on subjective (active) and objective (passive) positions which prevent individuals situated at the negative pole to access the object of desire, and therefore desire itself.

4 Conclusion: "Sexual Healing"

In Julien's film, the aquatic symbolism (i.e. the sound of the sea waves, the water that flows over the camera, and Beauty's listening to the conch shell) emphasises a black queer desire that is extremely ephemeral and expresses a fluid conception of identity and of masculinity. These symbols are linked to the Atlantic crossing and therefore to the Black Atlantic as a starting point for modernity and for the formation of Afro-diasporic cultures (Gilroy 1993). Hence the focus on a representation where past and present overlap and refuse to follow the temporal analytic process that displays the unfolding of a narrative either along an imaginary horizontal or vertical line (Kress and van Leeuwen 2006: 94) typical of Western historiography. Julien's alternative grammar of visual representation draws on a diasporic poetics that refuses monolithic and dominant readings (which are also stereotypical) to produce instead a text that creates meaning relationally. Likewise, Julien displaces the centrality of the visual by hybridising it with the sense of hearing and the evocation of the sense of touch. He liberates and heals black queer desire from a litany of racialised and sexualised violent representations, refusing to ground sexual acts in narratives of domination and submission. As bell hooks writes:

> Black males are in need of sexual healing. Such healing happens every time we create the culture of resistance where black male bodies and being are no longer held captive. A free black man, at home in his body, able to feel his sexual desire and to act with life-affirming agency, is the radical outlaw this nation fears. (hooks 2004: 78)

Empowered by the retrieval of a black queer genealogy and working against the grains of a reductionist, and at times homophobic, conception of black masculinity, Julien restores "the multiplicity of identities around colour, gender, sexuality, and class" (Riggs 1991: 394) which is part and parcel of the black experience. In his open depiction of a black queer desire, he brings to the fore the most feared radical outlaws in any racialised heteropatriarchy, demonstrating not only how naturalised knowledge can be deconstructed but also how (black) masculinity can be healed by recognising the multiplicity and complexity of its manifestations.

Notes

1. Like other independent film collectives, the *Sankofa* was born thanks to funding allocated by the British government as a way of reducing the increasing number of uprisings by the UK ethnic minorities that protested against their underrepresentation and misrepresentation within public discourse and the media (Kettle and Hodges 1982; Scarman 1982; Mercer 1994: 76). The name *Sankofa*—the Adinkra symbol meaning literally "go back and retrieve it"—served as a motto for the founders (black filmmakers involved in feminist and gay liberation movements) who were interested in retrieving hidden past histories with which to interrogate the present. This is a concept that also lies at the base of *Looking for Langston* which was re-screened on 7 and 15 October 2017 at The Museum of Modern Art (MoMA) in New York as part of the exhibition *Black Intimacy*.
2. Until November 2017, London-based Julien was present at the inaugural Diaspora Pavilion at the 57th edition of the Venice Biennale with *Western Union: Small Boats*. Previously, in 2015, he presented *Kapital* and directed *Das Kapital Oratorio* in the 56th edition of the Venice Biennale for the exhibition *All the World's Futures* curated by Okwui Enwezor, and was artist in residence at the American Academy in Rome to work on a project on the life and work of the Brazilian modernist architect Lina Bo Bardi.
3. Glissant's "passion for memory" is also recalled by another film produced by Julien: *The Passion of Remembrance* (1986). The importance of memory and creative reconstruction, furthermore, associates Julien's poetics to Romare Bearden's use of the collage technique to usher the past into

the present: "When I conjure these memories" said Bearden with reference to the collage fragments, "they are of the present to me, because after all, the artist is a kind of enchanter in time" (Ulaby 2003).

4. "Homosexuality was a sin against the race, so it had to be kept a secret, even if it was a widely shared one", states Stuart Hall in the film (Hall in Julien 1989).
5. Julien's investigation of black queer desire has been carried over subsequently in the film *Young Soul Rebels* (1991), and in the trilogy formed by the short film *The Attendant* (1993) and the installations *Trussed* (1996) and *Three* (1999).
6. Note Julien's use of the name "Beauty" (taken from Nugent's short story) to re-inscribe the stereotypical image of the black man as "beastly".
7. This interpretation is reinforced by Hemphill's words that read from his poem "If His Name Were Mandingo" while on the screen the exchange of money takes place: "He speaks good damn English to me/[...] I don't suppose you ever hear him clearly?/You're always busy,/seeking other things of him./His name isn't important./It would be coincidence/if he had a name,/a face, a mind./If he's not hard-on/then he's hard up/and either way you watch him" (Hemphill 1992: 141).
8. In *Reading Images* (2006) Kress and van Leeuwen develop a theory for reading images based on Halliday's theory of language. According to Halliday (1973) all meaning-making systems perform three main functions: ideational, interpersonal, and textual. The ideational function refers to the expression of ideas and the making of meanings about the individual's inner and outer worlds; the interpersonal function has to do with the enactment of interpersonal relationships between the speakers; and the textual function, which mediates between the previous two, indicates the creation of coherence and cohesion in the text. To these linguistic functions Kress and van Leeuwen match respectively a representational, interactive, and compositional one, which they use for the interpretation of images as part of a grammar of visual representation.
9. The untitled photograph by George Platt Lynes portrays three men (two are naked: one is lying on a bed and the other, standing, is undressing the third man). It is dated 1942 and can be found in Leddick (1997: 21).
10. The room seems to be a more or less intentional intertextual reference to another famous room, the one that David and Giovanni share in the novel *Giovanni's Room* (1956) by James Baldwin, whose *ménage à trois* (David-Giovanni-Hella) recalls, in turn, the one in Nugent's short story (Alex-Beauty-Melva).

11. The timeless aspect of the film is also emphasised by the black and white shooting that allows Julien to introduce very rare original moving scenes of black people in 1920s–1930s (i.e. Oscar Micheaux's 1932 film *Ten Minutes to Live*) and by the choice of music, which shifts from the first voices to sing homosexual love in the African American blues tradition (i.e. Bessie Smith's "St. Louis Blues", George Hannah's "Freakish Man Blues", and Kokomo Arnold's "Sissy Man Blues") to 1980s ones (from Blackberri's "Blues for Langston" and "Beautiful Blackman" to the Chicago gay disco anthem "Can You Party" by Royal House), therefore connecting the blues poetics to queer desire.
12. Water symbolism is also present, among the others, in Julien's installations *Paradise Omeros* (2002) and *Ten Thousand Waves* (2010). In *Paradise Omeros*, inspired by Derek Walcott's *Omeros* (1990), the image of the sea connecting opposite shores with its back and forth movement makes the spectator ponder over the "passage" between the self and the other, love and hate, good and evil, never fully antithetic but always coexisting. More recently in *Ten Thousand Waves*, Julien remembers the Morecambe Bay tragedy of 2004, in which more than 20 Chinese cockle pickers drowned on a flooded sandbank off the coast in northwest England, by poetically weaving together stories linking China's ancient past and present.

References

Allen, J. S. (2012). Black/Queer/Diaspora at the Current Conjuncture. *GLQ: A Journal of Lesbian and Gay Studies, 18*(2–3), 211–248.

Bateman, J. A., & Schmidt, K.-H. (2011). *Multimodal Film Analysis. How Films Mean*. New York: Routledge.

Brathwaite, E. K. (1999). *ConVERSations with Nathaniel Mackey*. New York: We Press.

Chambers, I. (2001). *Culture after Humanism. History, Culture, Subjectivity*. London: Routledge.

Connell, R. W. (1995). *Masculinities*. Berkeley: University of California Press.

De Ferrari, G. (2007). *Vulnerable States. Bodies of Memory in Contemporary Caribbean Fiction*. Charlottesville: University of Virginia Press.

Fanon, F. (2008 [1952]). *Black Skin White Masks* (C. L. Markmann, Engl. Trans.). London: Pluto Press.

Gilroy, P. (1993). *The Black Atlantic. Modernity and Double Consciousness.* London: Verso.

Glissant, É. (1997 [1990]). *Poetics of Relation* (B. Wing, Engl. Trans.). Michigan: University of Michigan Press.

Hall, S. (1997). The Spectacle of the "Other". In S. Hall (Ed.), *Representation. Cultural Representations and Signifying Practices* (pp. 223–290). London: Sage.

Halliday, M. A. K. (1973). *Explorations in the Functions of Language.* London: Arnold.

Halttunen, K. (1995). Humanitarianism and the Pornography of Pain in Anglo-American Culture. *The American Historical Review, 100*(2), 303–334.

Hemphill, E. (1991). Looking for Langston. An Interview with Isaac Julien. In E. Hemphill (Ed.), *Brother to Brother. New Writings by Black Gay Men* (pp. 174–180). Boston: Alyson Publications.

Hemphill, E. (1992). *Ceremonies. Prose and Poetry.* New York: Plume.

hooks, b. (2004). *We Real Cool. Black Men and Masculinity.* New York: Routledge.

hooks, b. (2015 [1990]). *Yearnings. Race, Gender, and Cultural Politics.* New York: Routledge.

hooks, b., & Julien, I. (1991). States of Desire. *Transition, 53*, 168–184.

Hunter, A. G., & Davis, J. E. (1994). Hidden Voices of Black Men: The Meaning, Structure and Complexity of Manhood. *Journal of Black Studies, 25*(1), 20–40.

Julien, I. (1989). *Looking for Langston.* Sankofa Film and Video Collective, UK.

Julien, I. interviewed by Molly Shinhat. (1990, June/July). Black History and Desire. *FUSE* Magazine.

Kettle, M., & Hodges, L. (1982). *Uprising! the Police, the People, and the Riots in Britain's Cities.* London: Pan.

Kress, G., & van Leeuwen, T. (2006 [1996]). *Reading Images. The Grammar of Visual Design* (2nd ed.). London: Routledge.

Leddick, D. (1997). *Naked Men. Pioneering Male Nudes 1935–1955.* New York: Universe Publishing.

Lorde, A. (1984). Uses of the Erotic. The Erotic as Power. In *Sister Outsider. Essays and Speeches* (pp. 53–59). Freedom, CA: The Crossing Press.

Machin, D. (2007). *Introduction to Multimodal Analysis.* Bloomsbury, USA: Hodder Arnold.

Mercer, K. (1994). *Welcome to the Jungle. New Positions in Black Cultural Studies.* New York: Routledge.

Milton, T. B. (2012). Class Status and the Construction of Black Masculinity. *Ethnicity and Race in a Changing World: A Review Journal, 3*(1), 17–31.
Mulvey, L. (1975). Visual Pleasure and Narrative Cinema. *Screen, 16*(3), 6–18.
Naylor, P. (1999). *Poetic Investigations: Singing the Holes in History*. Evanston: Northwestern University Press.
Nichols, B. (2010 [2001]). *Introduction to Documentary* (2nd ed.). Bloomington: Indiana University Press.
Parisi, L. (2004). La percezione della differenza nel digitale: Movimento e affetto. In L. Curti (Ed.), *La nuova Shahrazad. Donne e multiculturalismo* (pp. 321–332). Napoli: Liguori.
Ponzanesi, S. (2015). On the Waterfront. Truth and Fiction in Postcolonial Cinema from the South of Europe. *Interventions: International Journal of Postcolonial Studies, 18*(2), 1–17.
Pratt, M. L. (2008 [1992]). *Imperial Eyes. Travel Writing and Transculturation* (2nd ed.). New York: Routledge.
Riggs, M. T. (1991). Black Macho Revisited: Reflections of a Snap! Queen. *African American Review, 25*(2), 389–394.
Scarman, L. G. (1982). *The Scarman Report. The Brixton Riots Disorders 10–12 April 1981*. London: Penguin.
Shohat, E., & Stam, R. (1994). *Unthinking Eurocentrism. Multiculturalism and the Media*. New York: Routledge.
Silverman, K. (1996). *The Threshold of the Visible World*. New York: Routledge.
Staples, R. (1982). *Black Masculinity. The Black Male's Role in American Society*. San Francisco: The Black Scholar Press.
Staples, R. (2006). *Exploring Black Sexuality*. New York: Rowman & Littlefield Publishers.
Ulaby, N. (2003, September 14). The Art of Romare Bearden: Collages Fuse Essence of Old Harlem, American South. *NPR*. Retrieved November 30, 2015, from http://www.npr.org/templates/story/story.php?storyId=1428038
Van Leeuwen, T. (2005). *Introducing Social Semiotics*. New York: Routledge.
Walcott, D. (1974). The Caribbean: Culture or Mimicry? *Journal of Interamerican Studies and World Affairs, 16*(1), 3–13.
Walcott, D. (2007). The Sea Is History. In E. Baugh (Ed.), *Selected Poems* (pp. 137–139). New York: Farrar, Straus and Giroux.
Walcott, R. (2009). Queer Returns: Human Rights, the Anglo-Caribbean and Diaspora Politics. *Caribbean Review of Gender Studies, 3*, 1–19.

11

'You Cry Gay, You're In': The Case of Asylum Seekers in the UK

Maria Cristina Nisco

1 Introduction

Gender and sexuality, along with ethnicity, are pivotal categories that immigration law has regularly employed to bolster border control, either 'domesticating' or excluding migrants and asylum seekers who possess identities located outside dominant heteronormative conceptions (Millbank 2003; Berg and Millbank 2009; Jansen and Spijkerboer 2011). This chapter addresses the specific case of homosexual people claiming asylum from persecution in the UK on the basis of their sexual and gender identities. Such cases pose epistemological challenges regarding who is considered a subject in need of rescue (therefore having access to the social resources of the host country as a victim of violence), and who is made invisible, unrecognised, and unintelligible (therefore denied access to freedom from persecution). Fundamental questions are thus raised: what does it take to be a male gay asylum seeker? How 'gay' do you need to be

---

M.C. Nisco (✉)
Dipartimento di Scienze Motorie e del Benessere, Università degli Studi di Napoli "Parthenope", Napoli, Italy

P. Baker, G. Balirano (eds.), *Queering Masculinities in Language and Culture*, Palgrave Studies in Language, Gender and Sexuality,
https://doi.org/10.1057/978-1-349-95327-1_11

to satisfy immigration officials?[1] And what if some gay people do not appear to be gay? In order to gain entrance, homosexual asylum seekers must demonstrate codified and 'queering' versions of their masculinity so as to be recognisable and, thus, admissible to immigration and court officials.

The ways in which the cases of gay asylum seekers are interpreted and reported in both the institutional and media contexts offer important insights into how power and control are exercised to regulate those who are or are not to be incorporated into the nation-state through semiotic practices that first label subjects and then include them within or exclude them from national boundaries. Since the thematic areas linked to asylum, sexuality, and gender appear to be still profoundly under-researched (EUFRA 2009: 129), the present study takes the cue from the institutional background in which the policies and practices related to homosexual asylum seekers are conceived, to then move to how such issues are *mediated*, specifically by the British press, to the mainstream readership. Therefore, after the following section, which presents some of the most debatable provisions in asylum law at the international level, the chapter concentrates on the policies adopted to assess homosexuality within the European Union (EU) and, in particular, the UK. The central sections then examine how the British press reported the news concerning homosexual asylum seekers as emerging from the analysis and findings of the collection of articles under investigation. The concluding remarks discuss the semiotic production of narratives of gender identities that is enacted by the newspapers, and the epistemological challenges involved in news discourse when gender and ethnic diversity is at stake.

2 The International Institutional Landscape

Gay asylum seekers and their definition as refugees have long posed a difficult question for governments. Generally speaking, according to the Universal Declaration of Human Rights (1948, Art. 14), 'everyone has the right to seek and enjoy, in other countries, asylum from persecution'; in an attempt to be more precise, the UN Convention relating to the

Status of Refugees (1951, Art. 1)—also known as Geneva Convention—clarifies who a 'refugee' is:

> a person who owing to a well-founded fear of being persecuted for reasons of race, religion, nationality, membership of a particular social group or political opinion, is outside the country of his nationality and is unable or, owing to such fear, is unwilling to avail himself of the protection of that country; or who, not having a nationality and being outside the country of his former habitual residence as a result of such events, is unable or, owing to such fear, unwilling to return to it.

The fact that both documents do not specifically and explicitly include sexual orientation and gender identity among the reasons to seek protection from persecution has led governments in potential host countries to consider gay claimants' rights as debatable. Indeed, even acknowledging the encouraging recommendations set forth by the Universal Declaration of Human Rights and the Geneva Convention, sexuality and gender were not, in themselves, one of the grounds upon which an applicant could claim asylum.[2]

Indeed, this is a highly charged discursive field, where the main controversy surrounds one of the most contested provisions in refugee law: the provision for persecution on account of membership of a particular social group. According to McGhee (2003: 145), claims by homosexual (both male and female) applicants for refugee status involve some basic problems, among them the extent to which prosecution for 'sexual offences' can be considered a form of persecution, and whether groups whose associations are those of choice—rather than familial, tribal, or ethnic bonds—can be included in the wider label 'social group'. In fact, social groups (as minority groups) are mostly conceived as communities with the capacity of affiliating succeeding generations, so consanguinity and procreation are presented as their core biological characteristics. On the contrary, membership of a homosexual group is deemed, in itself, merely as a voluntary association—and such a voluntary nature is seen as a luxury other minority groups do not enjoy. As McGhee (2003: 146) aptly points out, '[t]he implication here is that not only are lesbians and gays an 'invisible' social group, they are also a purely voluntary social group, who should and could alter their behaviour in order to avoid their alleged persecution' (see also McGhee 2000, 2001).

Therefore, deeply embedded homophobic attitudes, combined with a lack of adequate legal protection against discrimination on grounds of sexual orientation and gender identity, expose gay people to constant violations of their human rights: they are harassed, stigmatised, beaten, sexually assaulted, tortured, and killed, heterosexuality being the only acceptable orientation.

At the time of writing, 80 countries around the world criminalise consensual sexual activities between same-sex adults. In most of them, homosexual contacts are a criminal act, and in seven of these countries, homosexual relations are punishable by death penalty—namely Iran, Mauritania, northern parts of Nigeria, Saudi Arabia, southern parts of Somalia, Sudan, and Yemen. In some of the remaining countries, homosexuality is not criminalised officially or explicitly, but it is nonetheless regarded as 'unnatural' or 'indecent' behaviour, and therefore persecuted. However, it is worth noting that while persecution may not be state-sponsored, it is often, nonetheless, socially accepted and enacted by non-state actors (relatives, neighbours, etc.), so that persecuted people see no choice other than fleeing their home countries.[3]

Each year, thousands of lesbian, gay, bisexual, transgender, and intersex (LGBTI) asylum seekers apply for international protection in the EU. The EU Member States have taken some concrete and positive steps—such as recognising sexual orientation as a persecution ground in Article 10 of the Qualification Directive (2004). Some States have also formally added gender identity as a persecution ground in their national legislation (which is the case in Portugal and Spain) or in their policy documents (as in Austria and the UK) (Jansen and Spijkerboer 2011: 7). Despite these improvements, there are considerable differences in the ways in which European States examine homosexual asylum applications. The creation of a Common European Asylum System, which is one of the EU's most urgent aims, is highly problematic. Indeed, the assumption according to which one common standard should be adopted in the application of refugee law (as prescribed by the Dublin Regulation 2003) is sadly illusory. Moreover, despite the work of the European Asylum Support Office which is meant to coordinate and identify good practices in the examination of LGBTI asylum applications, the European practice still appears below the standards required by international and European human rights and refugee law (Jansen and Spijkerboer 2011: 7). In fact, evidence worryingly shows that national authorities often rely on stereotypes when examining LGBTI asylum applications—which results in the exclusion of a series of 'non-conforming' applicants, such as lesbians who do not behave in a masculine way, non-effeminate gay men, or applicants who have been married or have children.[4] In this context, Judith Butler's theories, according to which certain gendered behaviours appear more 'natural' and are therefore more easily associated with femininity and masculinity, seem particularly relevant (Butler 1990a, b). While positing identity as a compelling illusion, an object of belief that is compelled by social sanctions and taboos, Butler purposely employs the term 'subject' (rather than 'person' or 'individual') to underline the linguistic nature of our position within what the famous psychoanalyst Jacques Lacan calls the symbolic order, namely the system of signs and conventions determining our perception of reality (1977).[5] The subject positions that people occupy in society are forged by a complex web of discursive practices which construe identities. Subjects negotiate their very existence through the norms of dominant discourses, the same norms that allow them to be intelligible. It is such intelligibility that enables individuals to become subjects. Similarly, gay asylum seekers are required to constitute themselves and their identity, by performing—literally, theatrically acting—artificial, but socially prescribed and acceptable versions of homosexuality, namely queer versions of masculinity, forcing them to conform to hegemonic, heterosexual formulations of identity.

Generally speaking, LGBTI asylum issues began to receive attention worldwide in the aftermath of some legislative developments. In 2006, 54 Member States presented a joint statement to the Human Rights Council (HRC), addressing the issue of violence based on sexual orientation and gender identity. Then, the Yogyakarta Principles—concerning the application of existing international human rights standards to issues of sexual orientation and gender identity—were drafted in 2007. One year later, in 2008, France and the Netherlands proposed a joint statement at the UN General Assembly, with the support of 66 additional States, and the UNHCR Guidance Note on Refugee Claims Relating to

Sexual Orientation and Gender Identity was also published. In 2011, South Africa successfully proposed a resolution in the HRC, requesting a study on discrimination and sexual orientation (see HRC 2011).

Nonetheless, since LGBTI asylum cases have only relatively recently become an object of debate, it is not surprising that divergent practices exist within the EU, which constitutes a problem for the implementation and harmonisation of European law and policy. In fact, if the standards in one or more States are below the minimum level set by the European Convention on Human Rights, this divergence may constitute a violation of the Convention itself. Unfortunately, the great majority of the EU Member States do not collect statistical data about the number of LGBTI asylum claimants; hence, it is not possible to give precise information. Since there are no reliable statistics, the provenance of LGBTI asylum claimants cannot be ascertained, although experts have identified 104 countries in the world in particular, which are involved in this phenomenon (Jansen and Spijkerboer 2011: 16).[6]

3 Assessing Homosexuality in Asylum Claims in the EU

Overall, there seems to be considerable incongruity between the EU Member States on how to deal with gay asylum applications; indeed, some of the practices that they have adopted in the last few decades appear rather problematic (to use an understatement) from the point of view of international human rights.

In the Netherlands, for instance, there was a tendency to label persecution by non-state actors simply as discrimination. When the test for discrimination was applied, in the attempt to determine whether someone's life was unbearable in his/her country of origin, all focus was on three factors in particular: access to work, health care, and housing. So even if people were raped or suffered other human rights violations, but they did not lose their job or house and still had access to health care, then their asylum application could be rejected.[7] To make things worse, research carried out by the Dutch gay rights organisation Cultuur en Ontspanningcentrum (COC) and the

Free University of Amsterdam (Jansen and Spijkerboer 2011) concluded that, even without applying the test for discrimination, asylum applications were regularly rejected when the applicant did not appear 'camp' enough. In fact, no later than 2012, the Dutch Immigration Minister, Geerd Leers, exhorted homosexual people facing problems of acceptance in their own countries to hide their homosexuality to avoid homophobic violence.[8]

In this context, credibility issues—involving the assessment of the genuineness of the narrative of the applicant's claim—are at the core of most asylum cases. Credibility has become a major topic in several refugee status determinations, despite their being notoriously difficult, since the applicants' statements are the main (and unique) source of evidence. Based on this, decision-makers have faced the onus of deciding whether the claim was truthful, i.e. credible. However, in the process of credibility assessment, some factors have played a worryingly central role. In various European States, remnants of the assumption that homosexual people are deviant in a medical, psychiatric, or psychological sense are still alive, although such notions have been formally abolished (and, therefore, the use of medical, psychiatric, or psychological expert opinions to prove the genuineness of an applicant's claims is not appropriate or legitimate). Medical examinations have been a common practice to establish whether or not the applicant is gay. Despite the fact that homosexuality has ceased to be considered as a medical or psychiatric condition since 1990—when the World Health Organisation (WHO) dropped it as a medical category—examinations performed by psychologists, psychiatrists, and sexologists were often reported in a number of EU Member States (namely Austria, Bulgaria, the Czech Republic, Germany, Hungary, Poland, Romania, and Slovakia). Whether or not sexual orientation and gender identity are regarded as medical issues is pivotal, because medical, psychiatric, and psychological examinations can be extremely intrusive, and even constitute a violation of a person's privacy. As Article 18 of the Yogyakarta Principles (2007) states:

> No person may be forced to undergo any form of medical or psychological treatment, procedure, testing, or be confined to a medical facility, based on sexual orientation and gender identity. Notwithstanding any classifications to the contrary, a person's sexual orientation and gender identity are not, in

> and of themselves, medical conditions and are not to be treated, cured or suppressed.[9]

Especially some of these measures are also held as violations of Articles 3 and 8 of the European Convention on Human Rights (ECHR 1953), according to which treatments considered as a therapeutic necessity cannot be viewed as degrading, but the therapeutic aim is absent in the asylum context; therefore the infringement of an individual's privacy cannot be justified.

Phallometric testing, a very controversial method, was applied in the Czech Republic (and introduced for the first time by the legal representative of an asylum seeker). In order to assess the applicants' credibility, authorities required additional proof to determine sexual and gender orientation in asylum processes, including an interview with a 'sexodiagnostic examination' and the so-called phallometric test.[10] This test was meant to measure sexual arousal by checking changes in genital blood flow in response to sexually explicit visual and audio stimuli (namely watching straight porn), using electrodes attached to the genitalia. If any of the applicants got aroused at the sight of men and women having heterosexual contact, they were automatically denied asylum rights. Such a practice—that was employed from 2007 to 2011—was harshly criticised as a breach of the ECHR and a degrading treatment of asylum seekers, interfering with the person's human dignity.

I will now consider another country within the EU at the time of writing, the United Kingdom. It is one of the 145 signatories of the UN Convention Relating to the Status of Refugees, and it adheres to the ECHR, which prevents the UK Border Agency (UKBA) from sending anyone to a country where there is a real risk that they will be exposed to torture, punishment, or inhuman or degrading treatment. However, Britain's approach to refugee claims by LGBTI people has been rather hostile and, as Millbank (2003) has noted, the UK has lagged behind other Western receiving countries—like Germany, the USA, Canada, and Australia—which extended eligibility to LGBTI claimants in the 1980s. The British immigration authorities often refused the idea that LGBTI people fleeing persecution could be regarded as refugees under the terms of the UN Convention. In fact, it is only since 1999 that the label 'particular social group' has included LGBTI people. An extremely high number of asylum claims were refused because the UKBA held that applicants would not be in danger if, once they returned to their countries of origin, they hid their homosexuality by being 'discreet'—but, of course, no 'discretion' requirement was imposed on other asylum claimants on the basis of religious or political persecution.[11]

Overall, in the UK, claims by homosexual applicants were invariably described as easy to make and impossible to disprove, and therefore addressed with suspicion by the legal system as much as the media. Credibility assessment appeared crucial (Millbank 2009a, b; Berg and Millbank 2009) because the claim to group membership rested entirely on the claimant's testimony rather than on an external proof. So credibility was a major battleground in determining positive or negative outcomes in asylum applications. UKBA officers were severely criticised for making unreasonable assumptions casting doubts on the applicants' credibility. Indeed, the process of determining asylum claims and credibility seemed totally arbitrary. Refugees had to submit themselves to cruel and protracted processes of judgement on whether or not they were genuine refugees, whose sufferings and experiences not only occurred but met the narrow criteria laid down by institutional documents. Explicitly or not, the main function of immigration officials was not to make clear and informed judgements, but rather to find reasons why a particular person should not be given refugee status and be deported. In other words, officials tended to seek out inconsistencies in the accounts given by applicants to undermine their credibility. A culture of disbelief seemed to affect all decisions concerning gay claimants' cases: significantly, the criteria behind acceptance or denial of such asylum applications appeared to shift from discretion to disbelief, where all emphasis was on the extent to which claimants could prove their homosexual identities.

What kinds of traits were UKBA officers searching for in order to 'probe' homosexuality? Or put another way, what types of gendered 'performances' were homosexual asylum seekers required to carry out in order to win their case? Surprisingly (and ridiculously), gay asylum seekers were asked some of the following questions, among others:

- Have you ever read any Oscar Wilde?
- Do you like the music of Kylie Minogue?
- Have you ever attended Heaven nightclub on Villiers Street?
- Can you name some famous gay people?[12]

What such questions reveal is a double set of assumptions. First is the generalising implication that all gay people are likely to have similar socio-cultural tastes in terms of literature, music, and attending a particular nightclub in London, and second, that people who identify as gay but are not from the UK will have adopted these supposed general interests of Western gay culture. The experience of gay people is thus 're-semiotised', it is recast and transformed into a stereotyped and clichéd semiotic form (where homosexual people are invariably expected to 'exhibit' certain traits and behaviours), which then provides the lens to trace and frame homosexuality according to hegemonic paradigms of masculinity.

Unfortunately, however, it is no laughing matter for those who find themselves facing an asylum interview when the questions they were asked featured a completely different tone, as shown by a UK Home Office document leaked in 2013:

- Did you put your penis into X's backside?
- When X was penetrating you, did you have an erection?
- Did X ejaculate inside you?
- What is it about men's backsides that attracts you?
- What is it about the way men walk that turns you on?
- Where is the medical evidence to prove penetrative sex?
- What kinds of sex toys do you use?[13]

Such questions epitomise the degrading treatment that gay asylum seekers have experienced in the UK in very recent times, with humiliating and offensive interviews 'inspired' by a toxic mix of homophobia and ignorance. Clearly, UKBA officers were not adequately prepared for the complexities of gender-based claims. In fact, they tried to assess 'genuine' homosexuality resorting to questions that almost exclusively revolved around the ideas of penis and the act of penetration—which, interestingly, bring to the fore a physical and symbolic representation of the phallus (in the words of Lacan).[14] Indeed, penetration has long been conceived as a male priority within the context of heterosexual hegemony (Butler 1993: 51). When it is linked to a gay male identity, it becomes the referent for a 'submissive' gay male identity, which seems to be the only admissible conceptualisation of homosexuality allowed by the UKBA. Gay asylum seekers are, therefore, required to construe their gender identity in compliance with the forms of queer masculinity recognised by a phallic order in which homosexuality is exclusively about being penetrated and using sex toys.

4 Gay Asylum Seekers and the British Press

July 2010 stands as a watershed, a major breakthrough in the UK asylum policy, due to the specific case of HT (from Cameroon) and HJ (from Iran), two gay men who had been denied asylum in the UK on the grounds that they could return to their home countries and avoid persecution if they concealed their sexuality, in line with the Home Office's most common policy, the so-called discretion test. Surprisingly, in 2010, the UK Supreme Court issued a judgment according to which the two men could not be expected to hide their sexuality; therefore, the application of the discretion test by the UKBA was declared unlawful. The decision quashed a key plank of asylum policy and it had a huge bearing on the way gay asylum seekers' applications were dealt with. Above all, two pivotal points were clarified by the ruling: firstly, it highlighted the importance that homosexual people were provided with the protection that was being denied to them by the state in their countries of origins and that they were entitled to under the terms of the Geneva Convention; secondly, it urged a more progressive understanding able to bring in wider issues of identity other than sexuality, thus stressing that, far from a sole focus on sexual behaviours and sex toys, homosexuality implied crucial issues of gender identity.

This critical ruling attracted extensive media coverage, which makes it particularly interesting for this investigation.

The key problem that needs to be faced when asylum issues and gay issues are combined is that the potential for misrepresentation grows exponentially. Of course, public misconceptions about gay asylum seekers are fuelled by media and press reporting, which heavily affects how societies construct what is normal or accepted behaviour—especially in relation to sexuality and gender. Questions of visibility and invisibility mostly relate to the fact that gay asylum seekers are a very vulnerable group within an already vulnerable group: they represent the 'Other' not only because of their ethnic identity but also because of their gender identity (Connely 2014). Therefore, those who are the victims of state-sanctioned violence end up becoming victims of a different kind of violence enacted by legal authorities in the countries where they seek protection (Morgan 2000): they are exposed not only to the normative gaze of the law but also to the judgemental and condemning gaze of mainstream media and audience.

Drawing on such assumptions as much as on the tricky nature of the topic (both in the institutional and media domains), the following analysis particularly concentrates on the British press reporting on the UK Supreme Court ruling. In particular, emphasis is given to the newspapers' responses to the legal decision and the implications in terms of how to assess 'genuine' homosexuality.

A collection of newspaper articles was therefore gathered from the most widely circulating British newspapers: *Daily Mail*, *Daily Mirror*, *Daily Record*, *Daily Star*, *The Express*, *The Sun*, *The Daily Telegraph*, *The Guardian*, *The Independent*, *The Times* (and their Sunday editions). The collection is balanced—since it comprised quality and popular papers, both left- and right-leaning in their political orientation—so it could be deemed as representative of the British press as a whole (Baker et al. 2008, 2013). The articles included in the set were selected searching for the keywords 'gay*', 'seeker*', and 'homosexual*',[15] over a time span ranging from 7 July to 15 July 2010, namely a whole week after the ruling was issued. The collection thus obtained comprises 30 news reports (see Tables 11.1 and 11.2).

Table 11.1 The popular press

Newspaper	*Daily Mail*	*Daily Mirror*	*Daily Record*	*Daily Star*	*The Express*	*The Sun*
No. of news reports	2	2	2	2	4	1

Table 11.2 The quality press

Newspaper	*The Daily Telegraph*	*The Guardian*	*The Independent*	*The Times*
No. of news reports	2	5	2	8

For the analysis of the collection, special attention is paid to how the main participants in the news reports are sketched by the press—especially in the headlines—with a positive or negative presentation (Fairclough 1995: 106).

More specifically, an investigation on participants can shed light on the representation of roles and on the discursive categories on which the construals of the 'self' and 'other' are based. What kinds of identities emerge from news reports and why they are conceptualised in a specific way can be interesting points to access a societal value-system and explain it. Starting from this assumption, van Leeuwen (1996) has suggested an analytical framework to account for the socio-semantic inventory of how participants can be represented in English. He has adopted the term 'social actors', highlighting that in any discourse people are evaluated through the way they are linguistically construed, and such construals depend upon culture. His taxonomy examines a wide range of linguistic devices and patterns that can be employed to represent social actors—just to mention a few: functionalisation, identification (which can be further developed into classification, relational identification, physical identification), nomination, appraisement, assimilation, individualisation, and so on (van Leeuwen 2008: 23–54). It therefore proved useful in the identification of the main discursive features through which asylum seekers were construed by the British press after the 2010 groundbreaking ruling.

5 Analysis

A qualitative reading of the news reports revealed that the judge, Lord Rodger, was the participant the press mostly concentrated on, especially on the days after the ruling was issued (07 July 2010). Harsh criticism could be noted in the great majority of the articles. What should have been heralded as a victory for human rights and fairness was generally greeted, instead, with warnings that gay asylum seekers had been given a 'get into Britain free card' (*Times*, 08 July 2010). Headlines clearly voiced the newspapers' stances on the question, as examples 1–3 show:

1. What planet is he on? (*Daily Mail*, 08 July 2010)
2. Gay asylum ruling is supreme stupidity (*Sunday Express*, 11 July 2010)
3. Absurd judgment on gay asylum seekers (*Express*, 14 July 2010)

The judge's sentence is humorously described as not practical or sensible (the judge being from another planet), since '[i]t sets the precedent that no gay man should be returned to a country which treats homosexuality harshly on the expectation they will 'act straight'' (*Daily Mail*, 08 July 2010). One newspaper interprets the decision by reworking a popular saying as 'You don't have to be gay to settle here, but it helps' (*Sunday Express*, 11 July 2010).[16] The critical issue that slowly but steadily surfaces is a conceptual opposition: acting straight is not admissible in the claimants' countries of origins but acting gay is acceptable in the UK to win protection. The Supreme Court ruling, therefore, sets itself as a pivotal turning point in the process to define the parameters on the basis of which homosexuality is defined and assessed.

Above all, a specific excerpt of the ruling was repeatedly quoted by the press. In Lord Rodger's words:

> To illustrate the point with trivial examples from British society: just as male heterosexuals are free to enjoy themselves playing rugby, drinking beer and talking about girls with their mates, so male homosexuals are to be free to enjoy going to Kylie concerts, enjoying exotically-coloured cocktails and talking about boys with their straight female mates.[17]

Although this statement was obviously meant to claim that the applicants' right to live freely and openly as gay men had to be protected, it reinforced stereotypes about gay masculinity, indicating how the judge's sentence reflected somewhat oppositional discourses. Despite ruling in favour of the two applicants, Lord Rodger still drew on the stereotyping discourses of homosexuality. In fact, he provided society with a legal formula of what gay masculinity should be expected to be; so the law itself, with its binding power, conflated such a queer description of homosexual asylum seekers.

Not surprisingly, the judgment was oversimplified and foregrounded by the great majority of the British newspapers (at the expense of more progressive arguments on asylum policy) with countless ironic comments which had the effect of misrepresenting not only the explanatory intentions of the judge, but also—and most importantly—gay asylum seekers themselves. In fact, as the other major participant in the news reports, asylum seekers were described, extremely frequently, solely in connection to their right to stay in the UK so that they could enjoy going to Kylie Minogue's concerts or drinking multi-coloured cocktails (see examples 4–5 below).

4. Gay refugees have the right to cocktails and Kylie, says judge (*Telegraph*, 08 July 2010).
5. Now being a fan of Kylie wins you the right to asylum (*Express*, 09 July 2010).

Despite the judge's attempt to somehow hedge his statement by clarifying that he was only illustrating his point with trivial examples, his claim was taken up by most of the press and even amplified, thus becoming the only suggested reading and interpretation of the issue. Indeed, strangely enough, this is the most recurrent discursive portrayal of gay masculinity emerging from the news reports following the Supreme Court ruling. While certainly being an effective way to catch the readers' attention and curiosity, it nonetheless conveyed an extremely narrow view not only of the homosexuality of asylum seekers, but also of the British (and, for that matter, Western) gay people.[18] Leaving aside the widespread worries about the huge number of asylum applications that might stem from the judgment, some concern is then aptly expressed in relation to the criteria to probe that claimants are actually gay: 'Does attendance to Kylie concerts guarantee a proof of homosexuality?' (*Express*, 14 July 2010). This question, that appears central for the purposes of the present case study, effectively sheds light on the complexities embedded in the process of codification that homosexuality seems to be put through: gay asylum seekers are expected to embody certain clichéd traits which are meant to 'queer' their masculinity. In other words, some criticism and disagreement clearly emerge in relation to the idea that access in the UK is only allowed after a stereotypical evidence of their overt queerness is assessed.

Moving further with the analysis of the construals of gay asylum seekers as a social actor, overall a widespread trend could be noted. When the newspapers report the specific case of HT and HJ—or some other cases they incidentally refer to—they tend to provide readers with full details concerning their stories and tragic experiences of homophobia in their countries of origins. In this regard, they mostly resort to a strategy that van Leeuwen defines as identification through classification: they are identified (and classified) through references to their gender, age, ethnicity, provenance, religion, and so on, as evident from examples 6–8.

6. One of them, known as T., aged 36, challenged a Court of Appeal ruling that he could return to Cameroon even though he said that he had been attacked by a mob after he was seen kissing a male partner. [...] The mob had stripped T. of his clothes and attempted to cut off his penis with a knife. [...] The other man, known as J., 40, from Iran, arrived in Britain in 2001. (*Times*, 08 July 2010)
7. One of the men involved, known as 'T', appealed against a decision that he could return to his native Cameroon, despite the fact that he was attacked by a mob after he was seen kissing a male partner. The other, 'J' from Iran, was told he could be expected to tolerate conditions arising from his homosexual relationship in his home country. (*Daily Mail*, 08 July 2010)
8. Punishments for homosexual acts in Cameroon range from six months to five years in jail. In Iran, home to the other man, known as J, homosexuals can be punished with flogging or execution. (*Daily Mirror*, 08 July 2010)

In such instances, the press provides readers with descriptions of what it is like to be homosexual in Cameroon and Iran, where people could be flogged, executed, or have their penis cut off in case of homosexual conduct, therefore acknowledging the circumstances of being gay in these countries.

However, several unfavourable generalisations are also made in relation to gay asylum seekers as a cohesive group through assimilation (using van Leeuwen's term). Some newspapers tend to follow a recurrent pattern labelling them as economic migrants making false claims to exploit the British welfare system, and thus avoid deportation. Indeed, these descriptions are usually 'loaded' with a negative connotation—something which is theorised as 'appraisement' in van Leeuwen's model: far from negatively evaluating straight claimants pretending to be gay, the majority of newspapers often depicts gay asylum seekers collectively in terms which evaluate them as bad, liars, bogus, and so forth, due to the fact that their claims are easy to make and impossible to disprove.

9. Opening the floodgates to gay asylum seekers is absolute madness. The idea is bound to be abused. Every illegal desperate to get into Britain will try claiming they're gay to ensure they stay here. Some people will do whatever it takes if it means a cushy life in Britain. (*Daily Star*, 08 July 2010)
10. The lure of British life is strong. It is not our liberal hearts migrants love but our stuffed wallets. [...] If you're from one of the evil 80, and you cry gay, you are in. (*Times*, 08 July 2010)
11. Already universally regarded as the softest of touches, Britain will now be seen as the ideal destination for homosexuals from around the world. Moreover, the judges' decision will have the effect of encouraging bogus refugees to make false claims about their sexuality in order to avoid deportation. (*Express*, 09 July 2010)

A quick look at the above-mentioned instances revealed that asylum seekers seem to be conceptualised mostly in association to the exploitation of British social welfare to gain access to an attractive lifestyle.

While additional discursive features also emerged from analysis but will not be discussed here since they are beyond the scope of this volume, the issue of passing (Sànchez and Schlossberg 2001; Alexander 2006) is certainly noteworthy. Gender attribution appears to be a difficult process in the context of asylum claims based on sexual orientation and gender identity. Applicants await officers to 'read' them, trying to exhibit gender cues which can be easily recognised in order to pass as 'queer' enough and have their application accepted. Passing thus seems to work on multiple levels: in the claimants' countries of origins, where queer identities are in danger, passing as straight can be the only way to save one's life; in a receiving country like Great Britain, passing as gay is the necessary requirement to achieve refugee status. In both cases, however, passing can be viewed as a form of self-protection and self-preservation enacted by societies to frame homosexuality, fitting it into narrow, heteronormative definitions.

Amid burning indignation concerning a 'piece of judicial arrogance' (*Express*, 09 July 2010) encouraging people to make false claims about their sexuality and the plea for Britain to 'open its liberal arms and give men [...] persecuted for their sexuality a great big gay hug' (*Times*, 08 July 2010), very little space was actually devoted to how to establish the very criteria to assess such asylum claims. Apart from the sarcastic suggestions and punchlines proposing 'attendance at Kylie concert' or 'talking loudly about boys', the British press could have offered a critical lens to more openly reflect on gender identities and the potential types of masculinities to be envisaged when assessing homosexuality. Instead, the position taken by most of the newspapers can be summarised as follows: 'Whereas the Home Office used to urge gays to pretend they were straight, now, thanks to our politically correct judges, straight asylum seekers will have every incentive to pretend they are gay' (*Express*, 09 July 2010). Leaving aside the implications of the heavily negative connotative value embedded in a lexical item like 'pretend'—which, in its modern use, has taken up the meaning of 'feign, put forward a false claim'[19]—the term closely recalls the concept of 'performativity' theorised by Judith Butler in relation to gender, which appears pivotal in this case study. In fact, applying the notion of 'performativity' to the asylum context, it could be argued that since the UKBA officers need to be sufficiently convinced of the claimants' sexuality and gender identity, asylum seekers find themselves in the position to *pretend* homosexuality even if they are truly gay. They must simulate the types of queer masculinity which are stereotypically conceptualised as gay; they have no choice but to act a mise-en-scène of the identity they are expected to have. They must play a masquerade in front of the officers in the attempt to prove something that cannot be actually assessed by resorting to whatever rigorous standard of proof the Home Office might adopt. What should be solely relied on is the oral testimony at the UKBA interview—which, of course, is affected by other relevant factors such as lack of words related to sexual issues (whether in English or their own language), reluctance to speak publicly about their sexuality, their trauma of violence and persecution, and so on. Still, such argumentations are often overtly and incisively addressed in most of the news reports.

6 Concluding Remarks

The European constructions of the 'refugee problem' on its doorstep and of the 'bogus' gay asylum seeker are far more telling of the European sense of self than of the reality of the migrants' experience. The EU seems to hold a crystallised vision of itself, of the kind of alterity it can cope with—provided it displays some 'manageable' traits—and of what is perceived as unacceptable since it does not fit the norm and must be expelled. As both foreigners and homosexuals, gay asylum seekers are the 'Other' par excellence; they are the subjects where ethnic and gender diversities combine. The need to acknowledge the demands placed upon them in the asylum process results in a forced semiotic production conceiving narratives of identities that are meant to be perfectly understandable and intelligible to decision-makers. The way asylum claims on the basis of sexual orientation and gender identity are interpreted and dealt with in asylum law as much as in the media context is fraught with epistemological challenges. Indeed, hegemonic discourses can be said to obscure certain subjectivities while creating the very labels that produce acceptable individuals: who is made visible as a subject and who is made invisible, unrecognised, and unintelligible? Authenticating refugees and their stories of persecution relies on culturally coded procedures (operating both in the legal and administrative context as well as in the media context) which actualise ethnocentric legal tropes of homosexual asylum seekers. This kind of imagery can be said to actively work within the European and, in this case, the British society to define the parameters fixing and discursively constructing gender identities which are not reducible to forms of non-mainstream or queer masculinities, sex toys, and genital penetration—not to mention the fact that a heteronormative Western knowledge is employed to recognise and normalise gay asylum seekers from a variety of different cultural contexts.

Despite the fact that this study is in an initial phase and it only constitutes a part of a wider research project,[20] some significant conclusions can be drawn from the data and findings resulting from analysis.

In the aftermath of the 2010 UK Supreme Court ruling, the most striking element emerging from investigation was a rather widespread sarcastic acceptance of the sentence, which was heralded as an absurd opening to abuse and false claims. While acknowledging the end of the Home Office's controversial policy of refusing asylum to gay claimants on the grounds that they could avoid persecution by pretending to be heterosexual, most of the British press promptly explicitated and anticipated the beginning of a new trend in asylum claims based on the pretence of being gay. While some newspapers expressed critical views, voicing their stances more or less straightforwardly, the references to Kylie Minogue's music, Oscar Wilde's works, and multi-coloured cocktails re-codify and re-semiotise homosexuality. As a matter of fact (and with the exception of *The Guardian* and *The Independent*), homosexuality was not only construed as camouflage and disguise, but, above all, it was turned into a clichéd semiotic form expecting gay people to feature the stereotyped traits of a 'queer' masculinity dictated by hegemonic paradigms. If we take a view that there should be a robust and fair asylum system, and that granting refugee status to those whose lives are at risk in homophobic regimes is morally justifiable, then implementation of the procedures would be advised not to rely on stereotypes based on cultural tropes linking homosexuality to effeminacy.

At the time of writing, potential scenarios for migrants and asylum seekers appear even more distressing in the UK. Indeed, given how contentious the issue of immigration has become, it is likely to be the most politically fraught area of policy post-Brexit. In a recent statement (March 2017) the Immigration Minister, Robert Goodwill, claimed that the UK may return tortured asylum seekers to the countries they fled, since the government—in its new anti-Europe surge—does not consider a person having been tortured reason enough alone to accept a claim of asylum.[21]

Within or without Europe, the asylum system might be improved, focusing on the identification of the abuses perpetrated on claimants, and the press could endorse a more complex discussion around stereotyping in the attempt to foster more progressive views.

Notes

1. 'How gay do you need to be to satisfy the Home Office?' was an ironic but effective test launched in 2015 by the *Daily Mirror* in relation to one particular case that provoked a storm of controversy: the case of a Nigerian asylum seeker, stating she feared imprisonment and death in her country because of her sexuality, who was accused by the Home Office's barrister of lying because she had children and 'you can't be heterosexual one day and a lesbian the next day. Just as you can't change your race' (see http://www.mirror.co.uk/news/ampp3d/home-office-think-youre-gay-5280895—unless otherwise specified, all websites were last accessed in December 2015).
2. The term 'asylum seeker' has become the established term of reference for those not yet accorded the official status of refugees. Unfortunately, this term is laden with connotations of a bogus status which the individual claiming asylum must seek to disprove through the legal process of having his/her claim assessed (see Hyland 2001).
3. Such cases are even trickier because effective protection should be granted by national authorities. However, persecution by non-state actors has been recognised as a relevant factor for asylum, if the State or de facto authorities are unable or unwilling to provide protection against harm. For further information on the criminalisation of homosexuality, see http://www.humandignitytrust.org/
4. For a discussion on the production of the dominant tropes on masculinity and the manifold processes of representation and semiotic re-configuration of male identities, see Balirano 2014.
5. In Lacan's view, once a child enters language and accepts the rules of society, she/he is able to deal with others, creating bonds which give him/her some recognition within the community.

6. These countries include the following: Afghanistan, Albania, Algeria, Angola, Armenia, Azerbaijan, Bangladesh, Barbados, Belarus, Bolivia, Bosnia-Herzegovina, Brazil, Burundi, Cameroon, Central African Republic, Chile, China, Colombia, Congo (DRC), Costa Rica, Croatia, Cuba, Dominica, Ecuador, Egypt, Eritrea, Estonia*, Ethiopia, Gambia, Georgia, Ghana, Guatemala, Guinea-Conakry, Guyana, Honduras, India, Indonesia, Iran, Iraq, Israel, Ivory Coast, Jamaica, Jordan, Kazakhstan, Kenya, Kosovo, Lebanon, Liberia, Libya, Lithuania*, Macedonia, Malawi, Malaysia, Mali, Mauritania, Mauritius, Mexico, Moldova, Mongolia, Morocco, Nepal, Nicaragua, Niger, Nigeria, Pakistan, Palestine, Panama, Paraguay, Peru, Philippines, Qatar, Romania*, Russia, Rwanda, Saudi Arabia, Senegal, Serbia, Sierra Leone, Slovakia*, Somalia, South Africa, Sri Lanka, St. Vincent & the Grenadines, Sudan, Syria, Tajikistan, Tanzania, Thailand, Togo, Trinidad & Tobago, Tunisia, Turkey, Turkmenistan, Uganda, Ukraine, United Arab Emirates, United States, Uzbekistan, Venezuela, Vietnam, Yemen, Yugoslavia (FRY), Zambia, Zimbabwe. Countries that are now the EU Member States have been marked with an asterisk.
7. http://www.migrazine.at/artikel/dutch-lgbt-asylum-policy-english
8. http://76crimes.com/2012/04/19/dutch-official-to-lgbt-asylum-seekers-stay-home-in-closet/
9. See www.yogyakartaprinciples.org
10. In medical terminology, phallometric testing of men is called penile plethysmography (PPG) while its counterpart for women is called vaginal photoplethysmography (VPG). Both PPG and VPG were used in the Czech Republic until 2011. They were also used in Slovakia in 2005.
11. A research report by the UK Lesbian and Gay Immigration Group (2010), a charity committed to assisting those seeking asylum on the basis of sexual and gender identity, found that, from 1999 to 2009, 98% to 99% of asylum claims made by lesbians and gay men were rejected compared to 73% of general asylum applications.
12. http://www.theguardian.com/uk-news/2014/feb/08/gay-asylum-seekers-humiliation-home-office
13. http://www.theguardian.com/uk-news/2014/feb/08/gay-asylum-seekers-humiliation-home-office. Not to mention the request to submit personal sex footage and photographic evidence in support of asylum applications.
14. Unlike Freud, Lacan distinguishes between the penis (the actual bodily organ) and the phallus (a signifier of sexual difference), the latter being

central in his theories on subjectivity and sexual difference. Lacan prefers to employ the term 'phallus' rather than 'penis' to emphasise the fact that what concerns psychoanalytic theory is not the male genital organ in its biological reality but the role it plays on the imaginary and symbolic level.

15. Such keywords were searched for when they occurred in headlines and leading paragraphs, through the online database LexisNexis (www.lexis-nexis.com).
16. The original saying reads: 'You don't have to be mad to work here, but it helps.'
17. http://www.bailii.org/uk/cases/UKSC/2010/31.html
18. It might be argued that newspapers used the judge's comments on Kylie Minogue and the multi-coloured cocktails to criticise the decision strategically. However, most of the news reports did not follow up the headlines with additional analysis on the stereotyping of gay men; they mainly tended to warn against the potential immigration surge. At the same time, it is worth noting that despite the overall trend, *The Guardian* (a left-leaning broadsheet) differentiated itself from the other newspapers by stressing other elements as shown in the following headlines: 'Milestone victory for gay refugees' (07 July 2010), 'Gay asylum seekers win protection from deportation' (07 July 2010), 'Gay refugees entitled to asylum, judge claims' (08 July 2010), among the others. Such instances highlight that a completely different focus was given to the issue in the news by this newspaper: while all references to cocktails and music are absent, the relevance of the ruling within the context of asylum law is aptly foregrounded.
19. See http://www.etymonline.com/index.php?allowed_in_frame=0&search=pretend
20. The study is part of a wider research project on the linguistic construals of gender and ethnic diversity in media and legal discourses.
21. http://www.independent.co.uk/news/uk/politics/asylum-seeker-torture-uk-refugee-immigration-minister-a7608206.html

References

Alexander, B. K. (2006). *Performing Black Masculinity: Race, Culture and Queer Identity*. Lanham and New York: Altamira Press.

Baker, P., Gabrielatos, C., Khosravinik, M., Krzyzanowski, M., McEnery, T., & Wodak, R. (2008). A Useful Synergy? Combining Critical Discourse Analysis and Corpus Linguistics to Examine Discourses of Refugees and Asylum Seekers in the UK Press. *Discourse and Society, 19*(3), 273–306.

Baker, P., Gabrielatos, C., & McEnery, T. (2013). *Discourse Analysis and Media Attitudes*. Cambridge: Cambridge University Press.

Balirano, G. (2014). *Masculinity and Representation: A Multimodal Critical Approach to Male Identity Constructions*. Napoli: Loffredo.

Berg, L., & Millbank, J. (2009). Constructing the Personal Narratives of Lesbian, Gay and Bisexual Asylum Claimants. *Journal of Refugee Studies, 22*(1), 1–17.

Butler, J. (1990a). *Gender Trouble*. London and New York: Routledge.

Butler, J. (1990b). Performative Acts and Gender Constitution: An Essay in Phenomenology and Feminist Theory. In S. E. Case (Ed.), *Performing Feminist Critical Theory and Theatre* (pp. 519–531). Baltimore: John Hopkins UP.

Butler, J. (1993). *Bodies That Matter. On the Discursive Limits of 'Sex'*. London and New York: Routledge.

Connely, E. (2014). *Queer, Beyond a Reasonable Doubt: Refugee Experiences of 'Passing' into 'Membership of a Particular Social Group'*. Research dissertation, University College London, UK.

Council of Europe. (1953). European Convention for the Protection of Human Rights and Fundamental Freedoms, as amended by Protocols Nos. 11 and 14, 4 November 1950, ETS 5.

Dublin Regulation. (2003). European Union: Council of the European Union, Council Regulation (EC) No 343/2003 of 18 February 2003 establishing the criteria and mechanisms for determining the Member State responsible for examining an asylum application lodged in one of the Member States by a third-country national, 18 February 2003, OJ L. 50/1-50/10; 25.2.2003, (EC)No 343/2003.

European Union Agency for Fundamental Rights (EUFRA). (2009). *Homophobia and Discrimination on Grounds of Sexual Orientation in the EU Member States – Part II – The Social Situation.*

European Union: Council of the European Union. (2004). Council Directive 2004/83/EC of 29 April 2004 on Minimum Standards for the Qualification and Status of Third Country Nationals or Stateless Persons as Refugees or as Persons Who Otherwise Need International Protection and the Content of the Protection Granted, 30 September 2004, OJ L. 304/12-304/23; 30.9.2004, 2004/83/EC.

Human Rights Council (HRC). (2011). *Human Rights, Sexual Orientation and Gender Identity*. A/HRC/17/L9/Rev.1, UN Human Rights Office of the High Commissioner.

Hyland, M. (2001). Refugee Subjectivity: 'Bare Life' and the Geographical Division of Labour. *The Physics Room* [Issue 13: *The Revolution Issue*]. Retrieved from http://physicsroom.org.nz/archive/log/archive/13/refugeesubjectivity/

International Panel of Experts in International Human Rights Law and on Sexual Orientation and Gender Identity. (2007). *Principles on the Application of International Human Rights Law in Relation to Sexual Orientation and Gender Identity*. Retrieved from www.yogyakartaprinciples.org

Jansen, S., & Spijkerboer, T. (2011). *Fleeing Homophobia*. COC Nederland: Vrije Universiteit Amsterdam.

Lacan J. (1977). *Écrits* (A. Sheridan, Trans.). New York: Norton.

McGhee, D. (2000). Accessing Homosexuality: Truth, Evidence and the Legal Practices for Determining Refugee Status. *Body & Society, 6*(1), 29–52.

McGhee, D. (2001). Persecution and Social Group Status: Homosexual Refugees. *Journal of Refugee Studies, 14*(1), 1–23.

McGhee, D. (2003). Queer Strangers: Lesbian and Gay Refugees. *Feminist Review, 73*, 145–147.

Millbank, J. (2003). Gender, Sex and Visibility in Refugee Claims on the Basis of Sexual Orientation. *Georgetown Immigration Law Journal, 18*, 71–110.

Millbank, J. (2009a). From Discretion to Disbelief: Recent Trends in Refugee Determinations on the Basis of Sexual Orientation in Australia and in the United Kingdom. *The International Journal of Human Rights, 13*(2), 391–414.

Millbank, J. (2009b). The Ring of Truth: A Case Study of Credibility Assessment in Particular Social Group Refugee Determinations. *International Journal of Refugee Law, 21*(1), 1–33.

Morgan, W. (2000). Queering International Human Rights Law. In C. Stychin & D. Herman (Eds.), *Sexuality in the Legal Arena* (pp. 208–225). London: Athlone.

Sànchez, M. C., & Schlossberg, M. (Eds.). (2001). *Passing. Identity and Interpretation in Sexuality, Race and Religion*. New York and London: New York University Press.

UN General Assembly. (1948). Universal Declaration of Human rights (217 [III] A). Paris.

UN General Assembly. (1951). Convention Relating to the Status of Refugees, 28 July 1951, United Nations, Treaty Series, vol. 189, p. 137.

UK Lesbian and Gay Immigration Group. (2010). *Failing the Grade. Home Office Initial Decisions on Lesbian and Gay Claims for Asylum*. London: UKLGI.

Van Leeuwen, T. (1996). The Representation of Social Actors. In C. R. Caldas-Coulthard & M. Coulthard (Eds.), *Texts and Practices* (pp. 32–70). London and New York: Routledge.
Van Leeuwen, T. (2008). *Discourse and Practice: New Tools for Critical Discourse Analysis*. Oxford: OUP.

12

The Object of Subordination Is Immaterial: Discursive Constructions of Masculinity in a Far-Right Online Forum

Andrew Brindle

1 Introduction

Building on Butler's (1990) view that gender is performative and can be understood to be produced, to a large extent, by language and discourse, Connell (1995) has argued that multiple masculinities exist, which intersect and interact in a gendered hierarchy of categories which include race, social class, and national and ethnic identity. Hegemonic masculinity is understood as the dominant and most honoured way of being a man. However, what is required of a man to be at the top of the masculine hierarchy is not universal or stable. This article attempts to analyse the masculine identities constructed on a white supremacist online forum called Stormfront. The data were taken from a thread centred on the topic of the mass-killing in Orlando, Florida of patrons of a gay nightclub perpetrated by a Muslim American. The study observes the ways in which the white supremacist members represent normal and subordinate

A. Brindle (✉)
Department of Applied English, St. John's University,
New Taipei City, Taiwan

P. Baker, G. Balirano (eds.), *Queering Masculinities in Language and Culture*,
Palgrave Studies in Language, Gender and Sexuality,
https://doi.org/10.1057/978-1-349-95327-1_12

ways of being a man, examining how such representations interact with other identity characteristics and how contestations and ambiguities around such constructions reveal much about the instability of categories of hegemonic masculinity. The ways that homophobia intersects with Islamophobia as part of a masculine hierarchy is also considered.

Performance, in gender studies, tends to follow Butler's model which views performance as "acting out" gender, based on repeating previously seen gendered behaviours, such as a deep voice for a man. However, performance in this chapter is also concerned about signalling stance (hatred of certain groups), as opposed to performing certain stereotypical gender-marked behaviours. Therefore, the performance of masculinity may be achieved by the subordination of other groups, which can be seen as a merging of the approaches of Butler and Connell.

Following Butler and Connell, masculinity is defined in this chapter as behaving in ways that are considered to be typical and acceptable for males by a particular social group. Masculinity, like gender, is also performed and therefore has to be continually constructed: males have to repetitively demonstrate their masculinity (Kimmel 2015). Masculinity is often demarcated in terms of what it is not. Therefore, it is often established relative to other identity components, predominantly femininity, but also non-hegemonic masculine identities. Additionally, sex, gender, and sexuality are often combined as a matrix which engraves preferable and problematic identities. A male is usually viewed as adequately masculine if he is also heterosexual. Thus heterosexuality becomes a key facet of masculinity (for men) and femininity (for women).

Masculine identities are effects of discursive practices; they are created within institutions and historically established. One way that the gender order is upheld is by associating concepts of appropriate and inappropriate (e.g. queer) gendered performances to different types of sexual identities. The notion that masculinity is a singular rather than multiple identity has been viewed as problematic, particularly where gender identities and power relations are contextualised practices. Whitehead (2002: 33–34) writes:

> It is no longer tenable, given recognition of the multiplicity, historicity and dynamism of gender representations, to talk of masculinity in the singular. Rather, we can see that masculinities are plural and multiple; they differ

> over space, time and context, are rooted only in the cultural and social moment, and are, thus, inevitably entwined with the powerful and influential variables such as sexuality, class, age and ethnicity.

In order to comprehend the multiplicity of masculinities, it is essential to study the relations, such as subordination and dominance, between the diverse forms of masculinity. These relationships are created through practices that may intimidate or exploit others (Kiesling 2006: 118). Masculinity is not a static characteristic, but a social process reliant upon restatement, and which, in various forms, encompasses language, thereby centrally situating linguistic concerns in gender theory. Men who heavily invest in a specific masculine identity will endeavour to communicate in a manner particular for that specific trait (Moita-Lopes 2006: 294). Masculinities are not removed from a social context, but embedded and associated in the lives of men. Thus Messerschmidt (2016) argues that the discourse of masculinity is dependent on a multitude of interlocking notions such as biology, performances, individual psychologies, and ideologies to form a web-like discourse. Such views propose that some of the central concepts in research on men and masculinities ought to be understood as part of this web.

I am predominantly interested in how members interpret and negotiate discourses of masculinity in white supremacist discourse and how this is manifested in the texts they produce. This topic is of particular relevance to research on masculinity because these groups are heavily invested in maintaining traditional hegemonic masculinity. Schlatter (2006) defines the white supremacist movement as overwhelmingly a movement of and for white men while Ferber (2000) maintains that white supremacism attempts to portray white men as victims who are oppressed by minority groups. She investigated the construction of masculinity in contemporary white supremacist discourse and likened it with that found in mythopoetic discourse, contending that both discourses share many features such as the portrayal of American men as de-masculinised, accrediting women and the women's movement for this, while endeavouring to encourage men to rediscover their absent masculinity and to reaffirm their authority.

2 Hegemonic Masculinities

As previously described, heterosexuality is critical to hegemonic masculinity. It is, however, dependent on subordinate masculinities, in particular homosexual forms, since it must oppose and challenge them.

The concept of hegemonic masculinity (Connell 1987) has significantly influenced current understandings of men, gender, and social hierarchy (Connell and Messerschmidt 2005: 829). Connell (1995) describes four tenets of masculinity. The first is hegemonic masculinity, (which differs from Gramsci's framework in that it concentrates on gender rather than social class), thereby controlling not only femininities, but also non-hegemonic masculinities. A typical example of hegemonic masculinity would be a married business executive from a developed nation like the United States. The majority of men do not hold this status but many would acknowledge it as being an ideal. The second tenet is subordination; of men over women and also between groups of men. This is of particular significance for this study, as not only are gay men one such subordinate group, but white supremacists would also be considered subordinate by mainstream society, although they would depict themselves as a dominant form of masculinity. The third tenet is complicity; while most men are not exemplars of hegemonic masculinity, Connell contends that they all benefit to differing degrees from the hierarchical gender system. The fourth tenet is marginalisation, which refers to the rejection of forms of masculinity that do not adhere to the hegemonic norm. Hegemonic masculinity is thus distinct from other masculinities, principally subordinated and marginalised forms.

Masculinity does not sit well within social structures as a monolithic set of static role demands and behavioural expectations (Mullins 2006: 152). Rather, any social location produces multiple masculinities that are defined in relation to each other. Thus certain masculinities can be elevated as hegemonic in relation to other subordinate masculinities if they are the most accepted within that particular context in relation to the subordinate masculinities (Benwell 2003: 181).

Donaldson (1993: 645–646) describes hegemonic masculinity as "exclusive, anxiety-provoking, internally and hierarchically differentiated, brutal and violent. It is pseudo-natural, tough, contradictory, crisis prone, rich and socially sustained". Such a portrayal of hegemonic masculinity does not fit well with the image of the international business executive, which shows the variability of notions held. In working class communities, hegemonic masculinity might be characterised by the man who is seen as the physically toughest or has the most confidence. According to Carrigan et al. (2006: 51) the ability of a specific form of masculinity to impose itself over other forms is recognised as hegemonic, consequently context is of overriding consequence.

Hegemonic standards ought to be recognised as defining a subject position in discourse that is taken up strategically by men in particular circumstances, therefore current research has tended to focus on hegemonic masculinities at the local level (Morris 2008, 2012). Hegemonic masculinity has multiple meanings and men can alternate between numerous meanings according to their interactional requirements. They can adopt hegemonic masculinity when it is required; but the same men can distance themselves strategically from hegemonic masculinity at other moments. Consequently, masculinity embodies not a particular type of man, but a means that men position themselves through discursive practices. From this approach, it can be understood how masculinities are constructed in discourse and also how they are sustained. It can also be understood how a locally hegemonic form of masculinity can be used for self-promotion.

3 Backlash and Homophobia

In the twentieth century, owing to the Women's Liberation and Gay Rights movements, according to Connell (2005: 244), "men were losing their cultural centrality". Gallagher (1995: 169) states, "…many whites see themselves as victims of the multicultural, pc, feminist onslaught". Men's patriarchal place within society, the separation of labour, and the status of men's sexuality have been affected and produced a sense of confusion as regards the perceptions of masculinity and whiteness initiated by the notion of loss of white, male privilege. Connell refers to Goode (1982) who contended that men resisted the changes brought on by these social movements because they were the advantaged group. Such a "backlash" against these changes is seen as cultural rather than political. Identities hitherto assumed as secure are challenged by the Civil Rights movement, women's movement, and gay and lesbian movements. One response to such instabilities by individuals or groups who feel their identity is being disputed is to reaffirm local gender hierarchies of masculine fundamentalism found within right-wing or white supremacist organisations which are able to appeal to white males who believe that their interests are not being represented. While the white supremacist movement is assumed to be primarily concerned with race issues, the roles of gender and the patriarchal position of men within the organisation are of vital significance (Ferber 2000).

Other researchers, such as Kimmel (2005, 2012), maintain that it is an opposition to globalisation and unattainable transnational hegemonic masculinities which has ensued the occurrence of local masculinities centred on the re-establishment of manhood founded on a domestic patriarchy from a previous era, which are entrenched within extremist groups. He writes (2005: 416), "Efforts to reclaim economic autonomy, to reassert political control, and to revive traditional domestic dominance thus take on the veneer of restoring manhood". Kimmel considers that such groups are populated by young men who have been adversely affected by the currents of globalisation; that they have responded to an erosion of public and domestic patriarchy with a renewal of masculine entitlement. Kimmel (2005: 418) claims:

> They believe themselves to be entitled to power—by a combination of historical legacy, religious fiat, biological destiny, and moral legitimacy—but they believe they have no power. That power has been surrendered by white men (their fathers) and stolen from them by a federal government controlled and staffed by legions of the newly enfranchised minorities, women, and immigrants, all in the service to the omnipotent Jews who control international economic and political life.

Accordingly, the masculinity of such individuals is founded on exclusion, racism, homophobia, sexism, and antisemitism. Thus, hegemonic masculinity exerts power over other masculinities and will dominate other forms in any particular historical and social setting (Van Kriekan et al. 2000: 413). A principle illustration in present-day western society is the dominance of heterosexual men and the subordination of homosexual men (Boler 2005: 262). This domination is more than cultural segregation of homosexuality, as gay men are subordinated to heterosexual men by material practices such as street violence, economic discrimination, and personal boycotts. Connell (2005: 78) writes:

> Oppression positions homosexual masculinities at the bottom of a gender hierarchy among men. Gayness, in patriarchal ideology, is the repository of whatever is symbolically expelled from hegemonic masculinity, the items ranging from fastidious taste in home decoration to receptive anal pleasure. Hence, from the point of view of hegemonic masculinity, gayness is easily assimilated to femininity. And hence—in view of some gay theorists—the ferocity of homophobic attacks.

An important outcome of this is that homophobia is used to control the boundaries of acceptable heterosexual male behaviour and identity as well as, overtly and at times violently, being used to control homosexual behaviour and identity (Mac an Ghaill and Heywood 2007: 130). Whitehead (2002: 166) writes, "men's complicity in sexist or homophobic behaviour arises not from their core sexuality, but from a desire not to be excluded from male groups; not to be cast out and declared 'not a male/man, like us'". Consequently, heterosexual masculinity is defined in opposition to racial and sexual minorities and women. Gorer (1964: 129) states, "The lives of most American men are bounded, and their interests daily curtailed by the constant necessity to prove to their fellows, and to themselves, that they are not sissies, not homosexuals". This, according to Kimmel (2001: 279), results in men inflating traditional rules of masculinity, a consequence of which is not only homophobic acts, but also the predation of women. Consequently, homophobia, racism, and sexism are closely interlinked, as women, gay men, and other minorities become the "other" against which heterosexual men construct their identities. Kimmel (2001: 284) writes:

> Others still rehearse the politics of exclusion, as if by clearing away the playing field of secure gender identity of any that we deem less than manly—women, gay men, non-native-born men, men of color—middle-class, straight, white men can regroup their sense of themselves without those haunting fears and that deep shame that they are unmanly and will be exposed by other men. This is the manhood of racism, of sexism, of homophobia.

Homophobia is one genre of subordination that most men are complicit in. Within the Stormfront community, this form of hatred interacts with hatred towards other minority groups to construct a hierarchy of hatred as the writers perform identity construction. Although white supremacism remains on the fringes of society, the group leaders continually attempt to become more mainstream, and with the increased prominence of right-wing populism both in Europe and North America, which makes such rhetoric increasingly common, studies such as this are of relevance.

4 Stormfront

Stormfront is a white supremacist Internet forum that is the Web's primary racial hate site (Daniels 2009). It was first founded as an online bulletin board in the early 1990s before developing into a website in 1996 by former Ku Klux Klan leader, Don Black. Its status within the extreme-right has increased since the 1990s, drawing scrutiny from watchdog organisations that oppose racism and antisemitism.

According to a 2014 two-year study by the Southern Poverty Law Center (SPLC)'s Intelligence Report, registered Stormfront users have been disproportionately accountable for some of the most fatal hate crimes and mass killings since the site was founded. In the previous five years before 2014, Stormfront members killed almost 100 people.[1] Of these, 77 were massacred by one Stormfront user, Anders Breivik, a Norwegian terrorist who committed the 2011 Norway attacks.

In 2006, the SPLC described a thread on Stormfront in which white nationalists were encouraged to join the U.S. military to learn the skills needed for winning a race war. The 2008 United States presidential candidacy of African-American Democrat Barack Obama was a cause of substantial apprehension for certain Stormfront members; the site received 2000 new members the day after Obama was elected as President and, due to an increased amount of visitors, went off-line temporarily.[2] Stormfront members considered that the election of Obama signified a new multicultural era in the United States which would end "white rule", and believed that he would encourage illegal immigration and affirmative action, and that he would facilitate making white people a minority group. During the 2016 election season, the Stormfront site once again experienced significant increase in traffic corresponding to controversial statements by Donald Trump, whose campaign is popular among white supremacists.

Don Black has continually attempted to increase the mainstream appeal of white supremacism. Black established Stormfront to amplify awareness of supposed anti-white discrimination and government actions allegedly unfavourable to white people and to construct a virtual community of white extremists. In addition to its propagation of white supremacism, antisemitism, and homophobia, Stormfront has increasingly become active in its dissemination of Islamophobia. At the time of writing, Stormfront claimed to have 315,447 members, while the website contained 933,850 threads and 12,058,136 posts. The vast majority of its members are, or claim to be, male. An event took place in June 2016, which highlighted the homophobic and Islamophobic ideologies of certain Stormfront members, and by studying an online discussion of this event, it is possible to gain insights into how such ideologies interact in the performance of hegemonic masculinities.

5 The Orlando Shooting

On June 12, 2016, Omar Mateen, a 29-year-old security guard killed 49 people and wounded 53 others in an attack inside Pulse, a gay nightclub in Orlando, Florida, United States. He was shot and killed by Orlando Police Department officers after a three-hour standoff. Pulse was hosting Latin Night and most of the victims were Latino. It was the deadliest incident of violence against LGBT people in United States history and the deadliest terrorist attack in the United States since the September 11 attacks in 2001.

In a 9-1-1 call shortly after the shooting began, Mateen swore allegiance to the leader of the Islamic State of Iraq, Abu Bakr al-Baghdadi. He later told a negotiator he had committed the massacre because of the American-led interventions in Iraq and in Syria, and that the negotiator should tell the United States to stop bombing ISIL.

Initial reports said Mateen may have been a patron of the nightclub and used gay dating websites and apps, but investigation officials said they have not found any credible evidence to substantiate these claims.

The aim of this study is to analyse how Stormfront members construct masculinities, to investigate if there are any contestations and ambiguities, and to observe the hierarchical structure of the out-groups. The following section will present the methodological approach.

6 Method

The data for this study were the postings made by Stormfront members on a single thread related to the Orlando shooting. The thread contained 1223 unique posts, which when collected, consisted of a corpus of 51,578 words. As with most online forums, some posters copied text from earlier postings in their messages. These quoted parts of texts were not counted in the analysis so as to maintain word frequency and keyword accuracy. The names and profiles of the members were not noted, as it was not my intention to expose individuals, but to study the discourses, identities, and ideologies they discursively constructed. At the time of writing, the thread had been viewed 84,414 times by both Stormfront members and site visitors.

This study combines methodologies of corpus linguistics and discourse analysis, a relationship which, according to Baker and McEnery (2015) has been developing for the past 25 years. Influential to the study were works such as Baker et al. (2008) which discussed the combination of corpus linguistics and the discourse historical approach (DHA) to critical discourse analysis (CDA) in order to undertake a study of the construction of refugees in the British media, which was followed by a more recent study (Baker et al. 2013), which examined the representation of Muslims and Islam in the British press. Another study of relevance for this research was Prentice et al. (2012), which utilised corpus methodologies to investigate the language of Islamic extremism.

In order to carry out the analysis of the corpus data, the online Corpus Query System, Sketch Engine (Kilgarriff et al. 2004) was used. Firstly, a study of word frequency was made in order to facilitate an understanding of the "aboutness" of the data, to understand the main themes discussed within the thread. This was followed by an investigation of keywords. Words that are considerably more frequent in one corpus when compared against another (often a much larger reference corpus) are known as keywords. The keyword procedure can therefore be used to identify the significantly different lexis between the Stormfront corpus and a larger general corpus.[3] A keyword list is a more useful approach in signifying lexical items that possibly will merit additional investigation than a raw frequency list as a keyword list provides a degree of prominence, instead of frequency alone (Baker 2014). To gain a more comprehensive insight into the data, high frequency words and keywords were then observed in context by undertaking a concordance analysis. A concordance analysis combines quantitative and qualitative analysis and therefore may be considered as more productive than relying on quantitative analysis alone.

Throughout the study, the discourse historical approach (Wodak 2015) has influenced the qualitative analysis. Such an approach focuses on discourse topics, discursive strategies, and argumentation schemes (Reisigl and Wodak 2001).

7 Analysis

Once the texts had been collected and duplicate messages removed, the corpus was converted into a computer readable format and the frequency and keyword data were analysed. Table 12.1 shows the 20 most frequent non-function words and the 20 keywords with the highest keyness values.

Table 12.1 Frequency and keyword data

Most frequent non-function words		Keywords		
Word	Frequency	Keyword	Keyness	Frequency
people	247	Mateen	934.16	57
white	208	gays	467.99	110
gay	154	Trump	420.19	108
Muslim	152	fags	415.75	31
Muslims	130	homos	372.31	24
gays	110	Isis	353.12	54
Trump	108	queers	291.62	22
guns	86	faggots	239.50	16
hate	73	muzzies	216.16	13
media	72	WN[a]	205.65	15
shooting	71	fag	186.30	17
Jews	70	Seddique	185.62	11
Orlando	69	muzzie	184.07	11
attack	67	shooter	166.49	58
control	66	degenerate	153.69	18
Islam	64	homosexuals	153.58	28
against	60	libtards	147.36	9
America	58	gunman	147.00	18
club	58	Omar	146.68	31
mass	58	shootings	126.80	21

[a]WN is an abbreviation for White Nationalism

By grouping the most frequent words into categories, it can been seen that some of the words are topic words related to the shooting: *guns*, *shooting*, *Orlando*, *attack*, *club*, and *mass*. Other words are associated with social groups and identification: *white*, *gay*, *gays*, *Muslim*, *Muslims*, *Jews*, and *Islam*. Other frequent words demonstrate the presence of discourses related to the media, Donald Trump, and gun control. When the keyword list is observed, and the most salient words grouped together, topic words related to the shooting include the following: *Mateen*, *Isis*, *Seddique*, *shooter*, *gunman*, *Omar*, and *shootings*. However, the majority of salient words function as derogatorily labelling out-groups as follows: *gays*, *fags*, *homos*, *queers*, *faggots*, *muzzies*, *fag*, *muzzie*, *degenerate*, *homosexuals*, and *libtards*.

The data highlight that there are discourses centred on the right to possess guns and the fear that the government will attempt to restrict gun ownership rights in light of the Orlando shooting. Other discourses are concerned with the presidential campaign of Donald Trump as many writers express their support of his candidacy. A further discourse is related to the media and how it is supposedly controlled by Jewish people and is biased against whites. However, these topics will not be specifically focused upon as the study is primarily concerned with the construction of masculinities. The following analysis will focus on the constructions of whites, Muslims, and gay men.[4]

Table 12.1 shows that the words *gay* and *gays* are among the most frequent non-function words. When the instances of *gay* and *gays* were studied, 24 depicted gay men as sexually aggressive or as a danger to children, 22 cases articulated a hatred or disgust of gay men, while 13 instances depicted them as a privileged group receiving disproportionate benefits from the government. Other, less frequent patterns were also present. Some posters ridiculed gay people while others portrayed them as innocent victims, or positively as decent people who didn't deserve to be murdered. A representative concordance line demonstrates an opinion commonly found in the texts written by Stormfront members:

1. There are the predator **gays** left who are very aggressive and pick on men and children.

In the above concordance line, gay men are labelled as *gays* and associated with being predators, thus being constructed as a threat to heterosexual men and their children. The writer constructs white heterosexual men as the protectors of white children, and by doing so perpetuates the patriarchal notion that the man is the protector of the family, in this instance, against the threat of the sexual predatory gay man. Ironically, this construction of gay men shares some stereotypical traits of hegemonic masculinity, e.g. the notion that men are more aggressive and sexually dominant. Furthermore, it depicts heterosexual men as victims.

The most salient keywords for gay men were *fags*, *homos*, *queers*, *faggots*, *fag*, and *degenerate*. The concordance lines for the most frequent label, *fag* and *fags*, an abbreviation of *faggot*, were studied further. This pejorative label was commonly used by posters, to further denigrate gay men:

2. But speaking for myself and Wife, we can not morn the dead **fags**. They are always in your face with their perversions.

Such a discursive strategy marginalises identities that have been stigmatized and positions gay men as the out-group. This is done by seeking segregation from undesirable identities and states indifference to the suffering or death of the group. The writer declares indifference to the murder of 49 innocent people. Thus, a defining feature of hate is an irrelevance to the suffering of the out-group that is so profound that the out-group could disappear completely and the individual would feel nothing for their ceased existence. Furthermore, gay men are constructed as deviant and aggressively intruding into the lives of the heterosexual in-group.

Another salient derogatory label was *queers*, which associated gay men with sexual deviancy and perversion:

3. Liberals love pushing sexual deviancy on the masses. Liberals love pushing mass mooslim immigration on the masses. Mooslim kills **queers**? What's a libtard to do?????? Blame guns, I suppose.

The political left is blamed for supporting two out-groups, which the writer ironically constructs as incompatible, then further criticises the left for using the excuse of guns, instead of their own policies for the resulting violence. Furthermore, each out-group is labelled disparagingly as follows: *Mooslim*, *queers*, and *libtard*.

The derogatory labelling of out-group members can be seen further in the following extract where the behaviour of two gay men is described as the provocative act which initiated the killings:

4. The Muslim saw two **fags** kissing and it triggered his **muzzie** senses. That is why he went on his **homo** Jihad.

When the 208 concordance lines of *white* were analysed, it was found that the most common discourse was related to constructing white people as victims. The corpus contained discourses relating to media being prejudiced against whites (20 occurrences), that whites were commonly the victims of physical violence perpetrated by members of minority groups (23), that immigration of minorities had an adverse effect on whites (18), and that white nations were on the decline (22). However, another discourse was present which constructed whites as superior to other races (23). When collocates of *white* were investigated, it was found that the most frequent were: *anti* (18) and *man/men* (14). The writers position themselves as victims with the notion of *anti-white*, as the following representative extract indicates:

> 5. Millions of White people have been stuck out of work for months, if not years while less qualified minorities took their jobs. These White victims suffered depression and had their lives severely harmed thanks to all this **anti-white** discrimination that the liberal and Jewish activists have put in place.

The writer employs the argumentation strategy that Jewish and liberal political and social actors have implemented a strategy to weaken the in-group by forcing them from their jobs and replacing them with out-group members who, according to the writer, are less qualified, thus the in-group has become displaced within their homeland. However, when the collocate *man* was studied a second discourse was present, which constructed the white race as superior to minority groups:

> 6. The **White Man** is not at the summit of civilization for being weak. But many of our kind have forgotten what it means, and are told you are NOT to feel proud of it. I reject that sentiment.

Therefore, there are contradictions around the construction of white men within the forum. Such men are depicted as victims, repressed by the Jewish-controlled government, and preyed upon by homosexual men whilst at other times they are constructed as at the pinnacle of civilisation and consequently positioned as hegemonic, although this supposed hegemony is considered to be something to be ashamed of by the mass media or government. Hence, this particular writer positions himself in opposition to the hypothetical opinion of society and constructs himself as proud of his white heritage.

A further example constructs white men with a differing identity:

> 7. I would rather see good paying jobs go to **White Men** who are trying to support their families as apposed to degenerates who support a perverse lifestyle.

Such a depiction of *white men* perpetuates the traditional patriarchal family structure which positions women as child producers and carers and men as breadwinners. The white man is constructed as dependable, heterosexual, and the supporter of a presumably white family, whereas the out-group members are portrayed as lacking such qualities, but are portrayed as deficient and deviant. This is further demonstrated in the following extended concordance line:

> 8. Puerto Ricans invaded and destroyed all the northwest side neigborhoods here in Chicago, they move into houses paid for by the government built by **white men** then have 20 kids they can't afford and lay back and collect the welfare and that's how they outbreed us and outnumber us **whites**. They outnumber us then stare us down, harass us, jump, rape, assault, shoot, talk smack too us, call us racial slurs like **white boy** and cracker and destroy the neighborhood forcing **whites** out.

A minority out-group is labelled as invading rather than immigrating, and as having *destroyed* the area in which they settled, *forcing* the indigenous whites to leave the area, thus immigration is described using metaphors of war and violence. White men are constructed as builders and workers in comparison to the out-group which are represented as living off the generosity of the American people, while taking advantage of this and again victimising and threatening the continued hegemony of the white race. The out-group families are hyperbolically depicted as having large numbers of children, which eventually will lead to whites becoming a minority race, thus threatening their hegemony. Not only are the out-group represented as having many children, but they are seen as having no means or desire to support such families, unlike the self-sufficient, hard-working white men. Once the whites have become outnumbered by the out-group, they are threatened, assaulted, and forced to leave.

The above poster uses a collective noun on himself, *whites*, in a similar strategy as labelling gay men as *gays*. Such a strategy may be understood as a means to establish in- and out-groups and then the context in which the labels are used will determine whether or not the term is derogatory.

Words related to Islam (*Muslim, Muslims*, and *Islam*, and the keywords *muzzie/muzzies*) were also frequent within the data, which is to be expected as the assailant was a Muslim and because of growing levels of Islamophobia on the Stormfront site. Furthermore, as the Orlando shooting involved two groups of "others" from the Stormfront members' perspective, there was the potential of multiple stances being taken for or against one or both of the groups. When the concordance lines of *Muslim/Muslims* were analysed, it was found that the principal discourses surrounding Muslims associated them with acts of violence, extremism, intolerance, and incompatibility, thus making them a danger to Western societies:

> 9. While I obviously don't approve of the gay 'lifestyle', the main point everyone needs to understand is that these people would be only too happy to do the same to any of the rest of us, whether we're 'gay', WN, Christian, Pagan, Atheist, Leftist, or whatever. That's why **Muslims** can never be trusted in civilized countries.

The above extract positions Muslims as the out-group and are stereotypically labelled as violent and unable to integrate into Western society or accept Western values. The extract, while first doing some positioning work to subordinate gay men, goes on to depict all social groups as being under threat from Muslims, not only gay men.

A derogatory label for Muslims, *Muzzies*, was used by certain writers to augment the pejorative construction of the out-group as the following extract demonstrates:

> 10. Still, it is better for decent human beings to be armed, so they can defend themselves against the Muslim savages!!! … or not, depending on how you regard cesspool America … Levity aside, it's a sad day when you simultaneously deplore and cheer the **Muzzies** for clearing out the faggots.

The above extract provides insights into the construction of both in-group and out-groups. In-group members, labelled positively as *decent human beings*, ought to and are in need for being armed in order to be able to defend themselves against the out-group, *Muslim savages*. America is described as a *cesspool*, a reflection of the writer's opinion of the state of American society. The writer also comments on the ambiguous response to the shootings by other Stormfront members, which has divided opinion on the board. There are those who commend the assailant's actions, as he murdered other out-group members, here derogatorily labelled faggots (a keyword in the data), while using the term *Muzzies* to further denigrate Muslims.

By studying the most frequent non-function words and keywords, it has been possible to gain insights into the central discourses within the data and to analyse the construction of the accepted masculine identity depicted in texts written by members of the Stormfront online community. Homophobia and anti-homosexual discourse are a prominent feature of the data. White heterosexual hegemonic masculinity strongly influences the online practices of Stormfront members. Thus individuals who participate on Stormfront construct their own identity online as racialised, gendered, and to a lesser extent, sexualised.

Heterosexual masculinity and whiteness are fundamental traits in the online communication of Stormfront. The realisation and development of Stormfront is an expression of a desire for a community which is articulated in a manner that relies on the construction of white, heterosexual males, and white supremacy. The analysis supports Connell's theory of hegemonic masculinity, with Stormfront members referencing gender identity in hierarchical ways, which involve subordinating certain groups, such as gay men and other minority groups, to white heterosexual men.

The linguistic study of the corpus of Stormfront texts has revealed that the forum members consider their collective identity as the norm, while excluding, repressing, and negating those groups they deem to be outside this norm. This is achieved by invoking claims to superiority and power, and the assumption of a good/bad opposition in which the "other" is depicted as inferior and deviant. The marking of difference as deficient is a social, political process that creates hierarchies along divisions of race and sexuality. Once an individual or group has been defined as inferior, a subordinated position is assigned in relation to the in-group. However, the Stormfront members also depict themselves as victims. Thus, there is a contradiction between the multiple constructions of the in-group. On the one hand, there is the powerful, normal in-group, but also evident is the group which is victimised by others.

When a qualitative analysis of each text of the thread is undertaken, it could be seen that the identity constructions performed by the majority of the Stormfront members are not universally accepted and repeated by all of the members; there is a continual construction of multiple identities and stances which contradict the norm, which are in turn refuted and contested further. Thus, masculinities of the white, heterosexual in-group, and the identities of the out-groups are in a constant state of flux and renegotiation. It would therefore be inaccurate to assign absolute identities and qualities to any of the social groups or to attempt to assign a single hierarchy of the out-groups, as the following data extract indicates:

> 11. The decadent West, enamored of filthy sodomites, now considers these disease spreaders and child molesters legit. Trump endorses this view, which explains why he was all on board with the tranny bathroom shtick. This, along with his judeophilia, makes him much less likely to perform up to the standard expected by the resident Trump dittoheads on this Board.
>
> The Muzzie that cleaned out the queer bar, for all his flaws, and despite the fact that neither he nor his co-religionists belong in the United States, is for all that a man. He has the strength of his convictions, and regards homos as a criminal class, as Americans once did as well within the lifetime of men now living.
>
> In short, Muslims are men. Most of those here in the West are merely children.
>
> Muslims are serious people. Americans (most of them) are clowns.
>
> The proximate cause of the slaughter was not the presence of Muslims in Florida, but the homos displaying their disgusting practices in full public view.
>
> But you ain't going to hear that story on the evening news.
>
> The idea that Trump will "Make America Great Again" by enshrining faggotry as a legitimate force in American society is laughable on its face.

> Continuing down the path of decay and vice will only insure our own destruction.

This Stormfront member constructs a different stance from that previously described in the data. Firstly, western society and homosexual men are constructed negatively, which could be described as the accepted position of the majority of the posters. However, Trump is then described as promoting LGBT rights and a supporter of Jewish groups, thereby he is depicted as failing to live up to the expectations of certain forum members. Following this, the writer labels the assailant positively by describing him as *a man*, a term of honour, primarily for the fact that he committed an act of great violence, a mass-killing, against members of a despised out-group, thereby elevating his position within the out-group hierarchy to a position of greater esteem than other out-group social actors, and in-group members regardless of the fact that the writer believes that Muslims should not be allowed to live in the US. This clearly indicates how violence and the ability to inflict violence on others is a valued attribute of hegemonic masculinity for some individuals.

Such an approach was rejected by another writer, who states:

> 12. While I do not condone gay lifestyle, they were in their own club, not out flaunting themselves. It was a private place, where gays could congregate and enjoy life. They were human beings, with families who loved them.

Thus, the victims of the attack were defended, and although not fully condoned or accepted by the writer (a distancing strategy seen in posts analysed earlier), they were not labelled with negative attributes as has been the strategy employed by the majority of Stormfront members, which evidently indicates the existence of multiple layers of identities and ideologies within the in-group. Further evidence of this stance can be found in the following extract, which takes an even more sympathetic stance towards gay people:

> 13. do any of you vilifying the victims who happen to be gay …. have any relatives, or associates at work who are gay?

do you believe they all deserve to die? i think you're hypocrites. most people have acquaintances who are gay who are decent hardworking human beings.

instead of condemning the muslim scum bag, many here are laughing and stating that the victims deserved to die.

you make us look like fools.

Consequently, it can be seen that there is no single position accepted by all of the members. In the above extract, the writer criticises those who demean the victims and construct their indifference or hatred towards those killed in the attack. The writer identifies gay people as potential relatives or workmates and labels them positively (*decent, hard-working human beings*), which is in contrast to the constructions found in previous data presented. However, this construction is contested by another member who replies:

14. I have no family members, friends, ect who are sexual deviants.

When sexual deviants have a very open agenda to confuse and indoctrinate our children as young as possible into sexual debauchery, do not expect me to shed a tear when some other POS offs what can only be considered another enemy of my people.

And i am not laughing. I am not celebrating. I am just not upset, either. Therefore if you look like a fool, place the blame on the man in the mirror who would sympathize with creatures hoping to sodomize our sons.

The writer reiterates the widely accepted construction of gay men on Stormfront (as predatory sexual deviants) in response to the previous poster who defended the victims of the attack. It is thus evident that there is no single construction of identities, no single performance which remains static, regardless of whether it is accepted by the majority or not. Each identity trait of the in-group and the out-groups has to be continually discursively performed and restated in order for it to be maintained, each position is challenged and contested throughout the thread. This appears to indicate that within the Stormfront membership, there are multiple contesting ideologies held, and it is the cumulative performance of certain identity traits which creates a structure of dominance and subordination.

8 Conclusion

Hegemonic masculinity has no meaning outside its relationship to non-hegemonic masculinity, particularly at a local level. However, as none of the forms of masculinities are static, but understood as a constant shifting of qualities and attributes, the meaning of either hegemonic or non-hegemonic masculinity must be repetitively reaffirmed. To a certain degree, the differing of opinions and contestation found in the data may be attributed to multiple localised hegemonic masculinities colliding in an online environment, thus this may indicate the importance of localised masculinity in a more general nature.

There is considerable talk about families and children, especially white children, yet the archetypical families focus on the power hierarchies at work between men and women. White heterosexual men are viewed as normal, and this is a stance which is not contested by any of the Stormfront members regardless of the level or lack of sympathy depicted towards the gay men who were victims of the attack.

However, white heterosexual men were also constructed as victims—of modernisation, globalisation, mass-immigration, and rights movements. Thus the threads are populated by like-minded individuals who, to an extent, but not uniformly, support the notion of victimhood at the hands of various out-groups and government.

Analysis of the data has highlighted that a great deal of anger is constructed through the notion of entitlement. White men consider themselves to be entitled to a patriarchal position. Although it could be argued that there is generally a widely held consensus on some of the fundamental tenets of Stormfront, at other times, there are clearly different ideological positions. Stormfront posters were homophobic and Islamophobic to different degrees and disagreed about how the victims of the massacre and Muslims ought to be treated. This may reflect different levels of awareness or concern among individual members about how Stormfront represents itself as an organisation to the outside world. On the other hand, it may suggest that some members view homosexuality as a central issue to Stormfront, while others view it as more peripheral, with race being the most important focus. The lack of homogeneity on multiple issues which have been highlighted throughout the analysis of the data certainly demonstrates a degree of openness and fluidity, and ambiguity as the accepted constructions of hegemonic and non-hegemonic masculinities. This has created a context in which the constructions of white heterosexual men, gay men, and other social groups does not go unchallenged, but are contested and rearticulated through the participatory nature of the discussion boards.

Perhaps the most important conclusion to draw from the analysis is that hegemonic masculinity sustains itself through subordination, but that the object of subordination is perhaps less important than the subordination itself. Indeed, arguing about who should be subordinated helps to contribute towards a performance of hegemonic masculinity in terms of posters engaging in conflict with one another and attempting to jockey for position. Hegemonic masculinity is endlessly adaptable then, and ironically has something in common with queer theory's propensity to avoid "naming the subject". Just as queer can be defined as anything which is "against the normal" Warner (1993: xxvi), so does hegemonic masculinity allows for versatility in naming the object of its subordination.

Notes

1. White Homicide Worldwide: Southern Poverty Law Center. https://www.splcenter.org/20140401/white-homicide-worldwide (Retrieved 16/09/2016).
2. http://www.webcitation.org/5cKwkrbTe (Retrieved 16/09/2016).
3. The reference corpus used in this study was enTenTen12, a 12 billion word, web crawled corpus of English texts.
4. Although a large number of the victims were Latino, reference to this ethnic group was not among the most frequent words or keywords.

References

Baker, P. (2014). *Using Corpora to Analyze Gender*. London: Bloomsbury.

Baker, P., & McEnery, T. (2015). Who Benefits When Discourse Gets Democratised? Analysing a Twitter Corpus Around the British Benefits Street Debate. In P. Baker & T. McEnery (Eds.), *Corpora and Discourse Studies: Integrating Discourse and Corpora* (pp. 244–265). London: Palgrave Macmillan.

Baker, P., Gabrielatos, C., Khosravinik, M., Krzyzanowski, M., McEnery, T., & Wodak, R. (2008). A Useful Methodological Synergy? Combining Critical

Discourse Analysis and Corpus Linguistics to Examine Discourses of Refugees and Asylum Seekers in the UK Press. *Discourse & Society, 19*(3), 273–306.

Baker, P., Gabrielatos, C., & McEnery, E. (2013). *Discourse Analysis and Media Attitudes*. Cambridge: Cambridge University Press.

Benwell, B. (2003). *Masculinity and Men's Lifestyle Magazines*. Oxford: Blackwell.

Boler, M. (2005). Masculinity on Trial: Undressing Homophobia in the Bible Belt. *Men and Masculinities, 7*, 261–269.

Butler, J. (1990). *Gender Trouble*. New York and London: Routledge.

Carrigan, T., Connell, R. W., & Lee, J. (2006). Hard and Heavy: Toward a New Sociology of Masculinity. In S. W. Whitehead (Ed.), *Men and Masculinities: Critical Concepts in Sociology* (Vol. 1, pp. 15–63). Oxford: Routledge.

Connell, R. W. (1987). *Gender and Power: Society, the Person and Sexual Politics*. Stanford, CA: Stanford University Press.

Connell, R. W. (1995). *Masculinities*. Berkeley, CA: University of California Press.

Connell, R. W. (2005). *Masculinities* (2nd ed.). Cambridge: Polity Press.

Connell, R. W., & Messerschmidt, J. W. (2005). Hegemonic Masculinity: Rethinking the Concept. *Gender & Society, 19*(6), 829–859.

Daniels, J. (2009). *Cyber Racism: White Supremacy Online and the New Attack on Civil Rights*. New York: Rowman & Littlefield.

Donaldson, M. (1993). What Is Hegemonic Masculinity? *Theory and Society, 22*, 643–657.

Ferber, A. L. (2000). Racial Warriors and Weekend Warriors: The Construction of Masculinity in Mythopoetic and White Supremacist Discourse. *Men and Masculinities, 3*, 30.

Gallagher, C. (1995). White Reconstruction in the University. *Socialist Review, 24*(1/2), 165–187.

Goode, W. J. (1982). Why Men Resist. In B. Thorne & M. Yalon (Eds.), *Rethinking the Family* (pp. 131–150). New York: Longman.

Gorer, G. (1964). *The American People: A Study in National Character*. New York: Norton.

Kiesling, S. F. (2006). Playing the Straight Man. In D. Cameron & D. Kulick (Eds.), *The Language and Sexuality Reader* (pp. 118–131). Oxford: Routledge.

Kilgarriff, A., Rychly, P., Smrz, P., & Tugwell, D. (2004). The Sketch Engine. *Proceedings of Euralex* (pp. 105–116). Lorient, France.

Kimmel, M. S. (2001). Masculinity as Homophobia: Fear, Shame and Silence in the Construction of Gender Identity. In S. M. Whitehead & F. J. Barrett (Eds.), *The Masculinities Reader* (pp. 266–287). Cambridge: Polity.

Kimmel, M. S. (2005). Globalization and Its Mal(e)contents: The Gendered Moral and Political Economy of Terrorism. In M. S. Kimmel, J. Hearn, & R. W. Connell (Eds.), *Handbook of Studies on Men & Masculinities* (pp. 414–431). London: Sage.

Kimmel, M. S. (2012). *Manhood in America* (3rd ed.). Oxford, NY: Oxford University Press.

Kimmel, M. S. (2015). *Angry White Men*. New York: Nation Books.

Mac an Ghaill, M., & Heywood, C. (2007). *Gender, Culture and Society: Contemporary Femininities and Masculinities*. London: Palgrave Macmillan.

Messerschmidt, J. W. (2016). *Masculinity in the Making*. New York: Rowman & Littlefield.

Moita-Lopes, L. P. (2006). On Being White, Heterosexual and Male in a Brazilian School: Multiple Positionings in Oral Narratives. In A. de Fina, D. Schiffrin, & M. Bamberg (Eds.), *Discourse and Identity* (pp. 288–313). Cambridge: Cambridge University Press.

Morris, E. W. (2008). Rednecks, 'Rutters' and Rithmetic: Social Class, Masculinity, and Schooling in a Rural Context. *Gender & Society, 22*(6), 728–751.

Morris, E. W. (2012). *Learning the Hard Way: Masculinity, Place, and the Gender Gap in Education*. New Brunswick, NJ: Rutgers University Press.

Mullins, C. W. (2006). *Holding Your Square: Masculinities, Streetlife and Violence*. Devon: Willan Publishing.

Prentice, S., Rayson, P., & Taylor, P. (2012). The Language of Islamic Extremism: Towards an Automated Identification of Beliefs, Motivations and Justifications. *International Journal of Corpus Linguistics, 17*(2), 259–286.

Reisigl, M., & Wodak, R. (2001). *Discourse and Discrimination: Rhetorics of Racism and Antisemitism*. London and New York: Routledge.

Schlatter, E. A. (2006). *Aryan Cowboys: White Supremacists and the Search for a New Frontier 1970–2000*. Austin: University of Texas Press.

Van Kriekan, R., Smith, P., & Holborn, M. (2000). *Sociology: Themes and Perspectives* (2nd ed.). Sydney: Pearson Education Australia.

Warner, M. (Ed.). (1993). *Fear of a Queer Planet*. Minneapolis, MN: University of Minnesota Press.

Whitehead, S. M. (2002). *Men and Masculinities: Key Themes and New Directions*. Cambridge: Polity Press.

Wodak, R. (2015). *The Politics of Fear*. London: Sage.

Index

P. Baker, G. Balirano (eds.), *Queering Masculinities in Language and Culture*, Palgrave Studies in Language, Gender and Sexuality,
https://doi.org/10.1057/978-1-349-95327-1

S

V

W

Y